FREE Study Skills Videos

Dear Customer,

Thank you for your purchase from Mometrix! We consider it an honor and a privilege that you have purchased our product and we want to ensure your satisfaction.

As part of our ongoing effort to meet the needs of test takers, we have developed a set of Study Skills Videos that we would like to give you for FREE. These videos cover our *best practices* for getting ready for your exam, from how to use our study materials to how to best prepare for the day of the test.

All that we ask is that you email us with feedback that would describe your experience so far with our product. Good, bad, or indifferent, we want to know what you think!

To get your FREE Study Skills Videos, you can use the **QR code** below, or send us an **email** at studyvideos@mometrix.com with *FREE VIDEOS* in the subject line and the following information in the body of the email:

- The name of the product you purchased.
- Your product rating on a scale of 1-5, with 5 being the highest rating.
- Your feedback. It can be long, short, or anything in between. We just want to know your impressions and experience so far with our product. (Good feedback might include how our study material met your needs and ways we might be able to make it even better. You could highlight features that you found helpful or features that you think we should add.)

If you have any questions or concerns, please don't hesitate to contact me directly.

Thanks again!

Sincerely,

Jay Willis
Vice President
jay.willis@mometrix.com
1-800-673-8175

SCAN HERE

SSAT
Middle Level
Prep Book 2025-2026

3 Full-Length Practice Tests

SSAT Secrets Study Guide
Covering Quantitative (Math),
Verbal (Vocabulary),
and Reading

5th Edition

Written and edited by Matthew Bowling

Printed in the United States of America

This paper meets the requirements of ANSI/NISO Z39.48-1992 (Permanence of Paper).

Mometrix offers volume discount pricing to institutions. For more information or a price quote, please contact our sales department at sales@mometrix.com or 888-248-1219.

Mometrix Media LLC is not affiliated with or endorsed by any official testing organization. All organizational and test names are trademarks of their respective owners.

Paperback
ISBN 13: 978-1-5167-2783-4
ISBN 10: 1-5167-2783-5

DEAR FUTURE EXAM SUCCESS STORY

First of all, **THANK YOU** for purchasing Mometrix study materials!

Second, congratulations! You are one of the few determined test-takers who are committed to doing whatever it takes to excel on your exam. **You have come to the right place.** We developed these study materials with one goal in mind: to deliver you the information you need in a format that's concise and easy to use.

In addition to optimizing your guide for the content of the test, we've outlined our recommended steps for breaking down the preparation process into small, attainable goals so you can make sure you stay on track.

We've also analyzed the entire test-taking process, identifying the most common pitfalls and showing how you can overcome them and be ready for any curveball the test throws you.

Standardized testing is one of the biggest obstacles on your road to success, which only increases the importance of doing well in the high-pressure, high-stakes environment of test day. Your results on this test could have a significant impact on your future, and this guide provides the information and practical advice to help you achieve your full potential on test day.

Your success is our success

We would love to hear from you! If you would like to share the story of your exam success or if you have any questions or comments in regard to our products, please contact us at **800-673-8175** or **support@mometrix.com**.

Thanks again for your business and we wish you continued success!

Sincerely,
The Mometrix Test Preparation Team

> **Need more help? Check out our flashcards at:**
> **http://mometrixflashcards.com/SSAT**

TABLE OF CONTENTS

Introduction

Thank you for purchasing this resource! You have made the choice to prepare yourself for a test that could have a huge impact on your future, and this guide is designed to help you be fully ready for test day. Obviously, it's important to have a solid understanding of the test material, but you also need to be prepared for the unique environment and stressors of the test, so that you can perform to the best of your abilities.

For this purpose, the first section that appears in this guide is the **Secret Keys**. We've devoted countless hours to meticulously researching what works and what doesn't, and we've boiled down our findings to the five most impactful steps you can take to improve your performance on the test. We start at the beginning with study planning and move through the preparation process, all the way to the testing strategies that will help you get the most out of what you know when you're finally sitting in front of the test.

We recommend that you start preparing for your test as far in advance as possible. However, if you've bought this guide as a last-minute study resource and only have a few days before your test, we recommend that you skip over the first two Secret Keys since they address a long-term study plan.

If you struggle with **test anxiety**, we strongly encourage you to check out our recommendations for how you can overcome it. Test anxiety is a formidable foe, but it can be beaten, and we want to make sure you have the tools you need to defeat it.

Secret Key #1 – Plan Big, Study Small

There's a lot riding on your performance. If you want to ace this test, you're going to need to keep your skills sharp and the material fresh in your mind. You need a plan that lets you review everything you need to know while still fitting in your schedule. We'll break this strategy down into three categories.

Information Organization

Start with the information you already have: the official test outline. From this, you can make a complete list of all the concepts you need to cover before the test. Organize these concepts into groups that can be studied together, and create a list of any related vocabulary you need to learn so you can brush up on any difficult terms. You'll want to keep this vocabulary list handy once you actually start studying since you may need to add to it along the way.

Time Management

Once you have your set of study concepts, decide how to spread them out over the time you have left before the test. Break your study plan into small, clear goals so you have a manageable task for each day and know exactly what you're doing. Then just focus on one small step at a time. When you manage your time this way, you don't need to spend hours at a time studying. Studying a small block of content for a short period each day helps you retain information better and avoid stressing over how much you have left to do. You can relax knowing that you have a plan to cover everything in time. In order for this strategy to be effective though, you have to start studying early and stick to your schedule. Avoid the exhaustion and futility that comes from last-minute cramming!

Study Environment

The environment you study in has a big impact on your learning. Studying in a coffee shop, while probably more enjoyable, is not likely to be as fruitful as studying in a quiet room. It's important to keep distractions to a minimum. You're only planning to study for a short block of time, so make the most of it. Don't pause to check your phone or get up to find a snack. It's also important to **avoid multitasking**. Research has consistently shown that multitasking will make your studying dramatically less effective. Your study area should also be comfortable and well-lit so you don't have the distraction of straining your eyes or sitting on an uncomfortable chair.

 The time of day you study is also important. You want to be rested and alert. Don't wait until just before bedtime. Study when you'll be most likely to comprehend and remember. Even better, if you know what time of day your test will be, set that time aside for study. That way your brain will be used to working on that subject at that specific time and you'll have a better chance of recalling information.

Finally, it can be helpful to team up with others who are studying for the same test. Your actual studying should be done in as isolated an environment as possible, but the work of organizing the information and setting up the study plan can be divided up. In between study sessions, you can discuss with your teammates the concepts that you're all studying and quiz each other on the details. Just be sure that your teammates are as serious about the test as you are. If you find that your study time is being replaced with social time, you might need to find a new team.

Secret Key #2 – Make Your Studying Count

You're devoting a lot of time and effort to preparing for this test, so you want to be absolutely certain it will pay off. This means doing more than just reading the content and hoping you can remember it on test day. It's important to make every minute of study count. There are two main areas you can focus on to make your studying count.

Retention

It doesn't matter how much time you study if you can't remember the material. You need to make sure you are retaining the concepts. To check your retention of the information you're learning, try recalling it at later times with minimal prompting. Try carrying around flashcards and glance at one or two from time to time or ask a friend who's also studying for the test to quiz you.

To enhance your retention, look for ways to put the information into practice so that you can apply it rather than simply recalling it. If you're using the information in practical ways, it will be much easier to remember. Similarly, it helps to solidify a concept in your mind if you're not only reading it to yourself but also explaining it to someone else. Ask a friend to let you teach them about a concept you're a little shaky on (or speak aloud to an imaginary audience if necessary). As you try to summarize, define, give examples, and answer your friend's questions, you'll understand the concepts better and they will stay with you longer. Finally, step back for a big picture view and ask yourself how each piece of information fits with the whole subject. When you link the different concepts together and see them working together as a whole, it's easier to remember the individual components.

Finally, practice showing your work on any multi-step problems, even if you're just studying. Writing out each step you take to solve a problem will help solidify the process in your mind, and you'll be more likely to remember it during the test.

Modality

Modality simply refers to the means or method by which you study. Choosing a study modality that fits your own individual learning style is crucial. No two people learn best in exactly the same way, so it's important to know your strengths and use them to your advantage.

For example, if you learn best by visualization, focus on visualizing a concept in your mind and draw an image or a diagram. Try color-coding your notes, illustrating them, or creating symbols that will trigger your mind to recall a learned concept. If you learn best by hearing or discussing information, find a study partner who learns the same way or read aloud to yourself. Think about how to put the information in your own words. Imagine that you are giving a lecture on the topic and record yourself so you can listen to it later.

For any learning style, flashcards can be helpful. Organize the information so you can take advantage of spare moments to review. Underline key words or phrases. Use different colors for different categories. Mnemonic devices (such as creating a short list in which every item starts with the same letter) can also help with retention. Find what works best for you and use it to store the information in your mind most effectively and easily.

Secret Key #3 – Practice the Right Way

Your success on test day depends not only on how many hours you put into preparing, but also on whether you prepared the right way. It's good to check along the way to see if your studying is paying off. One of the most effective ways to do this is by taking practice tests to evaluate your progress. Practice tests are useful because they show exactly where you need to improve. Every time you take a practice test, pay special attention to these three groups of questions:

- The questions you got wrong
- The questions you had to guess on, even if you guessed right
- The questions you found difficult or slow to work through

This will show you exactly what your weak areas are, and where you need to devote more study time. Ask yourself why each of these questions gave you trouble. Was it because you didn't understand the material? Was it because you didn't remember the vocabulary? Do you need more repetitions on this type of question to build speed and confidence? Dig into those questions and figure out how you can strengthen your weak areas as you go back to review the material.

 Additionally, many practice tests have a section explaining the answer choices. It can be tempting to read the explanation and think that you now have a good understanding of the concept. However, an explanation likely only covers part of the question's broader context. Even if the explanation makes perfect sense, **go back and investigate** every concept related to the question until you're positive you have a thorough understanding.

As you go along, keep in mind that the practice test is just that: practice. Memorizing these questions and answers will not be very helpful on the actual test because it is unlikely to have any of the same exact questions. If you only know the right answers to the sample questions, you won't be prepared for the real thing. **Study the concepts** until you understand them fully, and then you'll be able to answer any question that shows up on the test.

It's important to wait on the practice tests until you're ready. If you take a test on your first day of study, you may be overwhelmed by the amount of material covered and how much you need to learn. Work up to it gradually.

On test day, you'll need to be prepared for answering questions, managing your time, and using the test-taking strategies you've learned. It's a lot to balance, like a mental marathon that will have a big impact on your future. Like training for a marathon, you'll need to start slowly and work your way up. When test day arrives, you'll be ready.

Start with the strategies you've read in the first two Secret Keys—plan your course and study in the way that works best for you. If you have time, consider using multiple study resources to get different approaches to the same concepts. It can be helpful to see difficult concepts from more than one angle. Then find a good source for practice tests. Many times, the test website will suggest potential study resources or provide sample tests.

4

Practice Test Strategy

If you're able to find at least three practice tests, we recommend this strategy:

UNTIMED AND OPEN-BOOK PRACTICE

Take the first test with no time constraints and with your notes and study guide handy. Take your time and focus on applying the strategies you've learned.

TIMED AND OPEN-BOOK PRACTICE

Take the second practice test open-book as well, but set a timer and practice pacing yourself to finish in time.

TIMED AND CLOSED-BOOK PRACTICE

Take any other practice tests as if it were test day. Set a timer and put away your study materials. Sit at a table or desk in a quiet room, imagine yourself at the testing center, and answer questions as quickly and accurately as possible.

Keep repeating timed and closed-book tests on a regular basis until you run out of practice tests or it's time for the actual test. Your mind will be ready for the schedule and stress of test day, and you'll be able to focus on recalling the material you've learned.

Secret Key #4 – Pace Yourself

Once you're fully prepared for the material on the test, your biggest challenge on test day will be managing your time. Just knowing that the clock is ticking can make you panic even if you have plenty of time left. Work on pacing yourself so you can build confidence against the time constraints of the exam. Pacing is a difficult skill to master, especially in a high-pressure environment, so **practice is vital**.

Set time expectations for your pace based on how much time is available. For example, if a section has 60 questions and the time limit is 30 minutes, you know you have to average 30 seconds or less per question in order to answer them all. Although 30 seconds is the hard limit, set 25 seconds per question as your goal, so you reserve extra time to spend on harder questions. When you budget extra time for the harder questions, you no longer have any reason to stress when those questions take longer to answer.

Don't let this time expectation distract you from working through the test at a calm, steady pace, but keep it in mind so you don't spend too much time on any one question. Recognize that taking extra time on one question you don't understand may keep you from answering two that you do understand later in the test. If your time limit for a question is up and you're still not sure of the answer, mark it and move on, and come back to it later if the time and the test format allow. If the testing format doesn't allow you to return to earlier questions, just make an educated guess; then put it out of your mind and move on.

On the easier questions, be careful not to rush. It may seem wise to hurry through them so you have more time for the challenging ones, but it's not worth missing one if you know the concept and just didn't take the time to read the question fully. Work efficiently but make sure you understand the question and have looked at all of the answer choices, since more than one may seem right at first.

Even if you're paying attention to the time, you may find yourself a little behind at some point. You should speed up to get back on track, but do so wisely. Don't panic; just take a few seconds less on each question until you're caught up. Don't guess without thinking, but do look through the answer choices and eliminate any you know are wrong. If you can get down to two choices, it is often worthwhile to guess from those. Once you've chosen an answer, move on and don't dwell on any that you skipped or had to hurry through. If a question was taking too long, chances are it was one of the harder ones, so you weren't as likely to get it right anyway.

On the other hand, if you find yourself getting ahead of schedule, it may be beneficial to slow down a little. The more quickly you work, the more likely you are to make a careless mistake that will affect your score. You've budgeted time for each question, so don't be afraid to spend that time. Practice an efficient but careful pace to get the most out of the time you have.

Secret Key #5 – Have a Plan for Guessing

When you're taking the test, you may find yourself stuck on a question. Some of the answer choices seem better than others, but you don't see the one answer choice that is obviously correct. What do you do?

The scenario described above is very common, yet most test takers have not effectively prepared for it. Developing and practicing a plan for guessing may be one of the single most effective uses of your time as you get ready for the exam.

In developing your plan for guessing, there are three questions to address:

- When should you start the guessing process?
- How should you narrow down the choices?
- Which answer should you choose?

When to Start the Guessing Process

Unless your plan for guessing is to select C every time (which, despite its merits, is not what we recommend), you need to leave yourself enough time to apply your answer elimination strategies. Since you have a limited amount of time for each question, that means that if you're going to give yourself the best shot at guessing correctly, you have to decide quickly whether or not you will guess.

Of course, the best-case scenario is that you don't have to guess at all, so first, see if you can answer the question based on your knowledge of the subject and basic reasoning skills. Focus on the key words in the question and try to jog your memory of related topics. Give yourself a chance to bring the knowledge to mind, but once you realize that you don't have (or you can't access) the knowledge you need to answer the question, it's time to start the guessing process.

It's almost always better to start the guessing process too early than too late. It only takes a few seconds to remember something and answer the question from knowledge. Carefully eliminating wrong answer choices takes longer. Plus, going through the process of eliminating answer choices can actually help jog your memory.

Summary: Start the guessing process as soon as you decide that you can't answer the question based on your knowledge.

7

How to Narrow Down the Choices

The next chapter in this book (**Test-Taking Strategies**) includes a wide range of strategies for how to approach questions and how to look for answer choices to eliminate. You will definitely want to read those carefully, practice them, and figure out which ones work best for you. Here though, we're going to address a mindset rather than a particular strategy.

Your odds of guessing an answer correctly depend on how many options you are choosing from.

Number of options left	5	4	3	2	1
Odds of guessing correctly	20%	25%	33%	50%	100%

You can see from this chart just how valuable it is to be able to eliminate incorrect answers and make an educated guess, but there are two things that many test takers do that cause them to miss out on the benefits of guessing:

- Accidentally eliminating the correct answer
- Selecting an answer based on an impression

We'll look at the first one here, and the second one in the next section.

To avoid accidentally eliminating the correct answer, we recommend a thought exercise called **the $5 challenge**. In this challenge, you only eliminate an answer choice from contention if you are willing to bet $5 on it being wrong. Why $5? Five dollars is a small but not insignificant amount of money. It's an amount you could afford to lose but wouldn't want to throw away. And while losing $5 once might not hurt too much, doing

it twenty times will set you back $100. In the same way, each small decision you make—eliminating a choice here, guessing on a question there—won't by itself impact your score very much, but when you put them all together, they can make a big difference. By holding each answer choice elimination decision to a higher standard, you can reduce the risk of accidentally eliminating the correct answer.

The $5 challenge can also be applied in a positive sense: If you are willing to bet $5 that an answer choice *is* correct, go ahead and mark it as correct.

Summary: Only eliminate an answer choice if you are willing to bet $5 that it is wrong.

Which Answer to Choose

You're taking the test. You've run into a hard question and decided you'll have to guess. You've eliminated all the answer choices you're willing to bet $5 on. Now you have to pick an answer. Why do we even need to talk about this? Why can't you just pick whichever one you feel like when the time comes?

The answer to these questions is that if you don't come into the test with a plan, you'll rely on your impression to select an answer choice, and if you do that, you risk falling into a trap. The test writers know that everyone who takes their test will be guessing on some of the questions, so they intentionally write wrong answer choices to seem plausible. You still have to pick an answer though, and if the wrong answer choices are designed to look right, how can you ever be sure that you're not falling for their trap? The best solution we've found to this dilemma is to take the decision out of your hands entirely. Here is the process we recommend:

Once you've eliminated any choices that you are confident (willing to bet $5) are wrong, select the first remaining choice as your answer.

Whether you choose to select the first remaining choice, the second, or the last, the important thing is that you use some preselected standard. Using this approach guarantees that you will not be enticed into selecting an answer choice that looks right, because you are not basing your decision on how the answer choices look.

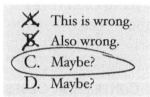

This is not meant to make you question your knowledge. Instead, it is to help you recognize the difference between your knowledge and your impressions. There's a huge difference between thinking an answer is right because of what you know, and thinking an answer is right because it looks or sounds like it should be right.

Summary: To ensure that your selection is appropriately random, make a predetermined selection from among all answer choices you have not eliminated.

Test-Taking Strategies

This section contains a list of test-taking strategies that you may find helpful as you work through the test. By taking what you know and applying logical thought, you can maximize your chances of answering any question correctly!

It is very important to realize that every question is different and every person is different: no single strategy will work on every question, and no single strategy will work for every person. That's why we've included all of them here, so you can try them out and determine which ones work best for different types of questions and which ones work best for you.

Question Strategies

☑ READ CAREFULLY

Read the question and the answer choices carefully. Don't miss the question because you misread the terms. You have plenty of time to read each question thoroughly and make sure you understand what is being asked. Yet a happy medium must be attained, so don't waste too much time. You must read carefully and efficiently.

☑ CONTEXTUAL CLUES

Look for contextual clues. If the question includes a word you are not familiar with, look at the immediate context for some indication of what the word might mean. Contextual clues can often give you all the information you need to decipher the meaning of an unfamiliar word. Even if you can't determine the meaning, you may be able to narrow down the possibilities enough to make a solid guess at the answer to the question.

☑ PREFIXES

If you're having trouble with a word in the question or answer choices, try dissecting it. Take advantage of every clue that the word might include. Prefixes can be a huge help. Usually, they allow you to determine a basic meaning. *Pre-* means before, *post-* means after, *pro-* is positive, *de-* is negative. From prefixes, you can get an idea of the general meaning of the word and try to put it into context.

☑ HEDGE WORDS

Watch out for critical hedge words, such as *likely, may, can, sometimes, often, almost, mostly, usually, generally, rarely,* and *sometimes.* Question writers insert these hedge phrases to cover every possibility. Often an answer choice will be wrong simply because it leaves no room for exception. Be on guard for answer choices that have definitive words such as *exactly* and *always.*

☑ SWITCHBACK WORDS

Stay alert for *switchbacks.* These are the words and phrases frequently used to alert you to shifts in thought. The most common switchback words are *but, although,* and *however.* Others include *nevertheless, on the other hand, even though, while, in spite of, despite,* and *regardless of.* Switchback words are important to catch because they can change the direction of the question or an answer choice.

☑ FACE VALUE

When in doubt, use common sense. Accept the situation in the problem at face value. Don't read too much into it. These problems will not require you to make wild assumptions. If you have to go beyond creativity and warp time or space in order to have an answer choice fit the question, then you should move on and consider the other answer choices. These are normal problems rooted in reality. The applicable relationship or explanation may not be readily apparent, but it is there for you to figure out. Use your common sense to interpret anything that isn't clear.

Answer Choice Strategies

⊘ ANSWER SELECTION

The most thorough way to pick an answer choice is to identify and eliminate wrong answers until only one is left, then confirm it is the correct answer. Sometimes an answer choice may immediately seem right, but be careful. The test writers will usually put more than one reasonable answer choice on each question, so take a second to read all of them and make sure that the other choices are not equally obvious. As long as you have time left, it is better to read every answer choice than to pick the first one that looks right without checking the others.

⊘ ANSWER CHOICE FAMILIES

An answer choice family consists of two (in rare cases, three) answer choices that are very similar in construction and cannot all be true at the same time. If you see two answer choices that are direct opposites or parallels, one of them is usually the correct answer. For instance, if one answer choice says that quantity x increases and another either says that quantity x decreases (opposite) or says that quantity y increases (parallel), then those answer choices would fall into the same family. An answer choice that doesn't match the construction of the answer choice family is more likely to be incorrect. Most questions will not have answer choice families, but when they do appear, you should be prepared to recognize them.

⊘ ELIMINATE ANSWERS

Eliminate answer choices as soon as you realize they are wrong, but make sure you consider all possibilities. If you are eliminating answer choices and realize that the last one you are left with is also wrong, don't panic. Start over and consider each choice again. There may be something you missed the first time that you will realize on the second pass.

⊘ AVOID FACT TRAPS

Don't be distracted by an answer choice that is factually true but doesn't answer the question. You are looking for the choice that answers the question. Stay focused on what the question is asking for so you don't accidentally pick an answer that is true but incorrect. Always go back to the question and make sure the answer choice you've selected actually answers the question and is not merely a true statement.

⊘ EXTREME STATEMENTS

In general, you should avoid answers that put forth extreme actions as standard practice or proclaim controversial ideas as established fact. An answer choice that states the "process should be used in certain situations, if..." is much more likely to be correct than one that states the "process should be discontinued completely." The first is a calm rational statement and doesn't even make a definitive, uncompromising stance, using a hedge word *if* to provide wiggle room, whereas the second choice is far more extreme.

⊘ BENCHMARK

As you read through the answer choices and you come across one that seems to answer the question well, mentally select that answer choice. This is not your final answer, but it's the one that will help you evaluate the other answer choices. The one that you selected is your benchmark or standard for judging each of the other answer choices. Every other answer choice must be compared to your benchmark. That choice is correct until proven otherwise by another answer choice beating it. If you find a better answer, then that one becomes your new benchmark. Once you've decided that no other choice answers the question as well as your benchmark, you have your final answer.

11

⊘ PREDICT THE ANSWER

Before you even start looking at the answer choices, it is often best to try to predict the answer. When you come up with the answer on your own, it is easier to avoid distractions and traps because you will know exactly what to look for. The right answer choice is unlikely to be word-for-word what you came up with, but it should be a close match. Even if you are confident that you have the right answer, you should still take the time to read each option before moving on.

General Strategies

⊘ TOUGH QUESTIONS

If you are stumped on a problem or it appears too hard or too difficult, don't waste time. Move on! Remember though, if you can quickly check for obviously incorrect answer choices, your chances of guessing correctly are greatly improved. Before you completely give up, at least try to knock out a couple of possible answers. Eliminate what you can and then guess at the remaining answer choices before moving on.

⊘ CHECK YOUR WORK

Since you will probably not know every term listed and the answer to every question, it is important that you get credit for the ones that you do know. Don't miss any questions through careless mistakes. If at all possible, try to take a second to look back over your answer selection and make sure you've selected the correct answer choice and haven't made a costly careless mistake (such as marking an answer choice that you didn't mean to mark). This quick double check should more than pay for itself in caught mistakes for the time it costs.

⊘ PACE YOURSELF

It's easy to be overwhelmed when you're looking at a page full of questions; your mind is confused and full of random thoughts, and the clock is ticking down faster than you would like. Calm down and maintain the pace that you have set for yourself. Especially as you get down to the last few minutes of the test, don't let the small numbers on the clock make you panic. As long as you are on track by monitoring your pace, you are guaranteed to have time for each question.

⊘ DON'T RUSH

It is very easy to make errors when you are in a hurry. Maintaining a fast pace in answering questions is pointless if it makes you miss questions that you would have gotten right otherwise. Test writers like to include distracting information and wrong answers that seem right. Taking a little extra time to avoid careless mistakes can make all the difference in your test score. Find a pace that allows you to be confident in the answers that you select.

⊘ KEEP MOVING

Panicking will not help you pass the test, so do your best to stay calm and keep moving. Taking deep breaths and going through the answer elimination steps you practiced can help to break through a stress barrier and keep your pace.

Final Notes

The combination of a solid foundation of content knowledge and the confidence that comes from practicing your plan for applying that knowledge is the key to maximizing your performance on test day. As your foundation of content knowledge is built up and strengthened, you'll find that the strategies included in this chapter become more and more effective in helping you quickly sift through the distractions and traps of the test to isolate the correct answer.

Now that you're preparing to move forward into the test content chapters of this book, be sure to keep your goal in mind. As you read, think about how you will be able to apply this information on the test. If you've already seen sample questions for the test and you have an idea of the question format and style, try to come up with questions of your own that you can answer based on what you're reading. This will give you valuable practice applying your knowledge in the same ways you can expect to on test day.

Good luck and good studying!

Writing Sample

Practice Makes Prepared Writers

Writing is a skill that continues to need development throughout a person's life. For some people, writing seems to be a natural gift. They rarely struggle with writer's block. When you read their papers, they have persuasive or entertaining ideas. For others, writing is an intimidating task that they endure. As you practice, you can improve your skills and be better prepared for writing a time-sensitive essay.

Remember that you are practicing for more than an exam. Two of the most valuable skills in life are the abilities to **read critically** and to **write clearly**. When you work on evaluating the arguments of a passage and explain your thoughts well, you are developing skills that you will use for a lifetime. In this overview of essay writing, you will find strategies and tools that will prepare you to write better essays.

Creative Writing

Take time to read a story or hear stories read aloud and use those opportunities to learn more about how stories are put together. This offers a frame for you to talk about a story with others and will help you to write better stories. With each new story that you read, try to predict what could happen in the story. Try to understand the setting by picturing the scenes and sounds that are described and the behaviors of characters. Then, try to summarize the events to understand more of the story.

If you need more help with understanding a story, you can try to relate narrative characters and events to your own life. For example, when reading a story, you can ask the following: Who is the main character in the story? What happened first? What happened next? What happened at the end of the story? Where does this story take place? And what is the theme or point of this story?

ESTABLISH A CONTEXT

When writing a narrative, an author must establish the context of the story. In other words, the stage needs to be set for the story to begin. Sometimes this is done by establishing the setting of the story and then introducing a narrator and characters. A character or the narrator can be introduced first. A narrator and/or characters can be introduced in many ways: through the use of dialogue, through description, or through the reactions of the narrator or characters to an event. Whatever means an that you choose, the beginning of a narrative must be compelling for your audience.

EXAMPLE

Discuss the introduction of the character in the following passage.

> Her parents named her Milagro, which means "miracle" in Spanish, but they called her Milly. She was a premature baby, very tiny, and it was a miracle that she survived. That was the beginning of her good fortune.

The author uses a dramatic way to introduce the character. Readers are told that *Milagro* means "miracle" in Spanish. Readers are told that it was a miracle that Milagro survived her birth because she was born prematurely. The way Milagro is introduced is dramatic because the author uses information to hint at what may come next. This is a form of foreshadowing. The author has established an interesting beginning with how the character is introduced, and this captures the attention of readers.

15

POINT OF VIEW

Point of view is the perspective from which writing occurs. There are several possibilities:

- **First person** is written so that the *I* of the story is a participant or observer. First-person narratives let narrators express inner feelings and thoughts. The narrator may be a close friend of the protagonist, or the narrator can be less involved with the main characters and plot.
- **Second person** is a device to draw the reader in more closely. It is really a variation or refinement of the first-person narrative. In some cases, a narrative combines both second-person and first-person voices, speaking of "you" and "I." When the narrator is also a character in the story, the narrative is better defined as first-person even though it also has addresses of "you."
- **Third person** may be either objective or subjective, and either omniscient or limited. Objective third-person narration does not include what the characters are thinking or feeling, while subjective third-person narration does include this information. The third-person omniscient narrator knows everything about all characters, including their thoughts and emotions; and all related places, times, and events. The third-person limited narrator may know everything about a particular character of focus, but is limited to that character. In other words, the narrator cannot speak about anything that character does not know.

SEQUENCE OF EVENTS

The sequence of events in a narrative should follow naturally out of the action and the plot. Rather than being forced, the sequence should follow the natural flow of a dialogue or plot and enhance what happens in the story. The only time that the sequence is not in the order that events naturally happen is when an author decides to use the literary device called flashback. In this case the action does not flow in sequence; instead, the action jumps back and forth in time. Events in a narrative are extremely important in helping the reader understand the intent or message of a narrative, which is why it is important to take note of the way in which the plot unfolds.

> **Review Video: Sequence of Events in a Story**
> Visit mometrix.com/academy and enter code: 807512

Remember from the Reading section that a plot shows the order of a story. The introduction is the beginning of the story. Next, the rising action, conflict, climax, and falling action are the middle. Then, the resolution or conclusion is the ending. So, stay focused on the goal of writing a story that needs those main parts: a beginning, a middle, and an ending.

AUTHOR TECHNIQUES

You can employ many techniques to make your narrative essay come alive in a fresh and interesting way. Dialogue is an important one. Often, dialogue is the means that helps readers understand what is happening and what a character is like. Equally important are the descriptions that you can use to help readers visualize a setting and what a character looks or acts like. Remember that you have limited time to write a whole story. So, don't be concerned with providing description for everything that you put in your story.

DEVELOPMENT OF CHARACTERS

Characters are important to a story, and the problems that they face make a story interesting and complex. As you write your story, be sure to show more information about the characters through their actions. The actions of characters are important to advancing the plot because they show the different stages of the story. If your story teaches a lesson, hey also help the reader understand the theme or lesson that the story teaches.

CONFLICT

A conflict is a problem that needs to be solved. Many stories include at least one conflict, and the characters' efforts to solve conflicts move the story forward. The protagonist is the character who has the main goal of solving the conflict. Conflicts can be external or internal to any of the characters. A major type of internal conflict is some inner personal battle that is called *man against himself*. This type of conflict is when a character struggles with his or her thoughts or emotions.

Major types of external conflicts include *man against nature*, *man against man*, and *man against society*. The man against nature conflict is

You can recognize conflicts in story plots by asking:

Who is the protagonist?

Who or what is the antagonist?

Why are the protagonist and antagonist in conflict?

What event(s) develop the conflict?

Which event is the climax?

TRANSITION WORDS

Transition words can be helpful when writing a narrative so that readers can follow the events in a seamless manner. Sequence words such as *first*, *second*, and *last* assist readers in understanding the order in which events occur. Words such as *then* or *next* also show the order in which events occur. *After a while* and *before this* are other sequence expressions.

Additionally, transition words can indicate a change from one time frame or setting to another: "We were sitting on a rock near the lake when we heard a strange sound." At this point we decided to look to see where the noise was coming from by going further into the woods." In this excerpt the phrase *at this point* signals a shift in setting between what was happening and what came next.

PRECISE LANGUAGE

Your use of precise language, phrases, and sensory language (i.e., language that appeals to the five senses) helps readers imagine a place, situation, or person in the way that you intended. Details of character's actions, the setting, and the events in a narrative help create a lively and thought-provoking story. Sensory language helps convey the mood and feeling of the setting and characters and can highlight the theme of your story.

Read the excerpt and analyze the language.

At dawn, in a stuffy and smoky second-class car in which five people had already spent the night, a bulky woman in deep mourning was hoisted in—almost like a shapeless bundle. Behind her, puffing and

17

moaning, followed her husband—a tiny man, thin and weakly, his face death-white, his eyes small and bright and looking shy and uneasy.

The language selected by the author is filled with fresh and precise words that describe and color the two passengers as well as the setting of the paragraph. The author describes the car as *stuffy and smoky*, *second-class*, and *in which five people had already spent the night*. All this conjures up a dreary train car. The author describes the woman as *a shapeless bundle*. Her husband is *tiny*, *thin*, and *weakly* with a *death-white* face. These words give a clear image of what the people look like for readers which should be a goal of your creative writing.

ROLE OF A CONCLUSION

The conclusion of a narrative is extremely important because it shapes the entire story and is the resolution of the characters' conflict(s). Some conclusions may be tragic (e.g., classic tragedies), and other endings may be lighthearted (e.g., classic comedies). Modern stories tend to have endings that are more complex than the clear-cut endings of classic literature. They often leave readers without a clear sense of how a character fares at the end. Nonetheless, this element can show how life is not always clear in its conclusions.

A student is writing a story about a boy who pushes himself to become an athlete. The student has written about how hard the boy has trained for an upcoming race. He has noted that winning has become a huge force in his life. Now, a conclusion is needed for the story. Describe what he should look for when he writes the conclusion.

The student should think about what the theme of the story is meant to be. Is it a story about someone who works hard and gets what he wants? Or is it about someone who loses an important race and how he deals with it? Then, the student should carry that theme through to the ending of the story which in this case would be whether he won or lost the race. A conclusion should bring the entire story to an appropriate ending so that readers have a sense of closure.

Traditional Essay Overview

A traditional way to prepare for the writing section is to read. When you read newspapers, magazines, and books, you learn about new ideas. You can read newspapers and magazines to become informed about issues that affect many people.

As you think about those issues and ideas, you can take a position and form opinions. Try to develop these ideas and your opinions by sharing them with friends. After you develop your opinions, try writing them down as if you were going to spread your ideas beyond your friends.

For your exam you need to write an essay that shows your ability to understand and respond to an assignment. When you talk with others, you give beliefs, opinions, and ideas about the world around you. As you talk, you have the opportunity to share information with spoken words, facial expressions, or hand motions. If your audience seems confused about your ideas, you can stop and explain. However, when you write, you have a different assignment. As you write, you need to share information in a clear, precise way. Your readers will not have the chance to ask questions about your ideas. So, before you write your essay, you need to understand the assignment. As you write, you should be clear and precise about your ideas.

BRAINSTORM

Spend the first few minutes brainstorming for ideas. Write down any ideas that you might have on the topic. The purpose is to pull any helpful information from the depths of your memory. In this stage, anything goes down on note paper regardless of how good or bad the idea may seem at first glance. You may not bring your own paper for these notes. Instead, you will be provided with paper at the time of your test.

Writing Sample

STRENGTH THROUGH DIFFERENT VIEWPOINTS

The best papers will contain several examples and mature reasoning. As you brainstorm, you should consider different perspectives. There are more than two sides to every topic. In an argument, there are countless perspectives that can be considered. On any topic, different groups are impacted and many reach the same conclusion or position. Yet, they reach the same conclusion through different paths. Before writing your essay, try to *see* the topic through as many different *eyes* as you can.

Once you have finished with your creative flow, you need to stop and review what you brainstormed. *Which idea allowed you to come up with the most supporting information?* Be sure to pick an angle that will allow you to have a thorough coverage of the prompt.

Every garden of ideas has weeds. The ideas that you brainstormed are going to be random pieces of information of different values. Go through the pieces carefully and pick out the ones that are the best. The best ideas are strong points that will be easy to write a paragraph in response.

Now, you have your main ideas that you will focus on. So, align them in a sequence that will flow in a smooth, sensible path from point to point. With this approach, readers will go smoothly from one idea to the next in a reasonable order. Readers want an essay that has a sense of continuity (i.e., Point 1 to Point 2 to Point 3 and so on).

START YOUR ENGINES

Now, you have a logical flow of the main ideas for the start of your essay. Begin by expanding on the first point, then move to your second point. Pace yourself. Don't spend too much time on any one of the ideas that you are expanding on. You want to have time for all of them. *Make sure that you watch your time.* If you have twenty minutes left to write out your ideas and you have four ideas, then you can only use five minutes per idea. Writing so much information in so little time can be an intimidating task. Yet, when you pace yourself, you can get through all of your points. If you find that you are falling behind, then you can remove one of your weaker arguments. This will allow you to give enough support to your remaining paragraphs.

Once you finish expanding on an idea, go back to your brainstorming session where you wrote out your ideas. You can scratch through the ideas as you write about them. This will let you see what you need to write about next and what you have left to cover.

Your introductory paragraph should have several easily identifiable features.

1. First, the paragraph should have a quick description or paraphrasing of the topic. Use your own words to briefly explain what the topic is about.
2. Second, you should list your writing points. What are the main ideas that you came up with earlier? If someone was to read only your introduction, they should be able to get a good summary of the entire paper.
3. Third, you should explain your opinion of the topic and give an explanation for why you feel that way. What is your decision or conclusion on the topic?

Each of your following paragraphs should develop one of the points listed in the main paragraph. Use your personal experience and knowledge to support each of your points. Examples should back up everything.

Once you have finished expanding on each of your main points, you need to conclude your essay. Summarize what you written in a conclusion paragraph. Explain once more your argument on the prompt and review why you feel that way in a few sentences. At this stage, you have already backed up your statements. So, there is no need to do that again. You just need to refresh your readers on the main points that you made in your essay.

Don't Panic

Whatever you do while writing your writing sample, do not panic. When you panic, you will put fewer words on the page and your ideas will be weak. Therefore, panicking is not helpful. If your mind goes blank when you see the prompt, then you need to take a deep breath. Remember to brainstorm and put anything on scratch paper that comes to mind.

Also, don't get clock fever. You may be overwhelmed when you're looking at a page that is mostly blank. Your mind is full of random thoughts and feeling confused, and the clock is ticking down faster. You have already brainstormed for ideas. Therefore, you don't have to keep coming up with ideas. If you're running out of time and you have a lot of ideas that you haven't written down, then don't be afraid to make some cuts. Start picking the best ideas that you have left and expand on them. Don't feel like you have to write on all of your ideas.

A short paper that is well written and well organized is better than a long paper that is poorly written and poorly organized. Don't keep writing about a subject just to add sentences and avoid repeating a statement or idea that you have explained already. The goal is 1 to 2 pages of quality writing. That is your target, but you should not mess up your paper by trying to get there. You want to have a natural end to your work without having to cut something short. If your essay is a little long, then that isn't a problem as long as your ideas are clear and flow well from paragraph to paragraph. Just be sure that your writing stays inside the assigned borders of the papers. Remember to expand on the ideas that you identified in the brainstorming session.

Leave time at the end (at least three minutes) to go back and check over your work. Reread and make sure that everything you've written makes sense and flows well. Clean up any spelling or grammar mistakes. Also, go ahead and erase any brainstorming ideas that you weren't able to include. Then, clean up any extra information that you might have written that doesn't fit into your paper.

As you proofread, make sure that there aren't any fragments or run-ons. Check for sentences that are too short or too long. If the sentence is too short, then look to see if you have a specific subject and an active verb. If it is too long, then break up the long sentence into two sentences. Watch out for any "big words" that you may have used. Be sure that you are using difficult words correctly. Don't misunderstand; you should try to increase your vocabulary and use difficult words in your essay. However, your focus should be on developing and expressing ideas in a clear and precise way.

The Short Overview

Depending on your preferences and personality, the essay may be your hardest or your easiest section. You are required to go through the entire process of writing a paper in a limited amount of time, which is very challenging.

Stay focused on each of the steps for brainstorming. Go through the process of creative flow first. You can start by generating ideas about the prompt. Next, organize those ideas into a smooth flow. Then, pick out the ideas that are the best from your list.

Create a recognizable essay structure in your paper. Start with an introduction that explains what you have decided to argue. Then, choose your main points. Use the body paragraphs to touch on those main points and have a conclusion that wraps up the topic.

Save a few moments to go back and review what you have written. Clean up any minor mistakes that you might have made and make those last few critical touches that can make a huge difference. Finally, be proud and confident of what you have written!

Grammar

SUBJECTS AND PREDICATES

SUBJECTS

Every sentence needs a subject and a predicate. The **subject** of a sentence names who or what the sentence is about. The subject may be directly stated in a sentence, or the subject may be implied. The **complete subject** includes the simple subject and any **modifiers**, such as adjectives, articles, prepositions, and adverbs, that go with it. To find the complete subject, ask *Who* or *What* before the verb to complete the question. The answer, including any modifiers, is the complete subject. To find the **simple subject**, remove all of the modifiers in the complete subject.

Examples:

simple
subject

The small, red car is the one that he wants for Christmas.

complete
subject

simple
subject

The young artist is coming over for dinner.

complete
subject

> **Review Video: Subjects in English**
> Visit mometrix.com/academy and enter code: 444771

An imperative sentence is a sentence that gives someone instructions or makes a request to someone. In **imperative** sentences, the verb's subject is understood, but is not actually present in the sentence. For example, this about the sentence *Drive to the store*. This sentence is a command, and the subject is *you*. If the subject were directly stated, the sentence would be *You, drive to the store*. Another fact to consider is that, normally, the subject comes before the verb. However, the subject comes after the verb in sentences that begin with *There are* or *There was*.

Direct:

John knows the way to the park.	Who knows the way to the park?	John
The cookies need ten more minutes.	What needs ten minutes?	The cookies
By five o'clock, Bill will need to leave.	Who needs to leave?	Bill
There are five letters on the table for him.	What is on the table?	Five letters
There were coffee and doughnuts in the house.	What was in the house?	Coffee and doughnuts

Implied:

Go to the post office for me.	Who is going to the post office?	You
Come and sit with me, please?	Who needs to come and sit?	You

PREDICATES

In a sentence, there is always a predicate and a subject. The subject tells what the sentence is about, and the **predicate** explains or describes the subject.

21

Think about the sentence *He sings*. In this sentence, we have a subject, *He*, and a predicate, *sings*. This is all that is needed for a sentence to be complete. Most sentences contain more information, but if this is all the information that is given in a sentence, then it is a complete sentence.

Now, let's look at another sentence: *John and Jane sing on Tuesday nights at the dance hall.*

subject   predicate
John and Jane sing on Tuesday nights at the dance hall.

SUBJECT-VERB AGREEMENT

Verbs **agree** with their subjects in number. In other words, singular subjects need singular verbs. Plural subjects need plural verbs. **Singular** is for **one** person, place, or thing. **Plural** is for **more than one** person, place, or thing. Subjects and verbs must also share the same point of view, as in first, second, or third person.

> **Review Video: Subject-Verb Agreement**
> Visit mometrix.com/academy and enter code: 479190

NUMBER AGREEMENT EXAMPLES:

singular singular
subject verb
Single Subject and Verb: Dan calls home.

Dan is one person. So, the singular verb *calls* is needed.

plural plural
subject verb
Plural Subject and Verb: Dan and Bob call home.

More than one person needs the plural verb *call*.

PERSON AGREEMENT EXAMPLES:

First Person: I *am* walking.

Second Person: You *are* walking.

Third Person: He *is* walking.

COMPLICATIONS WITH SUBJECT-VERB AGREEMENT
WORDS BETWEEN SUBJECT AND VERB

Words that come between the simple subject and the verb do not affect subject-verb agreement.

Examples:

singular   singular
subject   verb
The joy of my life returns home tonight.

The phrase *of my life* does not affect the verb *returns*.

singular   singular
subject   verb
The question that still remains unanswered is "Who are you?"

Don't let the phrase "*that still remains...*" confuse you. The subject *question* goes with the verb *is*.

COMPOUND SUBJECTS

A compound subject is formed when two or more nouns joined by *and*, *or*, or *nor* act together as the subject of the sentence.

JOINED BY AND

When a compound subject is joined by *and*, it is treated as a plural subject and requires a plural verb.

Examples:

plural subject / plural verb
You and Jon are invited to come to my house.

plural subject / plural verb
The pencil and paper belong to me.

JOINED BY OR/NOR

For a compound subject joined by *or* or *nor*, the verb must agree in number with the part of the subject that is closest to the verb.

Examples:

subject / verb
Today or tomorrow is the day.

subject / verb
Stan or Phil wants to read the book.

subject / verb
Neither the pen nor the book is on the desk.

subject / verb
Either the blanket or pillows arrive this afternoon.

INDEFINITE PRONOUNS AS SUBJECT

An indefinite pronoun is a pronoun that does not refer to a specific noun. Different indefinite pronouns are used as a singular noun, a plural noun, or change depending on how they are used.

ALWAYS SINGULAR

Pronouns such as *each*, *either*, *everybody*, *anybody*, *somebody*, and *nobody* are always singular. This is because these pronouns always stand in for one person, place, or thing.

Examples:

singular subject / singular verb
Each of the runners has a different bib number.

singular verb / singular subject
Is either of you ready for the game?

23

Note: The words *each* and *either* can also be used as adjectives. For example, *each* person is unique. When one of these adjectives modifies the subject of a sentence, it is always a singular subject.

singular
subject   singular
              verb
Everybody grows a day older every day.

singular   singular
subject   verb
Anybody   is   welcome to bring a tent.

ALWAYS PLURAL

Pronouns such as *both*, *several*, and *many* are always plural. This is because these pronouns always stand in for more than one person, place, thing, or idea.

Examples:

plural
subject   plural
                           verb
Both of the siblings were too tired to argue.

plural   plural
subject   verb
Many have tried, but none have succeeded.

DEPEND ON CONTEXT

Pronouns such as *some*, *any*, *all*, *none*, *more*, and *most* can be either singular or plural depending on what they are representing in the context of the sentence.

Examples:

singular
subject   singular
                           verb
All of my dog's food   was   still there in his bowl.

plural
subject   plural
                       verb
By the end of the night, all of my guests were already excited about coming to my next party.

OTHER CASES INVOLVING PLURAL OR IRREGULAR FORM

Some nouns are **singular in meaning but plural in form**: news, mathematics, physics, and economics.

The *news is* coming on now.

Mathematics is my favorite class.

Some nouns are plural in form and meaning, and have **no singular equivalent**: scissors and pants.

Do these *pants come* with a shirt?

The *scissors are* for my project.

Note: Look to your **dictionary** for help when you aren't sure whether a noun with a plural form has a singular or plural meaning.

EXAMPLE

Which word should go in the blank?

If Kelly if going to the party, Joan and Susan _____ going to the store.

a. Is
b. Are
c. Am
d. Was

Try using each choice in the sentence. Choice A, *is*, forms this sentence: If Kelly is going to the party, Joan and Susan is going to the store. There are two people, Joan and Susan, who are going to the store. This makes the subject of the clause plural. *Is* is a singular verb, meaning it does not agree with the subject and cannot be the answer.

Choice B, *are*, forms this sentence: If Kelly is going to the party, Joan and Susan are going to the store. The subject of the clause is still plural. But *are* is a plural verb! The subject and verb agree, so *are* is the correct answer.

Choice C, *am*, forms this sentence: If Kelly is going to the party, Joan and Susan am going to the store. *Am* is a singular verb, and it is also only used in first person, when the writer or speaker is referring to themself. The subject of the clause is plural, and the sentence is in third person, so *am* is not the correct answer.

Choice D, *was*, forms this sentence: If Kelly is going to the party, Joan and Susan was going to the store. *Was* is a singular verb, so it does not agree with the plural subject in this clause.

COMPLEMENTS

A complement is a noun, pronoun, or adjective that is used to give more information about the subject or verb in the sentence.

DIRECT OBJECTS

A direct object is a noun or pronoun that takes or receives the **action** of a verb. A complete sentence does not need a direct object, so not all sentences will have them. When you are looking for a direct object, find the verb and ask *who* or *what*.

Examples:

I took *the blanket*.

Jane read *books*.

INDIRECT OBJECTS

An indirect object is a word or group of words that show how an action had an **influence** on someone or something. If there is an indirect object in a sentence, then you always have a direct object in the sentence. When you are looking for the indirect object, find the verb and ask *to, for, whom,* or *what*.

Examples:

```
              indirect        direct
              object          object
We taught the old dog a new trick.
```

```
             indirect      direct
             object        object
I gave them a math lesson.
```

PRONOUN-ANTECEDENT AGREEMENT

The **antecedent** is the noun that has been replaced by a pronoun. A pronoun and its antecedent **agree** when they have the same number (singular or plural) and gender (male, female, or neutral).

Examples:

```
                  antecedent                pronoun
Singular agreement: John came into town, and he played for us.
```

```
                  antecedent                pronoun
Plural agreement: John and Rick came into town, and they played for us.
```

To determine which is the correct pronoun to use in a compound subject or object, try each pronoun **alone** in place of the compound in the sentence. Your knowledge of pronouns will tell you which one is correct.

Example:

Bob and (I, me) will be going.

Test: (1) *I will be going* or (2) *Me will be going.* The second choice cannot be correct because *me* cannot be used as the subject of a sentence. Instead, *me* is used as an object.

Answer: Bob and I will be going.

When a pronoun is used with a noun immediately following (as in "we boys"), try the sentence **without the added noun**.

Example:

(We/Us) boys played football last year.

Test: (1) *We played football last year* or (2) *Us played football last year.* Again, the second choice cannot be correct because *us* cannot be used as a subject of a sentence. Instead, *us* is used as an object.

Answer: We boys played football last year.

Writing Sample

A pronoun should point clearly to the **antecedent**. Here is how a pronoun reference can be unhelpful if it is puzzling or not directly stated.

Unhelpful: Ron and Jim went to the store, and he bought soda.

Who bought soda? Ron or Jim?

Helpful: Jim went to the store, and he bought soda.

The sentence is clear. Jim bought the soda.

EXAMPLE

Tom printed his ticket to the concert, but he forgot ____ at home.

Which pronoun should go in the blank?

a. It
b. Them
c. Him
d. He

What is the antecedent that the missing pronoun must match? There are only four nouns in the sentence. They are *Tom*, *ticket*, *concert*, and *home*. Which one should the missing pronoun refer to? Tom is the one who forgot something, so the pronoun does not refer to Tom. The concert is not at Tom's home, so he cannot forget the concert at home. It is also not logical to say that Tom forgot his home at home The antecedent must be *ticket*.

Choice A says that the missing pronoun is *it*. The pronoun refers to *ticket*, which is a singular noun. A ticket is also a nonliving thing. The missing pronoun is also the object in the second clause. *It* is singular, refers to nonliving nouns, and can be used as the object. Choice A is correct.

Choice B says that the missing pronoun is *them*. The pronoun refers to the singular noun *ticket*. While *them* can be used to refer to nonliving nouns and can be the object of a sentence, it is a plural pronoun. Choice B is incorrect.

Choice C says that the missing pronoun is *him*. The missing pronoun refers to a nonliving thing, not a human or animal. *Him* is an objective personal pronoun and is singular, but it only refers to living nouns. *Him* cannot represent *ticket*, so choice C is incorrect.

Choice D says that the missing pronoun is *he*. The missing pronoun refers to a nonliving noun and is the object of the second sentence. While *he* is a singular pronoun, it can only be used as the subject of a sentence and only refers to living nouns. Choice D is incorrect.

PHRASES

A phrase is a group of words that functions as a single part of speech, usually a noun, adjective, or adverb. A **phrase** is not a complete thought, and does not contain a subject, but it adds detail or explanation to a sentence, or renames something within the sentence.

CLAUSES

A clause is a group of words that contains both a subject and a predicate (verb). There are two types of clauses: independent and dependent. An **independent clause** contains a complete thought, while a **dependent (or subordinate) clause** does not. A dependent clause includes a subject and a verb, and may also contain additional information, but it cannot stand as a complete thought without being joined to an independent clause. Dependent clauses function within sentences as adjectives, adverbs, or nouns.

Example:

```
    independent                dependent
      clause                     clause
```
I am running because I want to stay in shape.

The clause *I am running* is an independent clause: it has a subject and a verb, and it gives a complete thought. The clause *because I want to stay in shape* is a dependent clause: it has a subject and a verb, but it does not express a complete thought. This is due to the fact that it begins with *because*, which shows that there is more information needed to complete the thought. This dependent clause adds detail to the independent clause to which it is attached.

> **Review Video: Independent and Dependent Clauses**
> Visit mometrix.com/academy and enter code: 556903

SENTENCE STRUCTURE

Sentence structure is based on the type and number of clauses in the sentence. Two common sentence structures are simple sentences and compound sentences:

SIMPLE

A simple sentence has one independent clause with no dependent clauses. A simple sentence may have a **compound subject** or a **compound verb**, or both.

Examples:

```
single     single
subject     verb
```
Judy watered the lawn.

```
compound         single
 subject          verb
```
Judy and Alan watered the lawn.

```
single   compound                   compound
subject    verb                       verb
```
Judy watered the lawn and pulled weeds.

```
compound        compound            compound
 subject          verb                verb
```
Judy and Alan watered the lawn and pulled weeds.

COMPOUND

A compound sentence has two or more independent clauses with no dependent clauses. Usually, the independent clauses are joined with a comma and a coordinating conjunction or with a semicolon.

Examples:

```
  independent            independent
    clause                 clause
```
The time has come, and we are ready.

```
  independent            independent
    clause                 clause
```
I woke up at dawn ; the sun was just coming up.

Writing Sample

COMPLEX

A complex sentence has one independent clause and at least one dependent clause.

Examples:

dependent clause	independent clause
Although he had the flu,	Harry went to work.

independent clause	dependent clause
Marcia got married	after she finished college.

> **Review Video: Sentence Structure**
> Visit mometrix.com/academy and enter code: 700478

SENTENCE FRAGMENTS

Recall that a group of words must contain at least one **independent clause** in order to be considered a sentence. If it doesn't contain even one independent clause, it is called a **sentence fragment**.

Choosing the best steps for **repairing** a sentence fragment depends on what type of fragment it is. If the fragment is a dependent clause, it can sometimes be fixed by simply removing a subordinating word, such as *when*, *because*, or *if*, from the beginning of the fragment. Alternatively, a dependent clause can be joined to a closely related neighboring sentence. If the fragment is missing some required part, like a subject or a verb, it may be fixed by simply adding the missing part.

Examples:

Fragment: Because he wanted to sail the Mediterranean.

Removed subordinating word: He wanted to sail the Mediterranean.

Combined with another sentence: Because he wanted to sail the Mediterranean, he booked a Greek island cruise.

EXAMPLE

Which of the following changes will NOT correct this sentence fragment?

Although she had found the coin first.

a. Remove *Although*.
b. Add a comma and *she let her brother keep it* after *first*.
c. Add *She let her brother keep the coin* before *although*.
d. Remove *first*.

Choice A suggests removing the word *although* to form the following sentence: She found the coin first. This option removes the subordinating conjunction to make the clause independent. The resulting sentence is complete, so removing *although* is an acceptable way to correct the fragment. Choice A is incorrect.

Choice B forms the following sentence: Although she had found the coin first, she let her brother keep it. A comma and an independent clause have been added to the sentence fragment to form a complex sentence. The resulting sentence is complete and written correctly, so choice B is incorrect.

Choice C forms the following sentence: She let her brother keep the coin although she had found the coin first. An independent clause has been added before the sentence fragment to form a complex sentence. This

29

sentence is correctly written and complete, so choice C is an acceptable way to correct the fragment. Choice C is incorrect.

Choice D removes the word *first*, leaving *Although she had found the coin*. This is still a sentence fragment, since it is a single dependent clause. Choice D does not correct the fragment, so D is correct.

RUN-ON SENTENCES

Run-on sentences consist of multiple independent clauses that have not been joined together properly. Run-on sentences can be corrected in several different ways:

Join clauses properly: This can be done with a comma and coordinating conjunction, with a semicolon, or with a colon or dash if the second clause is explaining something in the first clause.

Example:

> **Incorrect**: I went on the trip, we visited lots of castles.

> **Corrected**: I went on the trip, and we visited lots of castles.

Split into separate sentences: This correction is best to use when the independent clauses are very long or when they are not closely related.

Example:

> **Incorrect**: The drive to New York takes ten hours, my uncle lives in Boston.

> **Corrected**: The drive to New York takes ten hours. My uncle lives in Boston.

Make one clause dependent: This is the easiest way to make the sentence correct and more interesting at the same time. It's often as simple as adding a subordinating word between the two clauses or before the first clause.

Example:

> **Incorrect**: I finally made it to the store and I bought some eggs.

> **Corrected**: When I finally made it to the store, I bought some eggs.

Reduce to one clause with a compound verb: If both clauses have the same subject, remove the subject from the second clause, and you now have just one clause with a compound verb.

Example:

> **Incorrect**: The drive to New York takes ten hours, it makes me very tired.

> **Corrected**: The drive to New York takes ten hours and makes me very tired.

Note: While these are the simplest ways to correct a run-on sentence, often the best way is to completely reorganize the thoughts in the sentence and rewrite it.

COMMA SPLICES

A comma splice is a specific error that may appear in a run-on sentence. When a sentence has two independent clauses, but the clauses are joined with only a comma, a **comma splice** is formed. Remember that if two

Writing Sample

independent clauses are joined with a comma, a coordinating conjunction is also needed. Most of the solutions for fixing run-on sentences can also be used to correct a comma splice.

> **Review Video: Fragments and Run-on Sentences**
> Visit mometrix.com/academy and enter code: 541989

EXAMPLE

Rick wants to go see a movie tomorrow he would miss his sister's recital.

Identify the change that would NOT correct this run-on sentence.
a. Add a comma after *tomorrow*.
b. Split it into two sentences between *tomorrow* and *he*.
c. Add a comma and *but* after *tomorrow*.
d. Add a subordinating conjunction to make one of the clauses dependent.

Choice A says to add a comma after *tomorrow*. This forms the following sentence: Rick wants to go see a movie tomorrow, he would miss his sister's recital. A comma has been used to join two independent clauses, but there is no coordinating conjunction. This choice forms a comma splice, so it is not an acceptable correction for this sentence. Choice A is the correct answer.

Choice B says to split the sentence into two sentences. This forms the following two sentences: Rick wants to go see a movie tomorrow. He would miss his sister's recital. Both of these sentences are complete. This is an acceptable way to correct the run-on sentence, so choice B is incorrect.

Choice C says to add a coordinating conjunction after *tomorrow*. This forms the following sentence: Rick wants to go see a movie tomorrow, but he would miss his sister's recital. A comma and a coordinating conjunction have been added between the two independent clauses. This is an acceptable way to correct a run-on sentence. Choice C is incorrect.

Choice D says to add a subordinating conjunction to make one of the sentences dependent. There are many new sentences that could be created by adding a subordinating conjunction. For example, consider the following sentence: Although Rick wants to go see a movie tomorrow, he would miss his sister's recital. Alternatively, the following sentence could also be created: Rick wants to go see a movie tomorrow even though he would miss his sister's recital. Both of these sentences have an independent clause and a dependent clause. These sentences are both complete and written correctly, so choice D is incorrect.

EXAMPLE

Identify the sentence that has a comma splice.
a. Tom stopped at the store to buy supplies and his family met him at the campsite.
b. The ball rolled into the living room quietly, but it still startled the dog.
c. Theresa brought her mom some flowers, her mom did not have a vase.
d. Sweet potatoes, pecans, and brown sugar are all ingredients in my cousin's sweet potato casserole.

Choice A has two independent clauses joined by a coordinating conjunction. This is incorrect because there should be a comma before the coordinating conjunction. While the sentence is written incorrectly, there is no comma, so this sentence does not have a comma splice. Choice A is incorrect.

Choice B has two independent clauses joined by a comma and a coordinating conjunction. This is the correct way to write a compound sentence, so there is no error here. Choice B is incorrect.

Choice C has two independent clauses joined by a comma. This is incorrect because independent clauses should be joined together by a comma and a coordinating conjunction. When the comma is present without a coordinating conjunction between two independent clauses, a comma splice is formed. This means that choice C is correct.

Choice D is a simple sentence that contains one independent clause. The only commas used in this sentence are used to separate items in a list. There are no clauses that need to be joined or errors related to commas, so choice D does not contain a comma splice. Choice D is incorrect.

PARTS OF SPEECH
NOUNS
When you talk about a person, place, thing, or idea, you are talking about a **noun**. The two main types of nouns are **common** and **proper** nouns.

COMMON NOUNS
Common nouns are generic names for people, places, and things. Common nouns are not usually capitalized.

Examples of common nouns:

People: boy, girl, worker, manager

Places: school, bank, library, home

Things: dog, cat, truck, car

PROPER NOUNS
Proper nouns name specific people, places, or things. All proper nouns are capitalized.

Examples of proper nouns:

People: Abraham Lincoln, George Washington, Martin Luther King, Jr.

Places: Los Angeles, California; New York; Asia

Things: Statue of Liberty, Earth, Lincoln Memorial

Note: When referring to the planet that we live on, capitalize *Earth*. When referring to the dirt, rocks, or land, lowercase *earth*.

SINGULAR AND PLURAL NOUNS
Singular nouns name **one** person, place, thing, or idea. **Plural nouns** name **more than one** person, place, thing, or idea. Most nouns have both a singular and plural form. Many plural nouns are spelled like the singular noun with an -s at the end, but this is not true for all plural nouns. Singular nouns that already end in an *s, o, ch, sh*, or *x* usually end in -es when they are in the plural form. Singular nouns that end in a consonant followed by the letter *y* will usually lose the *y* and end in -ies in the plural form, and words that end with the letter *f* or *fe* will usually lose the *f* and end in -ves.

Some plural nouns have much different spellings than their singular form, and some plural nouns are spelled the same as their singular form. There are more rules for spelling plural nouns, but these are the most common spelling changes.

Examples of singular nouns:

Typical nouns: dog, pencil, girl, store, hope, stingray

Nouns ending in *s, o, ch, sh*, or *x*: mass, hero, lunch, polish, fox

32

Writing Sample

Nouns ending in a consonant and *y*: puppy, baby, fairy, sky

Nouns ending in *f* or *fe*: self, life, calf, hoof

Examples of plural nouns:

Typical nouns: dogs, pencils, girls, stores, hopes, stingrays

Nouns ending in *s*, *o*, *ch*, *sh*, or *x*: masses, heroes, lunches, polishes, foxes

Nouns ending in a consonant and *y*: puppies, babies, fairies, skies

Nouns ending in a vowel and *f* or *fe*: selves, lives, calves, hooves

COLLECTIVE NOUNS

Collective nouns are the names for a group of people, places, or things that function like singular nouns. The following are examples of collective nouns: *class, company, dozen, group, herd, team,* and *public.* Collective nouns usually require an article, such as *a, an,* and *the,* which shows that the noun is a single unit. For example, a choir is a group of singers. Even though there are many singers in a choir, the word choir describes a single group. If we refer to the members of the group, and not the group itself, it is no longer a collective noun.

Incorrect: The *choir are* going to compete nationally this year.

Correct: The *choir is* going to compete nationally this year.

Incorrect: The *members* of the choir *is* competing nationally this year.

Correct: The *members* of the choir *are* competing nationally this year.

PRONOUNS

Pronouns are words that are used to stand in for nouns. There are several different types of pronouns, but the two main types are subjective and objective pronouns. **Subjective** nouns and pronouns that those that are the subject of a sentence. **Objective** nouns and pronouns are those that are an object in a sentence. Another important type of pronoun is the personal pronoun, which refers to people. Personal pronouns can be subjective or objective. **Possessive** nouns and pronouns show possession or ownership. Pronouns can also be singular or plural.

Singular

Subjective	Objective	Possessive
I	Me	My, Mine
You	You	Your, Yours
He	Him	His
She	Her	Her, hers
It	It	Its
Who	Whom	Whose

Plural

Subjective	Objective	Possessive
we	us	our, ours
you	you	your, yours
they	them	their, theirs

33

Reflexive: Reflexive pronouns are pronouns that function as the object of a sentence and refer to the subject. Examples of reflexive pronouns include *myself, yourself, himself, herself, itself, ourselves, yourselves,* and *themselves.*

Indefinite: Indefinite pronouns are used to refer to multiple nouns or an undefined noun. Examples of indefinite nouns include *all, any, each, everyone, either/neither, one, some,* and *several.*

> **Relative**: Relative pronouns are used to connect relative clauses that specify or describe a noun to the rest of the sentence. Examples of relative pronouns include *which, who, whom,* and *whose.*

> **Review Video: <u>Nouns and Pronouns</u>**
> Visit mometrix.com/academy and enter code: 312073

VERBS

If you want to write a sentence, then you need a verb. Without a verb, you have no sentence. The verb of a sentence indicates action or being. In other words, the verb shows something's action or state of being or the action that has been done to something.

ACTION VERBS AND LINKING VERBS

Action verbs show what the subject is doing. In other words, an action verb shows action. **Linking verbs** link the subject of a sentence to a noun or pronoun. They can also link a subject to an adjective, so the linking verb helps create a description. You always need a verb if you want a complete sentence. However, linking verbs on their own cannot be a complete sentence. Any verb that shows a condition and connects to a noun, pronoun, or adjective that describes the subject of a sentence is a linking verb.

Action: He sings. | Run! | Go! | I talk with him every day. | She reads.

Linking:

> Incorrect: I am.

> Correct: I am John. | The roses smell lovely. | I feel tired.

> **Review Video: <u>Action Verbs and Linking Verbs</u>**
> Visit mometrix.com/academy and enter code: 743142

VERB TENSES

A verb **tense** shows the different form of a verb to point to the time of an action. The present and past tense are indicated by the verb's form. An action in the present, *I talk,* can change form for the past: *I talked.* However, for future tense, an auxiliary, or helping, verb is sometimes needed to show the change in form. When writing a composition, it is important to use verb tenses consistently. Choose the best tense for the composition and do not switch to a different tense unless it is necessary or appropriate for a particular sentence or paragraph.

> Present: I talk
> Past: I talked
> Future: I will talk

Present: The action happens at the current time.

> Example: He *walks* to the store every morning.

Past: The action happened in the past.

Example: He *walked* to the store an hour ago.

Future: The action is going to happen later.

Example: I *will walk* to the store tomorrow.

Review Video: <u>Verb Tenses</u>
Visit mometrix.com/academy and enter code: 269472

IRREGULAR VERBS

While most verbs gain the suffix -ed when used in the past tense, irregular verbs receive different spelling changes when they are written in the past tense. For example, *walk* is a regular verb, and it becomes *walked* when written in the past tense. However, *run* is an irregular verb because it becomes *ran* when written in the past tense.

EXAMPLE

My mother _____ me about the big nest of ants near the sandbox. I thanked her for telling me!

Which of the following verbs should go in the blank?
a. Warn
b. Warned
c. Will warn
d. Warns

First, look at the sentences. The first sentence does not have enough information to show which tense it is in. However, the second sentence says that the child thanked the mother. The verb here is *thanked*, which is the past-tense form of *thank*. Because the second sentence is in the past tense, it makes sense to say that the first sentence is also in past tense.

Choice A says that the missing verb is *warn*. *Warn* is a present-tense verb, but it can be used in the future tense if a helping verb is present. However, this sentence is in past tense, so it needs a past-tense verb. Choice A is wrong.

Choice B says that the missing verb is *warned*. *Warned* is a past-tense verb, and it logically completes the sentence. Choice B is correct!

Choice C says that the missing verb is *will warn*. *Will warn* is a future-tense verb, meaning that it describes an action that will occur in the future. However, since the speaker already thanked his or her mother for the warning, it is not logical to use a future-tense verb in the blank. Choice C is incorrect.

Choice D says that the missing verb is *warns*. *Warn* is usually used with plural subjects, and *warns* used with single subjects. *Warns* can be used in the future or present tense, but it cannot be used in the past tense. Since the sentence is in the past tense, it needs a past-tense verb, so D is incorrect.

ADJECTIVES

An **adjective** is a word that is used to modify a noun or pronoun. An adjective answers a question: *Which one? What kind?* or *How many?* Usually, adjectives come before the words that they modify, but they may also come after a linking verb.

Which one? The *third* suit is my favorite.

What kind? This suit is *navy blue.*

How many? I am going to buy *four* pairs of socks to match the suit.

> **Review Video: <u>Descriptive Text</u>**
> Visit mometrix.com/academy and enter code: 174903

COMPARISON WITH ADJECTIVES

Some adjectives are relative, and other adjectives are absolute. Adjectives that are **relative** can show the comparison between things. **Absolute** adjectives can also show comparison, but they do so in a different way. Let's say that you are reading two books. You think that one book is perfect, and the other book is not exactly perfect. It is not possible for one book to be more perfect than the other. Either you think that the book is perfect, or you think that the book is imperfect. In this case, perfect and imperfect are absolute adjectives.

Relative adjectives will show the different **degrees** of something or someone to something else or someone else. The three degrees of adjectives include positive, comparative, and superlative.

The **positive** degree is the normal form of an adjective.

Example: This work is *difficult.* | She is *smart.*

The **comparative** degree compares one person or thing to another person or thing.

Example: This work is *more difficult* than your work. | She is *smarter* than me.

The **superlative** degree compares more than two people or things.

Example: This is the *most difficult* work of my life. | She is the *smartest* lady in school.

> **Review Video: <u>Adjectives</u>**
> Visit mometrix.com/academy and enter code: 470154

ADVERBS

An **adverb** is a word that is used to **modify,** or describe, a verb, adjective, or another adverb. Usually, adverbs answer one of these questions: *When? Where? How?* and *Why?* The negatives *not* and *never* are considered adverbs. Adverbs that modify adjectives or other adverbs **strengthen** or **weaken** the words that they modify.

Examples:

He walks *quickly* through the crowd.

The water flows *smoothly* on the rocks.

Note: Adverbs are usually indicated by the suffix *-ly*, which has been added to the root word. For instance, *quick* can be made into an adverb by adding *-ly* to construct *quickly*. Some words that end in *-ly* do not follow this rule and can function as other parts of speech. Examples of adjectives ending in *-ly* include: *early, friendly,*

Writing Sample

holy, *lonely*, *silly*, and *ugly*. To know if a word that ends in *-ly* is an adjective or adverb, check your dictionary. Also, while many adverbs end in *-ly*, you need to remember that not all adverbs end in *-ly*.

Examples:

He is *never* angry.

You are *too* irresponsible to travel alone.

TYPES OF ADVERBS

Different types of adverbs are used to describe particular aspects of a verb, adjective, or other adverb. The following are examples of common types of adverbs:

Time: Some adverbs show when something was done, such as *yesterday*, *today*, or *in two days*.

Manner: Some adverbs show the way something was done, such as *hurriedly*, *neatly*, *grumpily*, or *loudly*.

Frequency: Some adverbs show how often something was done, such as *seldom*, *often*, *never*, or *often*.

Degree: Some adverbs show how much or to what degree something was done, such as *completely*, *barely*, *highly*, or *halfway*.

Conjunctive: Conjunctive adverbs are used similarly to conjunctions, as they connect different ideas, but they can connect ideas from different clauses or sentences. Some examples of conjunctive adverbs are *however*, *alternatively*, *likewise*, and *then*.

COMPARISON WITH ADVERBS

The rules for comparing adverbs are the same as the rules for adjectives.

The **positive** degree is the standard form of an adverb.

Example: He arrives *soon*. | She speaks *softly* to her friends.

The **comparative** degree compares one person or thing to another person or thing.

Example: He arrives *sooner* than Sarah. | She speaks *more softly* than him.

The **superlative** degree compares more than two people or things.

Example: He arrives *soonest* of the group. | She speaks the *most softly* of any of her friends.

Review Video: Adverbs
Visit mometrix.com/academy and enter code: 713951

EXAMPLE

Identify the conjunctive adverb in the following sentences.

Every night, Savannah's brother loudly gets up to get a glass of water. Consequently, she has started sleeping with earmuffs on so that he does not wake her up at night.

a. Every night
b. Loudly
c. Consequently
d. At night

Choice A says that *every night* is a conjunctive adverb. What does *every night* describe in this sentence? It describes how often Savannah's brother loudly gets a glass of water. This means that *every night* shows the frequency that Savannah's brother does this action. Since *every night* is an adverb that shows frequency, choice A is incorrect.

Choice B says that *loudly* is a conjunctive adverb. In this sentence, what does *loudly* describe? It describes the way that Savannah's brother gets a glass of water each night. This means that *loudly* is an adverb that shows manner. *Loudly* is not a conjunctive adverb, so choice B is incorrect.

Choice C says that *consequently* is a conjunctive adverb. What function does *consequently* have in this sentence? It shows the reason that Savannah started wearing earmuffs while she sleeps. It also shows a connection between the information in the first sentence and the information in the second sentence. Since *consequently* connects the ideas in these sentences, it is a conjunctive adverb. Choice C is correct.

Choice D says that *at night* is a conjunctive adverb. *At* and *night* work together to form an adverbial phrase. Which type of adverb do they form? In this sentence, *at night* shows when Savannah wants to avoid being woken up by her brother. This makes *at night* an adverb that shows time, meaning that *at night* is not a conjunctive adverb and choice D is incorrect.

PREPOSITIONS

A **preposition** is a word placed before a noun or pronoun that shows the relationship between an object and another word in the sentence.

Common prepositions:

about	before	during	on	under
after	beneath	for	over	until
against	between	from	past	up
among	beyond	in	through	with
around	by	of	to	within
at	down	off	toward	without

Examples:

The napkin is *in* the drawer.

The Earth rotates *around* the Sun.

The needle is *beneath* the haystack.

Can you find "me" *among* the words?

PREPOSITIONAL PHRASES

One important thing to know about prepositions is that they form special phrases, called prepositional phrases. A **prepositional phrase** begins with a preposition and ends with a noun or pronoun that is the object of the preposition. Normally, the prepositional phrase functions as an **adjective** or an **adverb** within the sentence.

Examples:

prepositional
phrase
The picnic is on the blanket.

prepositional
phrase
I am sick with a fever today.

prepositional
phrase
Among the many flowers, John found a four-leaf clover.

Be careful not to mistake the object in a prepositional phrase as the subject of a sentence. The subject of the sentence will not be found in a prepositional phrase because a prepositional phrase is used to describe how an object is related to the subject. Prepositional phrases do not influence subject-verb agreement.

Prepositional phrases do not influence subject-verb agreement. For example, consider the following sentence:

simple   prepositional
subject   phrase   verb
The basket of clothes is   on the floor in the laundry room.

This sentence contains a prepositional phrase between the simple subject and the verb. The simple subject is *basket*, which is a singular noun, and the verb is *is*, which is a singular verb. They are separated by the prepositional phrase "of clothes." Even though the plural noun *clothes* comes right before the singular verb *is*, this verb shows the action of the singular noun *basket*.

Review Video: Prepositions
Visit mometrix.com/academy and enter code: 946763

EXAMPLE
Which of the following could NOT complete the sentence?

She went ____ the cave.
a. Sadly
b. Into
c. From
d. Through

Choice A says that the missing word is *sadly*. The blank is between *went* and *the cave*, meaning that the missing word will connect these pieces of the sentence. While *sadly* could be used here to show how the girl felt, there would still be missing information. A preposition is needed here to show whether she entered, exited, or stood outside of the cave. *Sadly* is an adverb, so A is the correct answer.

Choice B says that *into* would complete the sentence. Does *into* complete the sentence without leaving missing information? To say *she went into the cave* is a logical, complete sentence. Choice B is incorrect.

Choice C says that the missing word is *from*. This creates the sentence *she went from the cave*. Since she could have left the cave to go somewhere else, this is also a logical, complete sentence. Choice C is incorrect.

Choice D says that *through* would complete the sentence. The sentence would read *she went through the cave*. Since she could have explored the whole cave or found an exit on the other side of it, *through* can logically complete the sentence. Choice D is incorrect.

<u>EXAMPLE</u>

Identify the prepositional phrase in the following sentence.

Mable visited the store to buy some vegetables.

a. To buy
b. Visited the store
c. The store to buy
d. To buy some vegetables

Remember the pieces of a prepositional phrase. Prepositional phrases should begin with a preposition and end with a noun or pronoun. Considering these rules, can any of the answer choices be eliminated? Choice B and choice C can be eliminated because neither choice begins with a preposition!

That leaves choices A and D. Choice A says that the prepositional phrase is *to buy*. This does start with a preposition, and it does give more information about Mable's trip to the store. However, it does not end with a noun or pronoun. Choice D says that the prepositional phrase is *to buy some vegetables*. Choice D begins with a preposition and ends with a noun, and it explains why Mabel went to the store.

Choice D is the only choice that has all of the pieces of a prepositional phrase, so D is correct!

<u>EXAMPLE</u>

Read the sentence below and answer the following question.

A band with 15 members _____ performing at my restaurant tonight.

Identify the verb that best completes the sentence.

a. Were
b. Is
c. Are
d. Are not

This question is asking which verb should go in the blank. There are a couple of reasons why choosing the correct verb for this sentence may be confusing. First of all, there are two nouns that appear before the verb. Second, one of these nouns is singular and one is plural.

The first step is to determine which noun goes with the verb. The two nouns are *band* and *members*. While *members* is closest to the blank, it is part of a prepositional phrase that describes *band*. The subject of the sentence is *band*, so the verb must agree with *band*.

Is *band* singular or plural? The sentence says that the band has multiple members, but there is only one band. *Band* is a collective noun, meaning that it is a singular noun. This means that the correct verb will also be singular. With this in mind, can any of the answer choices be eliminated?

Choices A, C, and D are all plural verbs. Even though the blank appears after a plural noun, this noun is part of a prepositional phrase. The verb should match the singular subject *band*. The only choice with a singular verb is choice B, so B is the correct answer.

CONJUNCTIONS

Conjunctions join words, phrases, or clauses and they show the connection between the joined pieces. **Coordinating conjunctions** connect equal parts of sentences. Coordinating conjunctions can also be used to create compound subjects and compound predicates, in addition to compound sentences.

Writing Sample

COORDINATING CONJUNCTIONS

The **coordinating conjunctions** include: *and, but, yet, or, nor, for,* and *so*

Compound Subjects:

compound subject
Terry *and* Marissa went to the movies last Saturday.

compund subject
Either pumpkin pie *or* apple pie would be a good dessert to bring to Thanksgiving dinner.

compound subject
Neither the clownfish *nor* the goldfish liked the new fish food very much.

Compound Predicates:

compound predicate
Veronica left school *and* picked up her sister from soccer practice.

compound predicate
The cat did not take a nap *or* play with the dog yesterday.

Compound Sentences:

The rock was small, *but* it was heavy.

She drove in the night, *and* he drove in the day.

Bill dressed nicely today, *for* he must give an important presentation this afternoon.

CORRELATIVE CONJUNCTIONS

Some examples of **correlative conjunctions** are: *either...or* | *neither...nor* | *not only...but also*. When one correlative conjunction is used, its matching correlative conjunction will be used later in the sentence.

Examples:

Either you are coming *or* you are staying.

He *not only* ran three miles *but also* swam 200 yards.

> **Review Video: Coordinating and Correlative Conjunctions**
> Visit mometrix.com/academy and enter code: 390329

SUBORDINATING CONJUNCTIONS

Subordinating conjunctions link dependent clauses, clauses with either a subject or a predicate, to independent clauses, clauses with both a subject and a predicate, to form a complex sentence. The subordinating conjunction will always be at the beginning of the dependent clause. When the dependent clause is at the beginning of the sentence, it will end with a comma. When the independent clause is at the beginning of the sentence, no comma is needed.

Common **subordinating conjunctions** include:

after	since	whenever
although	so that	where
because	unless	wherever
before	until	whether
in order that	when	while

Examples:

I am hungry *because* I did not eat breakfast.

He went home *when* everyone left.

While her brother ate dinner, she played his favorite video game.

┌───┐
│ **Review Video: Subordinating Conjunctions**   │
│ Visit mometrix.com/academy and enter code: 958913   │
└───┘

EXAMPLE

Which of the following is a complex sentence?
   a. Joseph went grocery shopping and put all of the groceries away at home.
   b. Joseph went grocery shopping, and he put all of the groceries away at home.
   c. Joseph went grocery shopping and put all of the groceries away when he got home.
   d. Joseph went grocery shopping; he put all of the groceries away at home.

Choice A contains one subject and a compound predicate. Because there is only one subject, Joseph, there is only one clause. Since the sentence is made of one independent clause and a prepositional phrase, it is a simple sentence, and choice A is incorrect.

Choice B contains two clauses. The clauses are separated by a comma and a coordinating conjunction, and both are independent clauses. This sentence contains a prepositional phrase and two independent clauses, so it is a compound sentence. Choice B is incorrect.

Choice C contains two clauses. There are two subjects in the sentence, *Joseph* and *he*. Even though one clause is much shorter than the other, these subjects each go with a different clause. The first clause is independent. The second clause is dependent, as it begins with the word *when*. Since the sentence is made of one independent clause and one dependent clause, it is a complex sentence. Choice C is correct.

Choice D contains two clauses. They are both independent clauses, because they both contain a subject and a predicate, and they both form complete thoughts. Since there is no coordinating conjunction, they are linked by a semicolon. Since the sentence is made from two independent clauses, it is a compound sentence. Choice D is incorrect.

EXAMPLE

Identify the sentence that contains correlative conjunctions.
   a. She can wait for her friend's letter to arrive, or she can call her now.
   b. He must leave now, or he will end up in heavy traffic when he gets on the highway.
   c. When your grandfather gets here, you can greet him with a handshake or a hug.
   d. I can't decide whether to go to my brother's concert or to study for my test tomorrow.

Read the answer choices carefully. Remember that correlative conjunctions appear in pairs, so there will be at least two conjunctions in the sentence. Additionally, these conjunctions will go together. The information given immediately after the first conjunction will make little sense without the information that comes after the second conjunction.

Choice A contains the conjunction *or*. Though *or* can be a correlative conjunction, in this sentence, it is used by itself to connect two independent clauses. This means it is a coordinating conjunction. There are no correlative conjunctions in this sentence, so choice A is incorrect.

Choice B contains the conjunctions *or* and *when*. Again, *or* can be a correlative conjunction. However, the sentence could end after *traffic*. The information beginning with *when* is not needed to complete the thought, and *or* and *when* do not form a pair of correlative conjunctions. Choice B is incorrect.

Choice C contains the conjunctions *when* and *or*. *When* is used to begin a dependent clause. *Or* is used to form a compound object by linking *handshake* and *hug*. These conjunctions do not work together in this sentence, so they are not correlative conjunctions. Choice C is incorrect.

Choice D contains the conjunctions *whether* and *or*. *Whether* is used to introduce one choice the speaker can make, and *or* is used to introduce an alternative choice. If the sentence ended before *or*, it would be an incomplete thought. The conjunctions *whether* and *or* go together in this sentence, and they are correlative conjunctions. Choice D is correct.

END PUNCTUATION
PERIODS

Use a period to end all sentences except direct questions and exclamations. Periods are also used for abbreviations.

Examples: 3 p.m. | 2 a.m. | Mr. Jones | Mrs. Stevens | Dr. Smith | Bill, Jr. | Pennsylvania Ave.

Note: An abbreviation is a shortened form of a word or phrase.

QUESTION MARKS

Question marks should be used following a **direct question**. A polite request can be followed by a period instead of a question mark.

Direct Question: What is for lunch today? | How are you? | Why is that the answer?

Polite Requests: Can you please send me the item tomorrow. | Will you please walk with me on the track.

> **Review Video: Question Marks**
> Visit mometrix.com/academy and enter code: 118471

EXCLAMATION MARKS

Exclamation marks are used after a word group or sentence that shows much feeling or has special importance. Exclamation marks should not be overused. They are saved for proper **exclamatory interjections**.

Example: We're going to the finals! | You have a beautiful car! | "That's crazy!" she yelled.

> **Review Video: Exclamation Points**
> Visit mometrix.com/academy and enter code: 199367

COMMAS

The comma is a punctuation mark that can help you understand connections in a sentence. Not every sentence needs a comma. However, if a sentence needs a comma, you need to put it in the right place. A comma in the wrong place or a missing comma will make a sentence's meaning unclear. These are some of the rules for commas:

Use Case	Example
Before a **coordinating conjunction** joining independent clauses in compound sentences	Bob caught three fish, and I caught two fish.
Between **items in a series**	I will bring the turkey, the pie, and the coffee.
After a **dependent clause** that **begins a complex sentence**	Before she left, Ashley turned off all of the lights in her house.
After **transition words**	Consequently, Joel's mother grounded him.
After an **introductory phrase**	After the final out, we went to a restaurant to celebrate.
After a **prepositional phrase** at the **beginning of a sentence**	At 10 in the evening, Georgia finally arrived home from work.
After an **adverbial clause**	Studying the stars, I was awed by the beauty of the sky.
Before and after **nonessential modifiers**	John Frank, who coaches the team, was promoted today.
Before and after **nonessential appositives**	Thomas Edison, an American inventor, was born in Ohio.
Before and after **nonrestrictive phrases** or **clauses**	His favorite movie, which premiered before he was born, is over three hours long.
After **absolute phrases**	Relieved the test was over, Leah dropped her pencil and slouched in her chair.

COMMAS FOR SETTING OFF NONESSENTIAL WORDS, PHRASES, AND CLAUSES

Identifying where to place commas for nonessential words, phrases, and clauses is sometimes tricky. If the word, phrase, or clause is necessary for the sentence to be complete or logical, then it is essential, or restrictive. Additionally, if the word, phrase, or clause cannot be removed without changing the meaning of the sentence, then it is essential. Nonessential words, phrases, and clauses are those that give unnecessary information or do not flow smoothly with the rest of the words in the sentence. These words usually can also be logically placed in more than one spot in the sentence. **Appositives** are often nonessential words or phrases. They are most often used to specify which person or thing is being discussed. An appositive is an additional name or description that may be essential or nonessential.

> **Review Video: <u>When To Use a Comma</u>**
> Visit mometrix.com/academy and enter code: 786797

EXAMPLE

Ella's favorite stuffed animal Rory used to be her mother's.

Which word in the sentence is nonessential and should be set off by commas?

   a. Be
   b. Stuffed
   c. Her
   d. Rory

Choice A says that *be* should be set off by commas. Since *be* is a verb, it is unlikely that it is a nonessential word. In this sentence, the subject is *stuffed animal*, and *be* is the verb that shows the subject's action. *Be* is essential to the sentence, so choice A is incorrect.

44

Choice B says that *stuffed* should be set off by commas. *Stuffed* is an adjective, so it may be nonessential. However, it affects the meaning of this sentence. The word *stuffed* shows that the sentence is about a toy, not a live animal. *Stuffed* is essential to the meaning of the sentence, so choice B is incorrect.

Choice C says that *her* should be set off by commas. *Her* is a personal pronoun, so it is unlikely that it is nonessential. This sentence uses the word *her* to identify whose mother previously owned the stuffed animal. *Her* is essential to show who is being discussed. Choice C is incorrect.

Choice D says that *Rory* should be set off by commas. *Rory* is a name, so it could be a nonessential word, or even an appositive. In this sentence, the word tells the reader the name of Ella's favorite stuffed animal. The sentence can only be about one stuffed animal, because Ella can only have one favorite. This means that the stuffed animal's name is extra, or nonessential, information. *Rory* is a nonessential appositive, so choice D is correct.

EXAMPLE

The singer growing more exhausted with every song decided to stop dancing and stood still while singing.

Identify the nonrestrictive phrase that should be set off by commas in the above sentence.
a. The singer growing more exhausted
b. Decided to stop dancing
c. Growing more exhausted with every song
d. Stop dancing and stood still

Choice A says that *the singer growing more exhausted* is the nonrestrictive phrase. Is the sentence still a complete sentence without this phrase? No, because choice A includes the subject, *the singer*. Choice A is not the nonrestrictive phrase.

Choice B says that *decided to stop dancing* is the nonrestrictive phrase. Does the sentence make sense without this phrase? No, removing this phrase leaves the following sentence: The singer growing more exhausted with every song and stood still while singing. This is not a logical sentence, so choice B is not the nonrestrictive phrase.

Choice C says that *growing more exhausted with every song* is the nonrestrictive phrase. Removing this phrase leaves the following sentence: The singer decided to stop dancing and stood still while singing. This sentence makes sense and has the same meaning as the original sentence. This phrase gives extra information that is not essential to the sentence, so choice C is the nonrestrictive phrase. Choice C is correct.

Choice D says that *stop dancing and stood still* is the nonrestrictive phrase. Removing this phrase leaves the following sentence: The singer growing more exhausted with every song decided to while singing. This sentence is now missing important information. What did the singer decide to do while singing? The remaining sentence is now missing the verb. Removing choice D makes the sentence incomplete, so choice D is not the nonrestrictive phrase.

EXAMPLE
Where should a comma be added in the following sentence?

Though the mountain is very steep he is not afraid to scale it.
a. After *Though*
b. After *mountain*
c. After *steep*
d. After *afraid*

45

Choice A says there should be a comma after *though*. In this sentence, *though* is a subordinating conjunction that begins a dependent clause. Remember that a comma goes at the end of a dependent clause that appears at the beginning of a sentence. *Though* is at the beginning of the clause, and there is no other need for a comma right after it. Choice A is incorrect.

Choice B says there should be a comma after *mountain*. *Mountain* is the subject of the dependent clause in this sentence. The comma should go at the end of the dependent clause. *Mountain* appears in the middle of the dependent clause, not at the end of it. Choice B is incorrect.

Choice C says there should be a comma after *steep*. *Steep* is the last word in the dependent clause that begins the sentence. Adding a comma here would correctly separate the dependent clause from the following independent clause. This is the correct place for the comma, so choice C is correct.

Choice D says there should be a comma after *afraid*. *Afraid* is the verb in the independent clause, and there is no need to separate it from the rest of the sentence. Choice D is incorrect.

SEMICOLONS

The semicolon is used to connect major sentence pieces of equal value. Some rules for semicolons include:

Use Case	Example
Between closely connected independent clauses **not connected with a coordinating conjunction**	You are right; we should go with your plan.
Between independent clauses **linked with a transitional word**	I think that we can agree on this; however, I am not sure about my friends.
Between items in a **series that has internal punctuation**	I have visited New York, New York; Augusta, Maine; and Baltimore, Maryland.

Review Video: How to Use Semicolons
Visit mometrix.com/academy and enter code: 370605

EXAMPLE

Which of the following sentences is NOT written correctly?

a. My sister burned the lasagna we were going to eat for dinner; we went out to eat instead of cooking something else.
b. The ball rolled into the ditch, therefore, it was muddy and wet when he retrieved it.
c. She has lived in many cities, including Nashville, Tennessee; San Diego, California; and Salt Lake City, Utah.
d. He hung the picture in the wrong spot; now there is a distracting hole in the wall.

Choice A is a compound sentence. The semicolon is used to separate two independent clauses. There is no coordinating conjunction in the sentence. This sentence correctly uses a semicolon, so choice A is incorrect.

Choice B is a compound sentence. In a compound sentence, either a coordinating conjunction or a semicolon can be used to separate the independent clauses. This sentence includes a transitional word, but it uses neither a semicolon nor a coordinating conjunction. To revise this sentence, *therefore* can be replaced by a coordinating conjunction, or the first comma can be replaced with a semicolon This sentence is written incorrectly, so choice B is the correct answer.

Choice C is a sentence that includes a list. Remember that semicolons can be used to separate items in a list when at least one of the items includes a comma. In this sentence, a list of cities is given. Since a comma is required to separate the name of a city from the name of the state it is in, each of the items in the list contain a

comma. This means that each full city name must be separated by a semicolon. This sentence is written correctly, so choice C is incorrect.

Choice D is a compound sentence and does not contain a coordinating conjunction. Semicolons can be used to separate independent clauses in a compound sentence instead of a coordinating conjunction. This sentence uses a semicolon correctly, so choice D is incorrect.

QUOTATION MARKS

Use quotation marks to close off **direct quotations** of a person's written or spoken words, which are also called **dialogue**. Do not use quotation marks around indirect quotations. An indirect quotation gives someone's message without using the person's exact words. Use **single quotation marks** to close off a quotation inside a quotation.

> **Direct Quote**: Nancy said, "I am waiting for Henry to arrive."

> **Indirect Quote**: Henry said that he is going to be late to the meeting.

> **Quote inside a Quote**: The teacher asked, "Has everyone read Martin Luther King's 'I Have a Dream' speech?"

Quotation marks should be used around the titles of **short works**: newspaper and magazine articles, poems, short stories, songs, television episodes, and radio programs. Titles of **long works** should be italicized when they are part of a typed composition or underlined when they are part of a handwritten composition.

Examples:

> "Rip Van Winkle" (short story by Washington Irving)

> "O Captain! My Captain!" (poem by Walt Whitman)

> **Review Video: Quotation Marks**
> Visit mometrix.com/academy and enter code: 884918

APOSTROPHES

An apostrophe is used to show **possession** or the **deletion of letters in contractions**. An apostrophe is not needed with the possessive pronouns *his, hers, its, ours, theirs, whose,* and *yours.*

> **Singular Nouns**: David's car | a book's theme | my brother's board game

> **Plural Nouns that end with -s**: the scissors' handle | boys' basketball

> **Plural Nouns that end without -s**: Men's department | the people's adventure

> **Review Video: Apostrophes**
> Visit mometrix.com/academy and enter code: 213068
>
> **Review Video: Punctuation Errors in Possessive Pronouns**
> Visit mometrix.com/academy and enter code: 221438

APOSTROPHES IN CONTRACTIONS

Contractions are combinations of words. Contractions involve taking two words, removing at least one letter from one of the words, putting an apostrophe in its place, and removing the space. For example, *does not* can be written as the contraction *doesn't.* The *o* is removed from *not* and is replaced with an apostrophe, which represents the removed letter, so it appears as *n't*. The space after does is then removed, turning *does not* into the contraction *doesn't*. Some more examples of contractions are listed below.

First Word	Second Word	Contraction
Can	Not	Can't
Do	Not	Don't
She	Will	She'll
They	Will	They'll
He	Is	He's
It	Is	It's
They	Are	They're
I	Am	I'm

Not all words can be used to form contractions, but many small, commonly used words can.

CAPITALIZATION

One important part of using correct grammar is properly capitalizing words. Usually, only nouns will be capitalized, but there are some exceptions. The most important capitalization rule is that the first word of every sentence, no matter what part of speech it is, should be capitalized. Another exception is that the pronoun *I* should always be capitalized.

Proper nouns are always capitalized, but sometimes it can be tricky to decide whether or not a noun is a proper noun. Some words that are usually common nouns may become proper nouns when used with other words or phrases. Also, when words that are not nouns are used with a noun, or when a group of words are used together as one noun, those words may also need to be capitalized.

TITLES OF BOOKS, STORIES, AND ESSAYS

Most of the words in titles of things like books, stories, and essays should be capitalized, but some should not. The very first word in a title should always be capitalized. Any other word in a title that is a noun, pronoun, adjective, verb or adverb should be capitalized. Articles, such as *a* or *the*, should not be capitalized. Short conjunctions and prepositions are usually not capitalized.

ABBREVIATIONS, INITIALS, AND ACRONYMS

Abbreviations are shortened versions of other words. When an abbreviation shortens, or abbreviates, a word that should be capitalized, the abbreviation's first letter should also be capitalized. When the shortened word is a noun that is not capitalized, the abbreviation should be in lowercase. Initials are usually written using the first letter from multiple words. For example, John Fitzgerald Kennedy is commonly referred to by his initials, JFK. Acronyms also use the first letter from multiple words, but they are different from initials because they form words on their own. For example, NASA is an acronym for National Aeronautics and Space Administration. Some acronyms, like NASA, omit small words, such as *and*, *of*, and *for*. When initials and acronyms are used for proper nouns, each letter should be capitalized.

The types of words and phrases in the chart below are proper nouns and should always be capitalized:

Writing Sample

	Description	Example
Historical Periods	A range of time in history that is related to specific events or circumstances	During the Romantic Period, many authors and poets wrote about their emotions.
Historical Events	Names of important events that happened in history	Napoleon Bonaparte led France after the French Revolution.
Historical Documents	Titles of important papers or compositions that are connected to historical events	The Mayflower Compact was written to create rules and expectations for the colony in Plymouth.
Languages	Names of the different languages that people speak	I want to learn to speak Cantonese, Spanish, and German.
Races and Ethnicities	Words often used to describe a person's heritage or cultural group	Malia taught her granddaughter how to hula so she could share a tradition of her Native Hawaiian heritage with her.
Nationalities	Words that describe which country a person is from	My teacher who moved to Canada last year is Romanian.
Organizations	Titles of official groups formed by people	Fewer than half of the states in America have a team in the National Basketball Association.

> **Review Video: Capitalization in Grammar**
> Visit mometrix.com/academy and enter code: 369678

EXAMPLE

Allison and Claire enjoy studying art from the beginning of the renaissance. They started a club so they and other students can learn more about it. Allison and Claire named the club Early Renaissance Art Club, which can be abbreviated to ERA Club. The students that joined elected Claire as the president and Allison as the vice president. The club's first meeting will take place after Christmas vacation.

Which of the following changes should be made in the passage?

a. In the first sentence, *Renaissance* should be capitalized.
b. In the third sentence, *ERA* should be written as *Era*.
c. In the fourth sentence, *president* and *vice president* should be capitalized.
d. In the last sentence, *Christmas* should be in lowercase.

Choice A says that *Renaissance* should be capitalized in the first sentence of the passage. The Renaissance is a historical period, so *Renaissance* is a proper noun that should always be capitalized. Choice A is correct.

Choice B says that *ERA* should be written as *Era*. In the third sentence of the passage, the word *era* is used as an acronym. Remember that all letters in an acronym should be capitalized. The correct capitalization is *ERA*, so choice B is incorrect.

Choice C says that *president* and *vice president* should be capitalized. Titles for people are capitalized when they are used as part of a person's name or in the place of a person's name. In this passage, these titles are not used as part of anyone's name or in place of anyone's name, so they should be in lowercase. Choice C is incorrect.

Choice D says that *Christmas* should be in lowercase. The passage says that the first meeting will be held after Christmas break. Even though *Christmas* is used to describe when the students are getting a vacation from school, it is the name of a holiday. Names of holidays are always capitalized, so choice D is incorrect.

Quantitative

Number Sense

NUMBERS AND THEIR CLASSIFICATIONS

There are several different kinds of numbers. When you learn to count as a child, you start with *Natural Numbers*. You may know them as counting numbers. These numbers begin with 1, 2, 3, and so on. *Whole Numbers* are all natural numbers and zero. *Integers* are all whole numbers and their related negative values (...-2, -1, 0, 1, 2...).

Aside from the number 1, all natural numbers are known as prime or composite. *Prime Numbers* are natural numbers that are greater than 1 and have factors that are 1 and itself (e.g., 3). On the other hand, *Composite Numbers* are natural numbers that are greater than 1 and are not prime numbers. The number 1 is a special case because it is not a prime number or composite number. *Rational numbers* include all integers, decimals, and fractions. Any terminating or repeating decimal number is a rational number.

Numbers are the basic building blocks of mathematics. These terms show some elements of numbers:

Integers – The set of positive and negative numbers. This set includes zero. Integers do not include fractions $\left(\frac{1}{3}\right)$, decimals (0.56), or mixed numbers $\left(7\frac{3}{4}\right)$.

Even number – Any integer that can be divided by 2 and does not leave a remainder.

Example: 2, 4, 6, 8, etc.

Odd number – Any integer that cannot be divided evenly by 2. For example: 3, 5, 7, 9, and so on.

Decimal number – a number that uses a decimal point to show the part of the number that is less than one. Example: 1.234.

Decimal point – a symbol used to separate the ones place from the tenths place in decimals. This symbol is used to separate dollars from cents in currency.

Decimal place – the position of a number to the right of the decimal point. In the decimal 0.123, the 1 is in the first place to the right of the decimal point. This is the place for tenths. The 2 is in the second place. This is the place for hundredths. The 3 is in the third place. This is the place for thousandths.

The decimal, or base 10, system is a number system that uses ten different digits (0, 1, 2, 3, 4, 5, 6, 7, 8, 9). Another system is the binary, or base 2, number system. This system is used by computers and uses the numbers 0 and 1. Some think that the base 10 system started because people had only their 10 fingers for counting.

Decimals, Fractions, and Percents

DECIMALS

DECIMAL ILLUSTRATION

Use a model to represent the decimal: 0.24. Write 0.24 as a fraction.

51

The decimal 0.24 is twenty four hundredths. One possible model to represent this fraction is to draw 100 pennies, since each penny is worth 1 one hundredth of a dollar. Draw one hundred circles to represent one hundred pennies. Shade 24 of the pennies to represent the decimal twenty four hundredths.

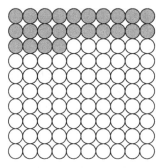

To write the decimal as a fraction, write a fraction: $\frac{\#\ shaded\ spaces}{\#\ total\ spaces}$. The number of shaded spaces is 24, and the total number of spaces is 100, so as a fraction 0.24 equals $\frac{24}{100}$. $\frac{24}{100}$ can then be reduced to $\frac{6}{25}$.

ADDING AND SUBTRACTING DECIMALS

When adding and subtracting decimals, the decimal points must always be aligned. Adding decimals is just like adding regular whole numbers.

Example: 4.5 + 2 = 6.5.

If the problem-solver does not properly align the decimal points, an incorrect answer of 4.7 may result. An easy way to add decimals is to align all of the decimal points in a vertical column visually. This will allow you to see exactly where the decimal should be placed in the final answer. Begin adding from right to left. Add each column in turn, making sure to carry the number to the left if a column adds up to more than 9. The same rules apply to the subtraction of decimals.

> **Review Video: Adding and Subtracting Decimals**
> Visit mometrix.com/academy and enter code: 381101

MULTIPLYING DECIMALS

Decimals can be multiplied using strategies involving **place value** or the **standard algorithm**. For example, when a decimal is multiplied by a power of 10, the decimal moves one place to the right. When a decimal is divided by a power of 10, the decimal moves one place to the left. This can be applied to situations involving money.

For example:

$4.55 \times 10 = \$45.50$
$4.55 \times 100 = \$455.00$
$45.50 \div 10 = \$4.55$
$455.00 \div 100 = \$4.55$

When decimals are multiplied by whole numbers that are not powers of 10, the standard algorithm can be used. Start by stacking the longer number on top of the smaller number. Shift the numbers to the right. There is no need to line up the decimals. For example, 2.74×6.1 becomes:

$$2.74$$
$$\times\ 6.1$$

Multiply the 1 by each digit in 2.74.
Add a place holder 0.
Multiply the 6 by each digit in 2.74
Find the sum.

Place the decimal. Count the total number of digits to the right of the decimal in 2.74 and 6.1 In this case, there is a total of 3 digits to the right of the decimal. Move the decimal 3 places to the left so that 16714 becomes 16.714. The product of 2.74 and 6.1 is 16.714.

$$
\begin{array}{r}
2.74 \\
\times\ \ 6.1 \\
\hline
274 \\
+\ 16440 \\
\hline
16.714
\end{array}
$$

Review Video: **Multiplying Decimals**
Visit mometrix.com/academy and enter code: 731574

EXAMPLE

A baker needs apples for an apple strudel recipe. The baker uses 4 apples that each weigh 3.5 ounces. How many ounces of apples were used?

14 ounces

The baker uses 4 apples that each weigh 3.5 ounces. This means there are 4 groups of 3.5. Multiplication can be used to determine the total number of ounces. Consider using partial products. 4×3.5 can be thought of as $(4 \times 3) + (4 \times 0.5)$. 4 groups of 3 is 12, and 4 groups of 0.5 is 2. Then, $12 + 2 = 14$. So, the baker used 14 ounces of apples for the strudel.

DIVIDING DECIMALS

The standard algorithm, commonly known as long division, can be used to divide decimals. For example, consider the division problem $65.35 \div 2.5$. The first thing to notice is that there is a decimal in the divisor. This needs to be adjusted. The divisor cannot contain a decimal. Get rid of this by multiplying both values by 10. 2.5 becomes 25, and 65.35 becomes 653.5. Now the problem can continue. Remember the 4-step process for long division.

Step 1: Divide
Step 2: Multiply

Step 3: Subtract
Step 4: Bring Down

Bring the decimal straight up into the answer line. The result is 26.14.

$$\begin{array}{r} 26.14 \\ 25\overline{)653.50} \\ -50 \\ \hline 153 \\ -150 \\ \hline 35 \\ -25 \\ \hline 100 \\ -100 \\ \hline 0 \end{array}$$

Review Video: Dividing Decimals
Visit mometrix.com/academy and enter code: 560690

EXAMPLE

A coach pours 28.4 gallons of sports drink into 8 containers. How many gallons of sports drink will be in each container?

3.55 gallons

Since we are dividing a whole into different parts, we will use division. Consider using the standard algorithm for long division. Follow the four-step process for long division: Divide, Multiply, Subtract, Bring Down. Then repeat. The result is 3.55 gallons.

$$\begin{array}{r} 3.55 \\ 8\overline{)28.40} \\ -24 \\ \hline 44 \\ -40 \\ \hline 40 \\ -40 \\ \hline 0 \end{array}$$

FRACTIONS

A fraction has one integer that is written above another integer with a dividing line between them: $\frac{x}{y}$. It represents the **quotient** of the two numbers "x divided by y." Also, this can be thought of as x out of y equal parts. The x and y in this fraction are known as variables. When the value for a symbol can change, a variable is given to that value. So, a number like 3 is a constant. A value that does not change is a constant.

The top number of a fraction is called the **numerator**. This number stands for the number of parts. The 1 in $\frac{1}{4}$ means that this is **one part** out of the whole. The bottom number of a fraction is called the **denominator**. This stands for the **total number** of equal parts. The 4 in $\frac{1}{4}$ means that the whole has four equal parts. A fraction cannot have a denominator of zero. This fraction is known as "undefined." The reverse of a fraction is known as the **reciprocal**. For example, the reciprocal of $\frac{1}{2}$ is 2, and the reciprocal of 3 is $\frac{1}{3}$.

CHANGING FRACTIONS

Fractions can be changed by multiplying or dividing the numerator and denominator by the same number. This will not change the value of the fraction. You cannot do this with addition or subtraction. If you divide both numbers by a common factor, you will **reduce** or **simplify** the fraction. Two fractions that have the same value but are given in different ways are known as equivalent fractions. For example, $\frac{2}{10}, \frac{3}{15}, \frac{4}{20}$, and $\frac{5}{25}$ are equivalent fractions. Also, they can be reduced or simplified to $\frac{1}{5}$.

Two fractions can be changed to have the same denominator. This is known as finding a common denominator. The number for the common denominator should be the least common multiple of the original denominators. Example: $\frac{3}{4}$ and $\frac{5}{6}$; the least common multiple of 4 and 6 is 12. So, you can change these fractions to have a common denominator: $\frac{3}{4} = \frac{9}{12}$ and $\frac{5}{6} = \frac{10}{12}$.

ADDING AND SUBTRACTING FRACTIONS

If two fractions have a common denominator, you can add or subtract the fractions with the two numerators. Example: $\frac{1}{2} + \frac{1}{4} = \frac{2}{4} + \frac{1}{4} = \frac{3}{4}$. If the two fractions do not have the same denominator, one or both of them must be changed to have a common denominator. This needs to be done before they can be added or subtracted.

MULTIPLYING FRACTIONS

Two fractions can be multiplied. The two numerators need to be multiplied to find the new numerator. Also, the two denominators need to be multiplied to find the new denominator. Example: $\frac{1}{3} \times \frac{2}{3} = \frac{1\times2}{3\times3} = \frac{2}{9}$. Two fractions can be divided. First, flip the numerator and denominator of the second fraction. Then multiply the numerators and denominators.

Example: $\frac{2}{3} \div \frac{3}{4}$ becomes $\frac{2}{3} \times \frac{4}{3}$. Now, $\frac{8}{9}$ is your answer.

A fraction with a denominator that is greater than the numerator is known as a proper fraction. A fraction with a numerator that is greater than the denominator is known as an improper fraction. Proper fractions have values less than one. Improper fractions have values greater than one.

A mixed number is a number that has an integer and a fraction. Any improper fraction can be rewritten as a mixed number. Example: $\frac{8}{3} = \frac{6}{3} + \frac{2}{3} = 2 + \frac{2}{3} = 2\frac{2}{3}$.

Also, any mixed number can be rewritten as an improper fraction. Example: $1\frac{3}{5} = 1 + \frac{3}{5} = \frac{5}{5} + \frac{3}{5} = \frac{8}{5}$.

A fraction that has a fraction in the numerator, denominator, or both is called a *Complex Fraction*. These can be solved in many ways. The easiest way to solve the equation is to use order of operations.

Quantitative

55

For example, $\frac{\frac{4}{7}}{\frac{5}{8}} = \frac{0.571}{0.625} = 0.914$. Another way to solve this problem is to multiply the fraction in the numerator by the reciprocal of the fraction in the denominator. For example, $\frac{\frac{4}{7}}{\frac{5}{8}} = \frac{4}{7} \times \frac{8}{5} = \frac{32}{35} = 0.914$.

MULTIPLYING FRACTIONS AND WHOLE NUMBERS

Modeling strategies can be helpful when multiplying a whole number by a fraction. For example, $4 \times \frac{2}{3}$ can be thought of as 4 groups of $\frac{2}{3}$. There are 8 thirds altogether, so $4 \times \frac{2}{3} = \frac{8}{3}$, or as a mixed number, $2\frac{2}{3}$.

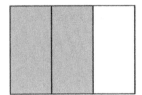 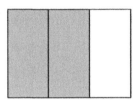 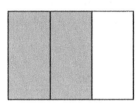 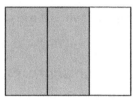

Multiplication is commutative, meaning the order does not matter. This same modeling strategy applies in situations where the fraction is listed first and the whole number is listed second.

DIVIDING FRACTIONS AND WHOLE NUMBERS

One way to visualize the concept of fraction division is to use a model. For example, when dividing a unit fraction by a whole number, start by drawing a model of the fraction. For example, for the problem $\frac{1}{8} \div 3$, start by modeling eighths, and then shade one share.

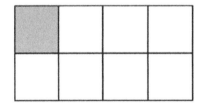

Now divide this shaded eighth into 3 equal shares. The size of one of these shares is now $\frac{1}{24}$ because dividing each eighth into 3 gives 24 total shares. This means that $\frac{1}{8} \div 3 = \frac{1}{24}$.

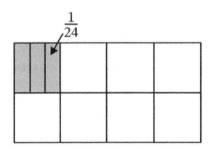

A similar process works when dividing a whole number by a unit fraction. For example,

56

Consider $4 \div \frac{1}{5}$. Start by drawing a model for 4. Then divide each whole into fifths. How many fifths are there altogether? In this case, there are 20. This means that $4 \div \frac{1}{5}$ is equal to 20.

EXAMPLE

A chef is making pizzas. The chef has 12 pounds of dough, and each crust requires $\frac{1}{7}$ pound of dough. How many pizza crusts can the chef make?

84 pizza crusts

There are 12 pounds of dough, and it needs to be divided into groups of $\frac{1}{7}$. To divide 12 by $\frac{1}{7}$, start by writing both values in fraction form. $12 \div \frac{1}{7}$ becomes $\frac{12}{1} \div \frac{1}{7}$. Now, follow the "flip and multiply" strategy. Change the division symbol to multiplication, and then flip the second fraction. $\frac{12}{1} \div \frac{1}{7}$ becomes $\frac{12}{1} \times \frac{7}{1}$. Now, multiply across and simplify if possible. $\frac{12}{1} \times \frac{7}{1}$ becomes $\frac{84}{1}$, or 84. The chef can make 84 pizza crusts.

EXAMPLE

Matt has $\frac{1}{4}$ of his birthday cake left over. Matt and two of his friends want to share the leftover cake. If he divides the leftover cake into 3 equal shares, what fraction of a whole cake will each person receive?

$\frac{1}{12}$

The scenario can be represented as a division problem. $\frac{1}{4}$ of the cake is being divided into 3 shares is $\frac{1}{4} \div 3$. To divide fractions and whole numbers, set up both values as a fraction. $\frac{1}{4} \div 3$ becomes $\frac{1}{4} \div \frac{3}{1}$. Follow the "flip and multiply" technique. Change the division symbol to multiplication and flip the second fraction. $\frac{1}{4} \div \frac{3}{1}$ becomes $\frac{1}{4} \times \frac{1}{3}$. Now, multiply straight across and simplify if possible, $\frac{1}{4} \times \frac{1}{3} = \frac{1}{12}$. So, each person will receive $\frac{1}{12}$ of the original whole cake.

> **Review Video: Overview of Fractions**
> Visit mometrix.com/academy and enter code: 262335

CONVERTING DECIMALS TO FRACTIONS

A fraction can be turned into a decimal and vice versa. In order to convert a fraction into a decimal, simply divide the numerator by the denominator. For example, the fraction $\frac{5}{4}$ becomes 1.25. This is done by dividing 5 by 4. The fraction $\frac{4}{8}$ becomes 0.5 when 4 is divided by 8. This remains true even if the fraction $\frac{4}{8}$ is first reduced to $\frac{1}{2}$. The decimal conversion will still be 0.5. In order to convert a decimal into a fraction, count the number of places to the right of the decimal. This will be the number of zeros in the denominator. The numbers to the right of the decimal will become the whole number in the numerator.

Example 1:

$$0.45 = \frac{45}{100}$$

$\frac{45}{100}$ reduces to $\frac{9}{20}$

Example 2:

$$0.237 = \frac{237}{1000}$$

Example 3:

$$0.2121 = \frac{2121}{10000}$$

PERCENTAGES

You can think of **percentages** as fractions that are based on a whole of 100. In other words, one whole is equal to 100%. The word percent means "per hundred." Fractions can be given as percents by using equivalent fractions with an amount of 100. Example: $\frac{7}{10} = \frac{70}{100} = 70\%$; Another example is $\frac{1}{4} = \frac{25}{100} = 25\%$. To give a percentage as a fraction, divide the percentage by 100. Then, reduce the fraction to its simplest possible terms. Example: $60\% = \frac{60}{100} = \frac{3}{5}$; $96\% = \frac{96}{100} = \frac{24}{25}$.

Converting decimals to percentages and percentages to decimals is as simple as moving the decimal point. To convert from a decimal to a percent, move the decimal point two places to the right. To convert from a percent to a decimal, move the decimal two places to the left.

Example: 0.23 = 23%; 5.34 = 534%; 0.007 = 0.7%; 700% = 7.00; 86% = 0.86; 0.15% = 0.0015.

A percentage problem can come in three main ways.

- Type 1: What percentage of 40 is 8?
- Type 2: What number is 20% of 40?
- Type 3: What number is 8 20% of?

The three parts in these examples are the same: a whole (W), a part (P), and a percentage (%).

To solve type (1), use the equation % = P/W.

To solve type (2), use the equation: P = W × %.

To solve type (3), use the equation W = P/%.

PERCENTAGE PROBLEMS

Percentage problems can be difficult because many are word problems. So, a main part of solving them is to know which quantities to use.

Example 1

In a school cafeteria, 7 students choose pizza, 9 choose hamburgers, and 4 choose tacos. Find the percentage that chose tacos.

To find the whole, you must add all of the parts: 7 + 9 + 4 = 20. Then, the percentage can be found by dividing the part by the whole (% = P/W): $\frac{4}{20} = \frac{20}{100} = 20\%$.

<u>Example 2</u>

At a hospital, 40% of the nurses work in labor and delivery. If 20 nurses work in labor and delivery, how many nurses work at the hospital?

To answer this problem, first think about the number of nurses that work at the hospital. Will it be more or less than the number of nurses who work in a specific department such as labor and delivery? More nurses work at the hospital, so the number you find to answer this question will be greater than 20.

40% of the nurses are labor and delivery nurses. "Of" indicates multiplication, and words like "is" and "are" indicate equivalence. Translating the problem into a mathematical sentence gives $40\% \cdot n = 20$, where n represents the total number of nurses. Solving for n gives $n = \frac{20}{40\%} = \frac{20}{0.40} = 50$.

Fifty nurses work at the hospital.

<u>Example 3</u>

A patient was given 40 mg of a certain medicine. Later, the patient's dosage was increased to 45 mg. What was the percent increase in his medication?

To find the percent increase, first compare the original and increased amounts. The original amount was 40 mg, and the increased amount is 45 mg, so the dosage of medication was increased by 5 mg (45 − 40 = 5). Note, however, that the question asks not by how much the dosage increased but by what percentage it increased. Percent increase $= \frac{\text{new amount} - \text{original amount}}{\text{original amount}} \cdot 100\%$.

So, $\frac{45 \text{ mg} - 40 \text{ mg}}{40 \text{ mg}} \cdot 100\% = \frac{5}{40} \cdot 100\% = 0.125 \cdot 100\% \approx 12.5\%$

The percent increase is approximately 12.5%.

Operations

There are four basic operations in math: addition, subtraction, multiplication, and division.

Addition increases the value of one number by the value of another number.

Example: 2 + 4 = 6; 8 + 9 = 17. The result is called the **sum**. With addition, the order does not matter. 4 + 2 or 2 + 4 equals 6. This is the **commutative property for addition**.

Subtraction decreases the value of one number by the value of another number. The result is called the **difference**. Example: 6 − 4 = 2 and 17 − 8 = 9. Note for subtraction that the order does matter. For example, 6 − 4 and 4 − 6 do not have the same difference.

Multiplication is like repeated addition. This operation tells how many times one number needs to be added to the other number. Example: 3 × 2 (three times two) = 2 + 2 + 2 = 6. With multiplication, the order does not matter. 2 × 3 (or 3 + 3) = 3 × 2 (or 2 + 2 + 2). This is the **commutative property for multiplication**.

Division is the opposite operation to multiplication. This operation shows how much of a number is in another number. The first number is known as the **dividend**. The second number is known as the **divisor**. The answer to the division problem is known as the **quotient**.

Example: 20 ÷ 4 = 5. If 20 is split into 4 equal parts, then each part is 5. With division, the order of the numbers does matter. 20 ÷ 4 and 4 ÷ 20 do not give the same result. Note that you cannot divide a number by zero. If you try to divide a number by zero, then the answer is known as undefined.

WORKING WITH POSITIVE & NEGATIVE NUMBERS

Addition: If the signs are the same, then add the absolute values of the addends and use the original sign with the sum. The addends are the numbers that will be added to have the sum. For example, $(+4) + (+8) = +12$ and $(-4) + (-8) = -12$. When the signs are different, take the absolute values of the addends and subtract the smaller value from the larger value. Then, put the original sign of the larger value on the difference. For example, $(+4) + (-8) = -4$ and $(-4) + (+8) = +4$.

Subtraction: For signed numbers, change the sign of the number after the minus symbol. Then, follow the same rules for addition. For example, $(+4) - (+8)$ becomes $(+4) + (-8) = -4$.

Multiplication: If the signs are the **same**, then the product is **positive**. For example, $(+4) \times (+8) = +32$ and $(-4) \times (-8) = +32$. If the signs are **different**, then the product is **negative**. For example, $(+4) \times (-8) = -32$ and $(-4) \times (+8) = -32$. When more than two factors are multiplied together, the sign of the product is decided by how many negative factors are in the equation. If there are an odd number of negative factors, then the product is negative. An even number of negative factors gives a positive product. For example, $(+4) \times (-8) \times (-2) = +64$ and $(-4) \times (-8) \times (-2) = -64$.

Division: The rules for dividing signed numbers are similar to multiplying signed numbers. If the dividend and divisor have the **same sign**, the quotient is **positive**. If the dividend and divisor have **opposite signs**, the quotient is **negative**. For example, $(-4) \div (+8) = -0.5$.

ORDER OF OPERATIONS

Follow the **order of operations** (PEMDAS) when simplifying numerical expressions.

P- parentheses and grouping symbols
E- exponents
M- multiplication
D- division
A- addition
S- subtraction

For example, consider the numerical expression $2[(9 + 21) \div 6]$. Start by simplifying the math inside the parentheses. $(9 + 21)$ simplifies to 30.

$$2[30 \div 6]$$

Now simplify the math inside the brackets. $[30 \div 6]$ simplifies to 5.

$$2[5]$$

Multiply 2 by 5. The result is 10, so $2[(9 + 21) \div 6]$ simplifies to 10.

Review Video: Order of Operations
Visit mometrix.com/academy and enter code: 259675

EXAMPLE

$$[(0.75 + 10) - 2 \times 5] + 8.25$$

9

When simplifying expressions, solve the math within grouping elements first. Remember to follow the order of operations within grouping elements, so first simplify the parentheses inside the brackets.

$$[10.75 - 2 \times 5] + 8.25$$

60

Then, simplify the multiplication inside the brackets.

$$[10.75 - 10] + 8.25$$

Now simplify the subtraction within the brackets.

$$0.75 + 8.25$$

Finally, add.

$$0.75 + 8.25 = 9$$

FACTORS AND MULTIPLES

Factors are numbers that are multiplied for a product. An example is the equation 2 × 3 = 6. The numbers 2 and 3 are factors. A **prime number** has only two factors: 1 and itself. Other numbers, called **composite numbers**, can have many factors.

Review Video: <u>Factors</u>
Visit mometrix.com/academy and enter code: 920086

A **common factor** is a number that divides exactly into two or more numbers. For example, the factors of 12 are 1, 2, 3, 4, 6, and 12. The factors of 15 are 1, 3, 5, and 15. So, the common factors of 12 and 15 are 1 and 3. A **prime factor** is a factor that is a prime number. Thus, the prime factors of 12 are 2 and 3. For 15, the prime factors are 3 and 5.

The **greatest common factor (GCF)** is the largest number that is a factor of two or more numbers. For example, the factors of 15 are 1, 3, 5, and 15. The factors of 35 are 1, 5, 7, and 35. So, the greatest common factor of 15 and 35 is 5.

A **multiple** of a number is the product of the number and some other integer. **Common multiples** are multiples that are shared by two numbers. The **least common multiple (LCM)** is the smallest number that is a multiple of two or more numbers. For example, the multiples of 3 are 3, 6, 9, 12, 15, etc. The multiples of 5 are 5, 10, 15, 20, etc. Therefore, the least common multiple of 3 and 5 is 15.

Review Video: <u>Multiples</u>
Visit mometrix.com/academy and enter code: 626738

ROUNDING

Rounding is changing a number to a different number that it is close to. The result will be less accurate, but it will be in a simpler form and will be easier to use. Whole numbers can be rounded to the nearest ten, hundred or thousand. Also, fractions and decimals can be rounded to the nearest whole number.

EXAMPLE

Round each number to the nearest ten: 11 | 47 | 118.

When rounding to the nearest ten, anything ending in 5 or greater rounds up.

So, 11 rounds to 10 | 47 rounds to 50 | 118 rounds to 120.

EXAMPLE

Round each number to the nearest hundred: 78 | 980 | 248.

When rounding to the nearest hundred, anything ending in 50 or greater rounds up.

So, 78 rounds to 100 | 980 rounds to 1000 | 248 rounds down to 200.

EXAMPLE

Round each number to the nearest thousand: 302 | 1274 | 3756.

When rounding to the nearest thousand, anything ending in 500 or greater rounds up.

So, 302 rounds to 0 | 1274 rounds to 1000 | 3756 rounds to 4000.

EXAMPLE

Round each number to the nearest whole number: $\frac{5}{8}$ | 2.12 | $\frac{14}{3}$.

When rounding fractions and decimals, anything half or higher rounds up.

So, $\frac{5}{8}$ rounds to 1 | 2.12 rounds to 2 | $\frac{14}{3}$ rounds to 5.

ESTIMATION

Estimation is the process of finding an **approximate answer** to a problem. Estimation may involve **rounding** to the nearest whole number to make addition or subtraction easier.

EXAMPLE

There are 24 people in an English class. Miss Foster decides to order three exam books for each student, plus 6 extras. She estimates that she should order 90 exam books. Identify if her solution is reasonable.

Write an expression to determine the total number of exam books to order. Since three books are ordered for each student, first multiply the number of books per student by the number of students: 3 books per student · 24 students = 72 books. Next, add the six extra exam books that Miss Foster would like to order. The total number of books to order is: 72 + 6 = 78 books. Her original estimate of 90 exam books is too large.

EXAMPLE

The following food items are available in a school cafeteria for lunch:

Sandwich: $3.15; Soup: $1.84

Salad: $2.62; Pretzels: $0.95

Milk: $0.40

Daniel has $4.00 and wants to purchase a milk, sandwich, and soup. Emily has $4.00 and wants to purchase a salad, pretzels, and milk. Estimate the cost of each student's lunch and determine if they have enough money to purchase the food they would like for lunch.

Daniel wants to purchase a milk, sandwich, and soup. Rounded to the nearest fifty cents, the cost of his items is $0.50, $3.00, and $2.00. The total for his three items would be approximately:

$$0.50 + 3.00 + 2.00 = 5.50$$

It will cost Daniel approximately $5.50 for his lunch. He does not have enough money to purchase the items he has selected.

Emily wants to purchase a salad, pretzels, and milk. Rounded to the nearest fifty cents, the cost of her items is $2.50, $1.00, and $0.50. The total for her three items would be approximately:

$$2.50 + 1.00 + 0.50 = 4.00$$

It will cost Emily approximately $4.00 for her lunch. She has approximately enough money to purchase the items she has selected.

MULTIPLYING MULTI-DIGIT NUMBERS

There are many ways to multiply multi-digit numbers. Some strategies include partial products, the distributive property, the lattice method, and the standard algorithm. The **standard algorithm** is a popular strategy because it is time effective. This process multiplies each digit in one number by each digit in the other number, based on place value. Start by lining up the ones digit for both numbers and stack the two numbers vertically with the larger number on top. For example, when multiplying 526×31, line up the ones digits, and stack the numbers with 526 on top.

$$\begin{array}{r} 526 \\ \times\ 31 \\ \hline \end{array}$$

Step 1: Multiply the 1 by all digits in 526. This is similar to the distributive property. The result is 526.

$$\begin{array}{r} 526 \\ \times\ \ 31 \\ \hline 526 \end{array}$$

Step 2: Write a "place holder zero" under the 6, and cross out the 1. The ones digit has been distributed, and the tens digit is next. The place holder zero will keep the columns aligned during the next round of multiplication.

$$\begin{array}{r} 526 \\ \times\ 3\cancel{1} \\ \hline 526 \\ 0 \end{array}$$

Step 3: Multiply the 3 by all digits in 526. Consider drawing loops over each digit to stay organized. $3 \times 6 = 18$. Notice how 18 is split up into ones and tens. The 1 is placed over tens column, and the 8 is placed under the answer line in the tens column.

$$\begin{array}{r} 1\ \ \\ 526 \\ \times\ 3\cancel{1} \\ \hline 526 \\ 80 \end{array}$$

Step 4: Move to the next digit: $3 \times 2 = 6$. Add the 1 (above). $6 + 1 = 7$, so write 7 under the answer line in the next spot (hundreds place).

$$\begin{array}{r} 1 \\ 5\cancel{2}6 \\ \times \ 3\cancel{1} \\ \hline 526 \\ 80 \end{array}$$

Step 5: Move to the last digit: $3 \times 5 = 15$. Write 15 under the answer line in the ten thousands and thousands place.

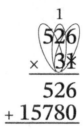

$$\begin{array}{r} 1 \\ 526 \\ \times \ 31 \\ \hline 526 \\ + \ 15780 \end{array}$$

Step 6: Use the standard algorithm to find the sum of the two rows of numbers under the answer line. The sum of 526 and 15,780 is 16,306. This means that the product of 526 and 31 is 16,306.

$$\begin{array}{r} 1 \\ 526 \\ \times \ 31 \\ \hline {}^{1}526 \\ {}_{1} \\ + \ 15780 \\ \hline 16,306 \end{array}$$

DIVIDING MULTI-DIGIT NUMBERS

The standard algorithm for multi-digit division is commonly referred to as **long division**. In this strategy, the **dividend** is placed under the division symbol, and the **divisor** is placed to the left of the division symbol. The answer will be placed above the symbol, and the work will occur under the symbol. For example, when dividing 3,190 by 58, place 3,190 under the symbol and 58 to the left of the symbol.

$3,190 \div 58$ becomes:

$$58\overline{)3190}$$

The standard algorithm follows a 4-step process.

Step 1: Divide
Step 2: Multiply
Step 3: Subtract
Step 4: Bring Down

Step 1: Figure out how many times the divisor can fit into the first digit of the dividend without going over it. In this case, 58 cannot go into 3 because 3 is too small. Include the next digit. Again, 58 cannot go into 31 because 31 is too small. Include the next digit. 58 can go into 319 because 319 is larger than 58. Use estimation to determine how many times 58 goes into 319. Round 58 to 60. Round 319 to 300. 60 goes into 300 5 times. This estimation can be used to determine how many times 58 goes into 319. Write 5 above the 9. Make sure the 5 is above the hundreds digit because this is the farthest place value considered in the estimation.

$$58)\overline{\begin{matrix} 5 \\ 3190 \end{matrix}}$$

Step 2: Multiply 5×58. The product of 5×58 is 290. Write 290 below the dividend.

$$58)\overline{\begin{matrix} 5 \\ 3190 \\ 290 \end{matrix}}$$

Step 3: Subtract $319 - 290 = 29$.

$$58)\overline{\begin{matrix} 5 \\ 3190 \\ -290 \\ \overline{29} \end{matrix}}$$

Step 4: Bring down the next digit and repeat the process.

$$58)\overline{\begin{matrix} 55 \\ 3190 \\ -290 \\ \overline{290} \\ -290 \\ \overline{0} \end{matrix}}$$

The last value is 0. This indicates that there is no remainder and that $3{,}190 \div 58 = 55$.

Ratios and Proportions

RATIOS

A ratio is a comparison of two numbers in a certain order. Example: There are 14 computers in a lab, and the class has 20 students. So, there is a student to computer ratio of 20 to 14. Normally, this is written as 20:14.

Ratios can be listed as *a to b*, *a:b*, or *a/b*. Examples of ratios are miles per hour (miles/hour), meters per second (meters/second), and miles per gallon (miles/gallon).

> **Review Video: Ratios**
> Visit mometrix.com/academy and enter code: 996914

PROPORTIONS AND CROSS PRODUCTS

A proportion is a relationship between two numbers. This relationship shows how one changes when the other changes. A direct proportion is a relationship where a number increases by a set amount with every increase in the other number.

Another way is for the number to decrease by that same amount for every decrease in the other quantity. Example: For every 1 sheet cake, 18 people can have cake. The number of sheet cakes and the number of people that can be served from them is a direct proportion.

Inverse proportion is a relationship where an increase in one number has a decrease in the other. This can work the other way where a decrease in a number has an increase in the other.

Example: The time needed for a car trip decreases as the speed increases. Also, the time for the trip increases as the speed decreases. So, the time needed for the trip is inversely proportional to the speed of the car.

Two equal ratios have cross products that are equal. This can be written as $\frac{m}{b} = \frac{w}{z}$. For example, Fred travels 2 miles in 1 hour, and Jane travels 4 miles in 2 hours. So, their speeds are proportional because $\frac{2}{1} = \frac{4}{2}$.

In a proportion, the product of the numerator of the first ratio and the denominator of the second ratio is equal to the product of the denominator of the first ratio and the numerator of the second ratio. In other words, you can see that $m \times z = b \times w$. So, $2 \times 2 = 1 \times 4$.

> **Review Video: <u>Proportions</u>**
> Visit mometrix.com/academy and enter code: 505355

Algebra and Functions

WRITING MATHEMATICAL EXPRESSIONS, EQUATIONS, AND PHRASES

EXPRESSIONS

Write "four less than twice *x*" as a mathematical expression.

Remember that an **expression** does not have an equal sign. "Less" indicates subtraction, and "twice" indicates multiplication by two. Four less than $2x$ is $2x - 4$. Notice how this is different than $4 - 2x$. You can plug in values for *x* to see how these expressions would yield different values.

EQUATIONS

Translate "three hundred twenty-five increased by six times $3x$ equals three hundred forty-three" into a mathematical equation. **Equations** do include equal signs.

The key words and phrases are "increased by," "times," and "equals."

Three hundred twenty-five increased by six times $3x$ equals three hundred forty-three:

$$325 + 6(3x) = 343$$

The mathematical equation is $325 + 6(3x) = 343$.

PHRASES

Write a **phrase** that represents this mathematical expression: $75 - 3t + 14^2$.

Because there are many words which indicate various operations, there are several ways to write this expression, including "seventy-five minus three times *t* plus fourteen squared."

MULTI-STEP WORD PROBLEMS WITH VARIABLES

Multi-step word problems can be solved algebraically These problems can be written as expressions or equations. In general, equations will consist of variables, coefficients, and constants. **Variables** are letters that represent unknown values. **Coefficients** are located in front of variables and signal multiplication. For example, $2x$ means 2 multiplied by the variable *x*. **Constants** are numbers that are not attached to variables. This means that constants are fixed values that do not change, regardless of the value of the variable.

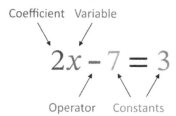

An equation is solved when the value of the variable is calculated. For example, if the equation states that $45 = 9 \times T$, the value of *T* is 5. This is considered a **one-step equation** because it is solved by dividing both sides of the equation by 9, which requires only one step. However, many equations require more than one step to solve. Consider the following scenario.

The temperature of water in a pool starts at 82°. The temperature rises 0.6 degrees every hour. Right now, the water temperature is 85°. How many hours have passed?

Quantitative

The word problem can be solved using an algebraic equation. Start by stating what is known.

- The water temperature is initially 82°.
- The temperature rises 0.6° each hour.
- Now the water temperature is 85°.

Then identify the unknown. Here, the unknown is the number of hours that have passed.
Since the number of hours is unknown, use h as the unknown variable. The goal is to set up a multi-step equation that can be solved for h.

The problem states that the water temperature will eventually be 85°, so start the equation with $85 =$.

$$85 =$$

The problem also states that the temperature will rise 0.6 degrees each hour. This can be represented as $(0.6) \times (h)$.

$$85 = (0.6) \times (h)$$

Since the water temperature starts at 82°, $(0.6) \times (h)$ should be added to 82°.

The result is the following equation.

$$85 = (0.6) \times (h) + 82$$

Solve for the variable h by subtracting 82 from both sides, and then use long division to divide by 0.6.

$$82 + (0.6) \times (h) = 85$$

$$(0.6) \times (h) = 3$$

$$h = 5$$

This means that 5 hours have passed.

EXAMPLE
Write and solve an equation to solve the following problem.

A school is taking a field trip. There are 331 students attending the field trip. 6 school busses are filled with an equal number of students, and 7 students will ride their bike to the field trip. How many students will be in each school bus?

54 students. $331 = 6b + 7$

Start by listing all the relevant facts.

- The total number of students is 331.
- 6 busses will be full, with an equal number of students on each bus.
- 7 students will ride their bikes

The equation will follow the format of Total Students = Bus Riders + Bikers. Fill in what is provided.

The total number of students is 331, so start the equation with $331 =$.

$$331 =$$

An equal number of bus riders will be placed on 6 buses. It is unknown how many riders will be on each bus. A variable can be substituted in for this unknown value. Use the variable b to represent the unknown number of riders on each bus. There are 6 buses, and b number of students on each bus. The expression $6 \times b$ or $6b$ can be used to describe "six buses with an equal number of students."

$$331 = 6(b)$$

The number of bikers is 7, so add a $+7$ to the end of the equation.

$$331 = 6(b) + 7$$

Now use the equation to solve for the unknown variable, b. The equation is solved in two steps. Subtract 7 from both sides, and then divide both sides by 6. These two steps are considered "inverse operations." Subtracting 7 is the inverse of adding 7, and dividing by 6 is the inverse of multiplying by 6.

$$331 = 6b + 7$$

$$324 = 6b$$

$$54 = b$$

This means that there will be 54 students on each bus.

PROPERTIES

The **commutative property of addition** is shown here, which states that you can add terms in any order.

$$2x + y = y + 2x$$

The **identity property of addition** is shown here, which states that adding 0 to any number or term does not change the value of that number or term.

$$s + 0 = s$$

The **associative property of addition** is shown here, which states that any group of numbers and/or variables can be grouped together in parentheses to be added first before adding the remaining numbers and/or variables.

$$10 + (6 + 1) = (10 + 6) + 1$$

The **commutative property of multiplication** is shown here, which states that you can multiply terms in any order.

$$6 \times m \times n = m \times n \times 6$$

The **identity property of multiplication** is shown here, which states that multiplying a number or term by 1 does not change its value.

$$3 \times 1 = 3$$

The **associative property of multiplication** is shown here, which states that any group of numbers and/or variables can be grouped together in parentheses to be multiplied first before multiplying by the remaining numbers and/or variables.

$$4 \times (5a) = (4a) \times 5$$

Quantitative

69

The **distributive property** is shown here, which states that a number multiplied to an expression in parentheses must be multiplied to every term in the parentheses.

$$5 \times (x + 1) = (5 \times x) + (5 \times 1)$$

COEFFICIENTS AND THE DISTRIBUTIVE PROPERTY

A **coefficient** is a number or symbol that is multiplied by a variable. For example, in the expression 2(ab), the number 2 is the coefficient of (ab). The expression can be written in other ways to have a different coefficient. For example, the expression can be 2a(b). This means that 2a is the coefficient of (b).

The **distributive property** can be used to multiply each addend in parentheses. Then, the products are added to reach the result. The formula for the distributive property looks like this:

$$a(b + c) = ab + ac$$

EXAMPLE

6(2+4)

First, multiply 6 and 2. The answer is 12.

Then, multiply 6 and 4. The answer is 24.

Last, we add 12 and 24. So, the final answer is 36.

ROOTS AND SQUARE ROOTS

A **square root** is a number that when multiplied by itself results in a real number. For example, $\sqrt{4} = +2$ and -2 because $(-2) \times (-2) = 4$ and $(2) \times (2) = 4$. Now, $\sqrt{9} = +3$ and -3 because $(-3) \times (-3) = 9$ and $(3) \times (3) = 9$. So, +2 and -2 are square roots of 4. Also, +3 and -3 are square roots of 9.

Instead of using a **superscript** (e.g., a^x), roots use the **radical symbol** (e.g., $\sqrt{}$) for the operation. A radical will have a number underneath the bar (i.e., radical symbol). Also, a number can be placed in the index. This is the upper left where n is placed: $\sqrt[n]{a}$. So, this is read as *the nth root of a*. There are two special cases for the use of n. When n = 2, this is a square root. When n = 3, this is a cube root.

If there is no number to the upper left, it is understood to be a square root (n = 2). Almost all of the roots that you will face will be square roots. A square root is the same as a number raised to the $\frac{1}{2}$ power. When we say that a is the square root of b ($a = \sqrt{b}$), we mean that the variable multiplied by itself equals b: (a × a = b).

A perfect square is a number that has an integer for its square root. There are 10 perfect squares from 1 to 100: 1, 4, 9, 16, 25, 36, 49, 64, 81, 100. These are the squares for integers: 1, 2, 3, 4, 5, 6, 7, 8, 9, and 10.

EXPONENTS AND PARENTHESES

A number like 7, 23, or 97 is a **base number**. A number that is connected to the base number, as in 7^3, 23^4, or 97^2 is a **superscript** number. An **exponent** is a superscript number placed at the top right of a base number. Exponents are a short form of a longer math operation. This superscript number shows how many times the base number is to be multiplied by itself.

For example, consider $a^2 = a \times a$ or $2^4 = 2 \times 2 \times 2 \times 2$. A number with an exponent of 2 is said to be **squared**. A number with an exponent of 3 is said to be **cubed**. The value of a number raised to an exponent is called its **power**. So, 8^4 is read as *8 to the 4th power* or *8 raised to the power of 4*. A negative exponent can be written as a fraction to have a positive exponent. Example: $a^{-2} = 1/a^2$.

LAWS OF EXPONENTS

The laws of exponents are as follows:

1. Any number to the power of 1 is equal to itself: $a^1 = a$.
    Examples: $2^1=2$ | $-3^1=-3$

2. The number 1 raised to any power is equal to 1: $1^n = 1$.
    Examples: $1^3=1$ | $1^{30}=1$

3. Any number raised to the power of 0 is equal to 1: $a^0 = 1$.
    Examples: $8^0=1$ | $(-10)^0=1$ | $(1/2)^0=1$

4. Add exponents to multiply powers of the same base number: $a^n \times a^m = a^{n+m}$.
    Example: $2^3 \times 2^4 = 2^{3+4} = 2^7 = 128$

5. Subtract exponents to divide powers of the same base number: $a^n \div a^m = a^{n-m}$.
    Example: $\frac{2^5}{2^3} = 2^{5-3} = 2^2 = 4$

6. When a power is raised to a power, the exponents are multiplied: $(a^n)^m = a^{n \times m}$.
    Example: $(3^2)^3 = 3^2 \times 3^2 \times 3^2 = 3^6 = 729$

7. Multiplication and division operations that are inside parentheses can be raised to a power. This is the same as each term being raised to that power: $(a \times b)^n = a^n \times b^n$; $(a \div b)^n = a^n \div b^n$.
    Multiplication: $(2 \times 3)^2 = 2^2 \times 3^2 = 4 \times 9 = 36$
    Division: $(4 \div 3)^3 = 4^3 \div 3^3 = 64 \div 27 = 2.37$

Note: Exponents do not have to be integers. Fractional or decimal exponents follow all the rules above as well.
Example: $5^{\frac{1}{4}} \times 5^{\frac{3}{4}} = 5^{\frac{1}{4}+\frac{3}{4}} = 5^1 = 5$.

> **Review Video: Laws of Exponents**
> Visit mometrix.com/academy and enter code: 532558

Parentheses are used to show which operation should be done first when there is more than one operation. Example: $4 - (2 + 1) = 1$. So, the first step for this problem is to add 2 and 1. Then, subtract the sum from 4.

SOLVING FOR A VARIABLE

Similar to order of operation rules, algebraic rules must be obeyed to ensure a correct answer. Begin by locating all parentheses and brackets, and then solving the equations within them. Then, perform the operations necessary to remove all parentheses and brackets. Next, convert all fractions into whole numbers and combine common terms on each side of the equation.

Beginning on the **left** side of the expression, solve operations involving multiplication and division. Then, work **left to right** solving operations involving addition and subtraction. Finally, cross-multiply if necessary, to reach the final solution.

EXAMPLE

$4a-10=10$

Constants are the numbers in equations that do not change. The variable in this equation is a. Variables are most commonly presented as either x or y, but they can be any letter. Every **variable** is equal to a number. One must solve the equation to determine what that number is. In an algebraic expression, the answer will usually be the number represented by the variable. In order to solve this equation, keep in mind that what is done to one side must be done to the other side as well. The first step will be to remove 10 from the left side by adding 10 to both sides. This will be expressed as $4a-10+10=10+10$, which simplifies to $4a=20$. Next, remove the 4 by dividing both sides by 4. This step will be expressed as $4a÷4=20÷4$. The expression now becomes $a=5$.

Quantitative

Since variables are the letters that represent an **unknown number**, you must solve for that unknown number in single variable problems. The main thing to remember is that you can do anything to one side of an equation as long as you do it to the other.

EXAMPLE

Solve for x in the equation 2x + 3 = 5.

First you want to get the "2x" isolated by itself on one side. To do that, first get rid of the 3. Subtract 3 from both sides of the equation 2x + 3 – 3 = 5 – 3 or 2x = 2. Now since the x is being multiplied by the 2 in "2x", you must divide by 2 to get rid of it. So, divide both sides by 2, which gives 2x / 2 = 2 / 2 or x = 1.

MANIPULATING EQUATIONS

Sometimes you will have variables missing in equations. So, you need to find the missing variable. To do this, you need to remember one important thing: whatever you do to one side of an equation, you need to do to the other side. If you subtract 100 from one side of an equation, you need to subtract 100 from the other side of the equation. This will allow you to change the form of the equation to find missing values.

EXAMPLE

Ray earns $10 an hour. This can be given with the expression $10x$, where x is equal to the number of hours that Ray works. This is the independent variable. The independent variable is the amount that can change. The money that Ray earns is in y hours. So, you would write the equation: $10x = y$. The variable y is the dependent variable. This depends on x and cannot be changed. Now, let's say that Ray makes $360. How many hours did he work to make $360?

$$10x = 360$$

Now, you want to know how many hours that Ray worked. So, you want to get x by itself. To do that, you can divide both sides of the equation by 10.

$$\frac{10x}{10} = \frac{360}{10}$$

So, you have: $x = 36$. Now, you know that Ray worked 36 hours to make $360.

FUNCTIONS
EXAMPLE

The table below is the value of each part of an ordered pair. An ordered pair is written as: (x, y)

x	y
2	6
4	12
6	18
8	24

You can find y if you know x. The number in the y column is three times the number in the x column. Multiply the x number by 3 to get the y number.

x	y
2	$2 \times 3 = 6$
4	$4 \times 3 = 12$
6	$6 \times 3 = 18$
8	$8 \times 3 = 24$

EXAMPLE

The table shows some data points for a linear function. What is the missing value in the table?

x	y
0	?
3	50
5	80

The data in the table represent a linear function. For a linear function, the rate of change is equal to the slope. To find the slope, calculate the change in y divided by the change in x for the two given points from the table:

$$m = \frac{80-50}{5-3} = \frac{30}{2} = 15$$

The rate of change of the linear function is 15. This means for each increase of 1 in the value of x, the value of y increases by 15. Similarly, each decrease of 1 in the value of x decreases the value of y by 15. The x-value 0 is 3 less than 3, so subtract $3 \cdot 15 = 45$ from 50 to get $y = 5$. This is the missing value in the table.

Quantitative

Geometry

CLASSIFYING TWO-DIMENSIONAL FIGURES

Two-dimensional shapes can be classified and sorted based on properties such as number of angles, edges, and vertices. **Polygons** are two-dimensional figures that are formed by straight lines on a flat surface. One way to sort polygons is based on the number of sides they have.

Graphic organizers can be helpful for sorting polygons into categories. Polygons can be split into three categories. One category contains three-sided polygons called **triangles**, one category contains four-sided polygons called **quadrilaterals**, and one category contains polygons with more than four sides. Notice how the number of sides is always the same as the number of angles and vertices.

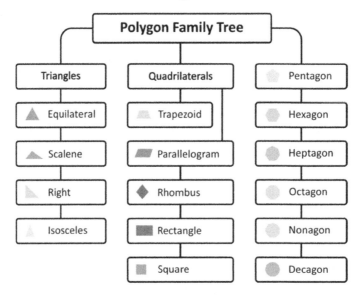

EXAMPLE

Franklin is sorting two-dimensional shapes. He places a rectangle, square, and rhombus into a group, and labels the group "parallelograms." Franklin's friend Henry says that this is incorrect because the group should also contain trapezoids. Is Henry correct?

Henry is not correct. Franklin has labeled the shapes correctly.

Rectangles, squares, and rhombi fall under the umbrella of parallelograms. Parallelograms are defined as four-sided figures with two pairs of opposite sides that are parallel. Trapezoids do not fall into this category because trapezoids only have one set of parallel sides. A trapezoid is shown below.

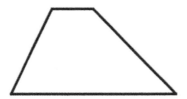

EXAMPLE

Elizabeth states that all squares can be classified as a rhombus, but not all rhombi are classified as squares. Ryan states that all rhombi can be classified as squares, but not all squares can be classified as rhombi. Who is correct?

Elizabeth is correct.

All squares can be classified as a rhombus, but not all rhombi are classified as squares. A square has four congruent sides and four right angles. This qualifies as a rhombus because a rhombus is a four-sided figure with four congruent sides. However, in a rhombus, the angles do not have to be 90 degrees. For example, both figures below can be classified as a rhombus, but only the figure on the left can be classified as a square.

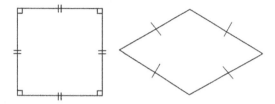

ANGLES

An **angle** is made when two lines or line segments meet at a point. The angle may be a starting point for a pair of segments or rays. Angles may also come from the intersection of lines. The symbol ∠ stands for angles. Angles that are opposite to one another are called vertical angles, and their measures are equal. The **vertex** is the point where two segments or rays meet to make an angle. Angles that are made from intersecting rays, lines, and/or line segments have four angles at the vertex.

An **acute angle** is an angle with a degree measure less than 90°. A **right angle** is an angle with a degree measure of exactly 90°. An **obtuse angle** is an angle with a degree measure greater than 90° but less than 180°. A **straight angle** is an angle with a degree measure of exactly 180°. A **reflex angle** is an angle with a degree measure greater than 180° but less than 360°. A **full angle** is an angle with a degree measure of exactly 360°.

> **Review Video: Angles**
> Visit mometrix.com/academy and enter code: 264624

Two angles with a sum of exactly 90° are known as **complementary**. The two angles may or may not be adjacent (i.e., *next to* or *beside*). In a right triangle, the two acute angles are complementary.

Two angles with a sum that is exactly 180° are known as **supplementary**. The two angles may or may not be adjacent. Two intersecting lines always make two pairs of supplementary angles. Adjacent supplementary angles will always make a straight line.

CONGRUENCY, SIMILARITY, AND SYMMETRY

Congruent figures are geometric figures that have the **same size and shape**. All corresponding angles are equal, and all corresponding sides are equal. Congruence is shown by the symbol ≅.

Congruent polygons

Quantitative

Similar figures are geometric figures that have the **same shape**, but may not have the same size. All corresponding angles are equal, and all corresponding sides are **proportional**. However, they do not have to be equal. Similarity is shown by the symbol ∼.

Similar polygons

Note that all congruent figures are also similar. However, not all similar figures are congruent.

The line that divides a figure or object into equal parts is a **line of symmetry**. Each part is congruent to the other. An object may have no lines of symmetry, one line of symmetry, or multiple (i.e., more than one) lines of symmetry.

Lines of symmetry:

 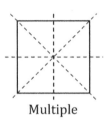

None   One   Multiple

RECTANGLES
PERIMETER OF A RECTANGLE
The perimeter of a **rectangle** can be found with two formulas $P = 2l + 2w$ or $P = 2(l + w)$, where l is the length, and w is the width.

EXAMPLE
You may have problems that give you the perimeter of a rectangle and ask you to find the width or length:

The perimeter of a rectangle is 100cm, and the length is 20cm. Find the width.

First: Set up the equation to set apart the width.

The equation is $100 = 2(20 + w)$

Second: Distribute the 2 across $(20 + w)$: $100 = 40 + 2w$

Then, subtract 40 from both sides: $100 - 40 = 40 + 2w - 40$

So, you are left with: $60 = 2w$. Then, divide both sides by 2: $\frac{60}{2} = \frac{2w}{2}$.

Now, you have $30 = w$.

AREA OF A RECTANGLE

The **area** of a polygon describes the total measure of the amount of space inside the polygon. We describe area using **square units** because area can be described as the number of squares that cover the inside of a polygon. A rectangle is a polygon with four sides, two sets of parallel sides, and four right angles.

If we have a rectangle that is 5 inches by 3 inches, we can count the number of square inches inside the rectangle to find the area.

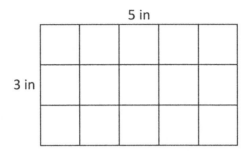

By counting the square inches in this rectangle, we can see that the area is 15 square units.

AREA FORMULA FOR RECTANGLES

We can also use formulas to find the area of a rectangle. Instead of counting the square units, we can find the area of a rectangle by multiplying the base and the height, or multiplying perpendicular sides. **Perpendicular sides** create right angles. Sides can be described as a base and a height, or length and width.

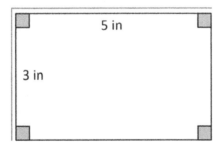

$$5 \text{ in} \times 3 \text{ in} = 15 \text{ sq in}$$

The side length that is 3 inches is perpendicular to the side length that is 5 inches, so the area is 15 square inches.

The area of a shape does not change if it is positioned differently. Consider the rectangle below.

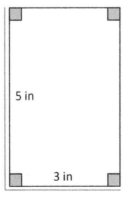

In this example, the base is 3 inches and the height is 5 inches. These sides are still perpendicular to each other, so we can still multiply the base and height to find the area.

$$\text{Area} = \text{base} \times \text{height}$$
$$A = b \times h$$
$$A = 3 \text{ in} \times 5 \text{ in}$$
$$A = 15 \text{ square inches}$$

The formula for finding the area of a rectangle is area equals the base times the height, or $A = b \cdot h$, where the base and height are perpendicular.

EXAMPLE

If we have a rectangle with a given area and a given side length, we can use the area formula to find a missing side length.

A rectangle has an area of 20 square units, and a base of 5 units, we can use the area formula to find the height.

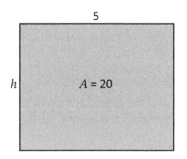

$$A = b \times h$$
$$\frac{20}{5} = \frac{5 \times h}{5}$$
$$\frac{20}{5} = h$$
$$h = 4$$

If we have a rectangle with an area of 20 square units, and a base of 5 units, the height is 4 units because 20 divided by 5 is 4.

We can use equivalent equations to find alternative area formulas. For example, to find a missing height, we can use the equation $h = \frac{A}{b}$, or to find a missing base, we can use the equation $b = \frac{A}{h}$. We can divide the total area by the side length to find the missing perpendicular side length.

$\frac{A}{b} = \frac{b \times h}{b}$ $\frac{A}{b} = h$ $h = \frac{A}{b}$	$\frac{A}{h} = \frac{b \times h}{h}$ $\frac{A}{h} = b$ $b = \frac{A}{h}$

TRIANGLES

ANGLES

There are a few rules about triangles that are important to remember that have to do with angles and side lengths. The first rule is that the angles in a triangle add up to **180 degrees**. You can remember this because we know that a square's angles add to 360 degrees because each angle in a square is a right angle, or 90 degrees, and $90° + 90° + 90° + 90° = 360°$. Half of a square is a triangle, so all angles in a triangle add up to half of 360 degrees, which is 180 degrees.

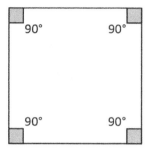
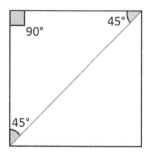

You can use this information to solve problems about angle measures of triangles. If we know two angle measurements, we can calculate the third. If we are given three angle measurements, we can conclude whether they could possibly create a triangle. Suppose a triangle has two angle measures, 90° and 45°, we can find the measure of the third angle. We know that all three angles of a triangle must add up to 180°, so the missing angle must measure 45°.

$$90° + 45° + x = 180°$$
$$x = 45°$$

SIDE LENGTHS

The second rule about triangles is about side lengths. For three sides to form a triangle, the sum of two side lengths must be greater than the length of the third side. This goes for any two sides in a triangle. This is true because if two side lengths are smaller than the third side, the triangle would form an open figure. Let's say we have three lengths: length A is 6 inches, length B is 3 inches, and length C is 1 inch. This can never make a triangle. We can see this mathematically. The sum of two side lengths must be greater than the third side length.

| 6 in ———— A |
| 3 in ——— B |
| 1 in — C |

$A + B > C$	$A + C > B$	$B + C > A$
$6 + 3 > 1$	$6 + 1 > 3$	$3 + 1 > 6$
$9 > 1$	$7 > 3$	$4 > 6$
TRUE	TRUE	FALSE

So, because the sum of length B and C is smaller than length A, these lengths can never form a triangle. The figures below show how the three sides cannot connect with the given lengths.

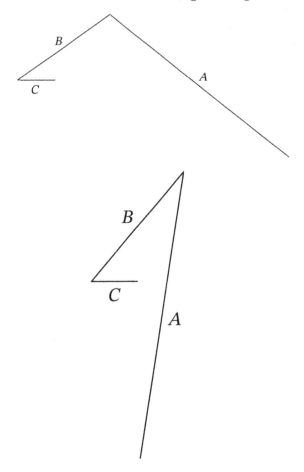

Neither of these are examples of triangles.

Now, if we had the lengths 6 inches, 3 inches, and 5 inches, we could make a triangle.

We can see this mathematically.

$A + B > C$	$B + C > A$	$A + C > B$
$6 + 3 > 5$	$3 + 5 > 6$	$6 + 5 > 3$
$9 > 5$	$8 > 6$	$11 > 3$
TRUE	TRUE	TRUE

And visually.

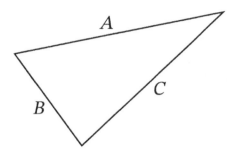

Review Video: <u>General Rules for Triangles</u>
Visit mometrix.com/academy and enter code: 166488

TYPES OF TRIANGLES

An **equilateral triangle** is a triangle with three congruent sides. Also, an equilateral triangle will have three congruent angles and each angle will be 60°. All equilateral triangles are acute triangles.

An **isosceles triangle** is a triangle with two congruent sides. An isosceles triangle will have two congruent angles as well.

A **scalene triangle** is a triangle with no congruent sides. Also, a scalene triangle will have three angles of different measures. The angle with the largest measure is opposite from the longest side. The angle with the smallest measure is opposite from the shortest side.

An **acute triangle** is a triangle whose three angles are all less than 90°. If two of the angles are equal, the acute triangle is also an isosceles triangle. If the three angles are all equal, the acute triangle is also an equilateral triangle.

A **right triangle** is a triangle with exactly one angle equal to 90°. A right triangle can never be acute or obtuse.

An **obtuse triangle** is a triangle with one angle greater than 90°. The other two angles may or may not be equal. If the two remaining angles are equal, the obtuse triangle is also an isosceles triangle.

PERIMETER OF A TRIANGLE

The perimeter of any triangle is found by adding the three side lengths $P = a + b + c$. For an equilateral triangle, this is the same as $P = 3s$, where s is any side length. The reason is that the three sides are the same length.

EXAMPLE

You may have problems that give you the perimeter of a triangle. So, you are asked to find one of the sides:

81

The perimeter of a triangle is 35 cm. One side length is 10 cm. Another side length is 20cm. Find the length of the missing side.

First: Set up the equation to set apart a side length.

Now, the equation is $35 = 10 + 20 + c$. So, you are left with $35 = 30 + c$.

Second: Subtract 30 from both sides: $35 - 30 = 30 - 30 + c$

Then, you are left with $5 = c$

AREA OF A TRIANGLE

We can dissect and rearrange simple shapes to find the areas of difficult shapes. The formula for the area of a rectangle is $A = b \cdot h$, and we can use this formula to help us model the area of a triangle.

A triangle has half of the area of a rectangle with the same base and height measurements as the triangle. We can represent this visually.

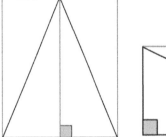 

When looking at an obtuse triangle in this way, the triangle will extend outside the rectangle formed by the base and height. But the area of the triangle is still equal to half the area of the rectangle made from the base and height.

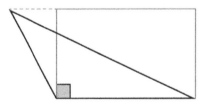

Remember, the base and height of a polygon will always be perpendicular and will create a right angle.

AREA FORMULA FOR TRIANGLES

Knowing that a triangle is half of a rectangle with the same base and height, we can determine that the area of a triangle can be found by multiplying the base and height of the triangle and dividing this product by 2.

When we multiply the base and height of a triangle, we are finding the area of the surrounding rectangle which is twice the area of the triangle. We need to divide this area by 2 to find the area of the triangle. The formula $A = \frac{1}{2}bh$ is used to find the area of a triangle.

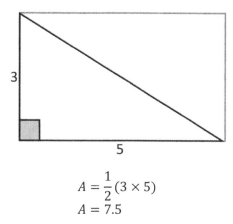

$$A = \frac{1}{2}(3 \times 5)$$
$$A = 7.5$$

The area of a rectangle with a base and height of 5 and 3 is 15 square units. A triangle with the same base and height will be half of that, so 7.5 square units.

> **Review Video: <u>Area and Perimeter of a Triangle</u>**
> Visit mometrix.com/academy and enter code: 853779

EXAMPLE

A triangle is pictured below. What is the area of the triangle in square meters?

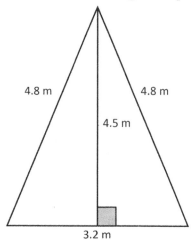

In this problem, we are given a picture of a triangle with the base, height, and all side lengths labeled. We need to first identify the base and the height out of all these measurements.

Remember, the base and height will always be perpendicular and will form a right angle, and only two measurements form a right angle, which is depicted by a square in the corner.

The base of the triangle is 3.2 meters and the height of the triangle is 4.5 meters.

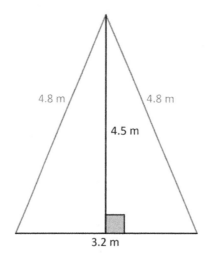

Now that we have identified the base and height of the triangle, we can use the triangle formula to find the area in square meters.

The triangle area formula is half of the base times the height, or half of the area of the surrounding rectangle. We can use the triangle area formula, input the given values, and solve.

$$A = \frac{1}{2}b \times h$$
$$A = \frac{1}{2}(3.2 \times 4.5)$$
$$A = \frac{1}{2}(14.4)$$
$$A = 7.2 \text{ m}^2$$

The area of the triangle is 7.2 square meters.

PARALLELOGRAMS

PERIMETER OF A PARALLELOGRAM

The perimeter of a **parallelogram** is found by the formula $P = 2a + 2b$ or $P = 2(a + b)$, where a and b are the lengths of the two sides.

EXAMPLE

You may have problems that give you the perimeter of a parallelogram. So, you are asked to find one of the sides:

The perimeter of a parallelogram is 100cm, and one side is 20cm. Find the other side.

First: Set up the equation to set apart one of the side lengths.

The equation is $100 = 2(20 + b)$

Second: Distribute the 2 across $(20 + b)$: $100 = 40 + 2b$

Then, subtract 40 from both sides: $100 - 40 = 40 + 2b - 40$

So, you are left with: $60 = 2b$. Then, divide both sides by 2: $\frac{60}{2} = \frac{2b}{2}$

Now, you have $30 = b$.

AREA OF A PARALLELOGRAM

The area of a parallelogram can be found by dissecting the shapes within the parallelogram. Within a parallelogram, there are rectangles and triangles. The area of a polygon remains the same whether it is decomposed or rearranged. Consider the following rectangle that is split into two squares.

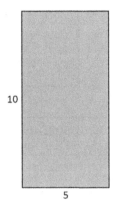 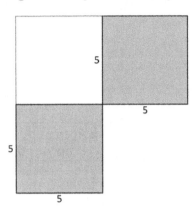

These shapes have the same area even though the area is decomposed, split apart, and rearranged, moved around. The shaded area is still 50 square units regardless of placement.

AREA FORMULA FOR PARALLELOGRAMS

When we are dealing with polygons, we can divide the shape into easier-to-calculate shapes and add these smaller areas together. The area of a polygon is the same as the sum of its parts, so we can use what we know about rectangles and triangles to find the area of the parallelogram.

A parallelogram has two sets of parallel sides. As you can see, this means that a parallelogram has two identical triangles on either side.

If we rearrange these "triangle ends" we can see that a rectangle with the same measurements is formed. We know that the area of a rectangle can be found using the formula $A = b \cdot h$, which is the same formula as a parallelogram. The area of a parallelogram is equivalent to the area of a rectangle with the same base and height measurements.

$$A = 5 \times 2$$

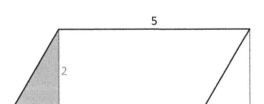 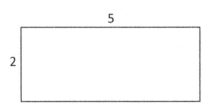

Remember, bases and heights are perpendicular, so the base and height of a parallelogram is the set of perpendicular measurements.

85

These parallelograms have the same area. The base and height are depicted. As you can see, the base and height can be found by identifying the base and height of the equivalent rectangle. The "slanted" side length is not used to find area.

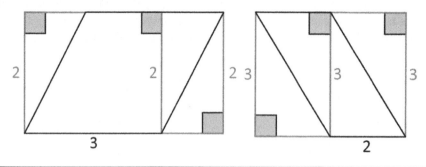

Review Video: <u>Area and Perimeter of a Parallelogram</u>
Visit mometrix.com/academy and enter code: 718313

EXAMPLE

A park is shaped like a parallelogram. The dimensions are shown below.

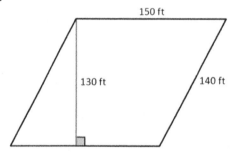

What is the total area of the parallelogram in square feet?

In this problem, we are given the dimensions of a parallelogram and need to calculate the total area in square feet.

The area of a parallelogram can be found using the formula $A = b \cdot h$, where the base and height are perpendicular lines.

In this diagram, the perpendicular pair is 150 feet and 130 feet. We will not use the 140 ft measurement because this side length is not part of a perpendicular pair. We will input these values in our formula and multiply.

$$A = b \times h$$
$$A = 150 \times 130$$
$$A = 19{,}500 \text{ ft}^2$$

The area of the park is 19,500 square feet.

TRAPEZOIDS

PERIMETER OF A TRAPEZOID

The perimeter of a **trapezoid** is found by the formula $P = a + b_1 + c + b_2$, where a, b_1, c, and b_2 are the four sides of the trapezoid.

EXAMPLE

The perimeter of a trapezoid is 50cm. B_1 is 20cm, B_2 is 10cm, and a is 5cm. Find the length of side c.

First: Set up the equation to set apart the missing side.

The equation is $50 = 5 + 20 + c + 10$. So, you have $50 = 35 + c$

Second: Subtract 35 from both sides: $50 - 35 = 35 + c - 35$.

So, you are left with $15 = c$

AREA OF A TRAPEZOID

A trapezoid can be viewed as a collection of rectangles and triangles. A trapezoid has two bases because there are two different sides that are perpendicular to the height.

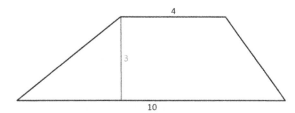

One way to find a formula for the area of a trapezoid is to suppose we have a second copy of the trapezoid. If we rotate one copy 180° and put it next to the original trapezoid, we get a parallelogram:

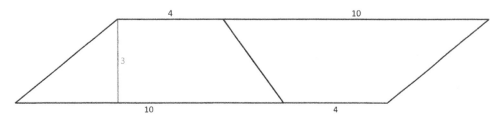

AREA FORMULA FOR TRAPEZOIDS

We have already seen that the area of a parallelogram is equal to its base times height. What are the base and height of the parallelogram made from the two trapezoids? The height is the same as the height of the trapezoid. The base is equal to the sum of the bases of the trapezoids, since the base of the parallelogram is made up of the large base of one trapezoid and the small base of the other.

We can use h to refer to the height of the trapezoid, b_1 to refer to the measurement of one of its bases, and b_2 to refer to the measurement of the other base. The height of the parallelogram is h and the base of the parallelogram is $b_1 + b_2$. The area of the parallelogram is $(b_1 + b_2) \times h$.

But the parallelogram is made up of two copies of the trapezoid. That means the area of the parallelogram is twice the area of the original trapezoid. To find the area of the trapezoid, we need to divide the area of the parallelogram by 2, or multiply it by $\frac{1}{2}$. This gives the formula: $A = \frac{1}{2}(b_1 + b_2) \times h$.

So, to find the area of the trapezoid shown above, we can substitute values into the formula and simplify.

$$A = \frac{1}{2}(b_1 + b_2) \times h$$
$$A = \frac{1}{2}(4 + 10) \times 3$$
$$A = \frac{1}{2}(14 \times 3)$$
$$A = \frac{1}{2}(42)$$

87

$$A = 21 \text{ units}^2$$

The area of the trapezoid is 21 square units.

Review Video: Area and Perimeter of a Trapezoid
Visit mometrix.com/academy and enter code: 587523

EXAMPLE
Calculate the area of the trapezoid.

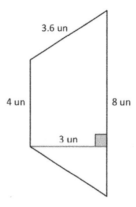

In this problem, we are given a diagram of a trapezoid and need to calculate the area.

First, we need to identify the area formula for a trapezoid. The area formula is $A = \frac{1}{2}(b_1 + b_2)h$.

Now, we need to identify the bases and the height of the trapezoid. The bases are always parallel to each other, and in the diagram, the line measuring 4 units and the line measuring 8 units are parallel. These are the values for our bases.

The height of a trapezoid is always perpendicular to the bases. In the diagram, the line measuring 3 units is perpendicular to the bases. This is the value for the height.

Now, we can substitute the given values and simplify.

$$A = \frac{1}{2}(b_1 + b_2) \times h$$
$$A = \frac{1}{2}(4 + 8) \times 3$$
$$A = \frac{1}{2}(12) \times 3$$
$$A = \frac{1}{2}(36)$$
$$A = 18 \text{ un}^2$$

We have calculated area, so the units are square units. The area of the trapezoid is 18 square units.

SOLVING FOR MEASUREMENTS OF CIRCLES

The relationships between the measurements of a circle are unique. A circle does not have any sides or angles. The perimeter of a circle is called the **circumference**, and the width of a circle is called the **diameter**. The

88

radius of a circle is the length from the center to any point along the circumference. The radius is half of the diameter.

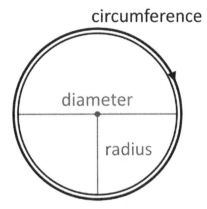

Pi, represented by the symbol π, is the constant for the proportional relationship between a circle's circumference and diameter. Pi is often rounded to 3.14. Formulas are used to find the circumference and area of circles and they all involve π.

CIRCUMFERENCE

The circumference of a circle can be found by multiplying the diameter by π. The formula to solve for the circumference of a circle is $C = \pi d$ where C represents the circumference and d represents the diameter.

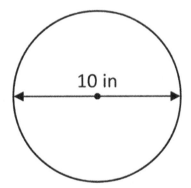

This circle has a diameter of 10 inches. We can use $C = \pi d$ to calculate the circumference.

$$C = \pi d$$
$$C = \pi \cdot 10$$
$$C = 10\pi$$

We could say that the circumference of the circle is 10π inches, or we can express the value as an approximate decimal.

$$C \approx 3.14 \cdot 10$$
$$C \approx 31.4$$

The circumference is about 31.4 inches. We say that it is about 31.4 inches because 3.14 is a rounded form of pi.

The diameter of a circle is twice the radius, so the circumference of a circle can also be found by multiplying the radius by 2 and π. An alternative circumference formula is $C = 2\pi r$, where r represents the radius.

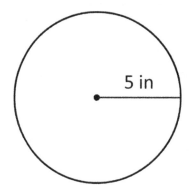

If a circle has a diameter of 10, then the radius is 5. We can use the radius to find the circumference of the circle.

$$C = 2\pi r$$
$$C = 2\pi(5)$$
$$C = 2 \cdot 5 \cdot \pi$$
$$C = 10\pi$$
$$C \approx 10 \cdot 3.14$$
$$C \approx 31.4$$

Both formulas find the circumference of the circle to be 10π inches or about 31.4 inches.

EXAMPLE

A circle has a radius of 6. Which measurement is closest to the circumference of the circle?

    a.   113.04 cm
    b.   37.68 cm
    c.   452.16 cm
    d.   18.84 cm

Each answer choice is a decimal, so we will substitute 3.14 for π in the circumference formula to solve.

$$C = 2\pi r$$
$$C \approx 2 \times 3.14 \times 6$$
$$C \approx 12 \times 3.14$$
$$C \approx 37.68$$

The circumference of the circle is about 37.68 centimeters. The correct answer is B.

AREA

The area of a circle can be found by multiplying π by the radius squared.

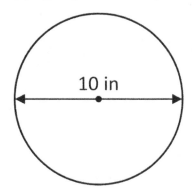

The diameter of this circle is 10 inches, so the radius of the circle is 5 inches. The formula for the area of a circle is $A = \pi r^2$.

$$A = \pi r^2$$
$$A = \pi \cdot 5^2$$
$$A = \pi \cdot 25$$
$$A = 25\pi$$

We can say that the area of the circle is 25π square inches, or we express the area as an approximate decimal by using 3.14 in place of π.

$$A \approx 25 \cdot 3.14$$
$$A \approx 78.5$$

The area of the circle is about 78.5 square inches.

EXAMPLE

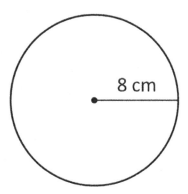

Which measurement is closest to the area of the circle?

    a. 25.12 cm^2
    b. 50.24 cm^2
    c. 200.96 cm^2
    d. 204.8 cm^2

Each answer choice is in decimal form, so we will substitute 3.14 for π in the circumference formula to solve.

$$A = \pi r^2$$
$$A \approx 3.14 \times 8^2$$

Quantitative

$$C \approx 3.14 \times 64$$
$$C \approx 200.96$$

The area of the circle is about 200.96 square centimeters. The correct answer is C.

> **Review Video: <u>Area and Circumference of a Circle</u>**
> Visit mometrix.com/academy and enter code: 243015

AREA OF COMPOSITE FIGURES

The **area** is a measurement of the total space a two-dimensional figure occupies. Area is described using square units. Rectangles, squares, triangles, parallelograms, trapezoids, and circles are examples of shapes.

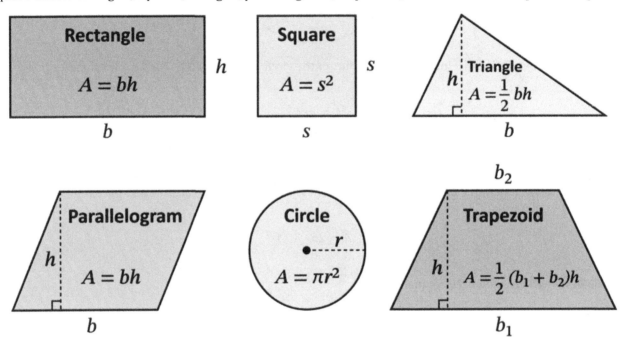

Figures that are made from a collection of shapes are called **composite figures**. Because composite figures are collections of shapes, we can find the areas of composite figures by combining known area formulas.

EXAMPLE

A window is comprised of a rectangle and a half circle.

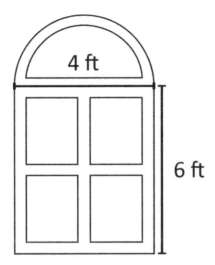

To find the area of the window, we can find the area of the rectangle and add this to the area of the half circle.

The formula for the area of a rectangle is $A = bh$. The base of the rectangle part of the window is 4 feet and the height is 6 feet.

$$A = bh$$
$$A = 4 \cdot 6$$
$$A = 24$$

The area of the rectangle part is 24 square feet, or 24 ft^2.

The formula for the area of a circle is $A = \pi r^2$. The window includes a half circle, so we can use the circle area formula and divide by 2 to find the area of the half circle. The diameter of the circle is 4 feet, which means that the radius is 2 feet.

$$A = \frac{\pi r^2}{2}$$
$$A = \frac{3.14 \cdot (2)^2}{2}$$
$$A = \frac{3.14 \cdot 4}{2}$$
$$A = \frac{12.56}{2}$$
$$A = 6.28$$

The area of the half circle is approximately 6.28 square feet, or 6.28 ft^2.

The area of the window is the sum of the two areas, $24 + 6.28 = 30.28$. So, the area of the window is approximately 30.28 square feet.

Quantitative

EXAMPLE

A bathroom counter is a trapezoid with a circle cut out for a sink.

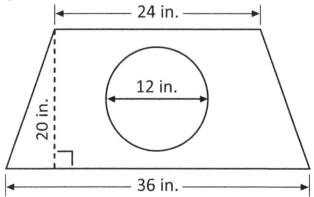

What is the best estimate of the area of the countertop that does not include the space for the sink?

This composite figure is made of a trapezoid with a circle removed. The area can be found by finding the area of the trapezoid and subtracting the area of the circle.

The formula to find the area of a trapezoid is $A = \frac{1}{2}(b_1 + b_2)h$. The trapezoid counter has two bases that measure 36 and 24 inches and a height of 20 inches.

$$A = \frac{1}{2}(b_1 + b_2) \cdot h$$
$$A = \frac{1}{2}(36 + 24) \cdot 20$$
$$A = \frac{1}{2}(60) \cdot 20$$
$$A = \frac{1}{2} \cdot 1{,}200$$
$$A = 600$$

The area of the trapezoid is 600 square inches.

The circle cut out of the trapezoid has a diameter of 12 inches, so it has a radius of 6 inches. The formula for the area of a circle is $A = \pi r^2$.

$$A = \pi r^2$$
$$A \approx 3.14 \times 6^2$$
$$A \approx 3.14 \times 36$$
$$A \approx 113.04$$

The area of the circle is about 113.04 square inches.

The area of the counter is the area of the trapezoid minus the area of the circle, $600 - 113.04 = 486.96$. So, the area of the counter is about 486.96 square inches.

VOLUME AND CUBIC UNITS

All three-dimensional figures occupy space. This space is defined as **volume**. Volume is also known as capacity. Spheres, prisms, pyramids, cylinders, cones, and cubes are common three-dimensional figures that have volume. The volume of a three-dimensional solid is measured in cubic units. For example, a cube has a length, width, and height. A cube that is 1 unit tall, 1 unit wide, and 1 unit deep is called a **unit cube**. The number of unit cubes that fills a solid determines its volume. The formula $V = l \times w \times h$, where l is length, w is width, and h is height, can be used to calculate the volume of a cube or rectangular prism.

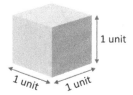

For example, a rectangular prism that is has a height of 4 units, a width of 3 units, and a depth of 6 units has a volume of 4 units $\times$ 3 units $\times$ 6 units, which is 72 units^3. Remember, this is *not* the volume formula for all three-dimensional solids. Each solid has its own volume formula.

Many solids will have dimensions that give specific units. For example, a cube might have side lengths measured in centimeters, which means the volume would be described as "cubic centimeters," not "cubic units."

Consider the cube below. The side lengths are all 4 centimeters. The volume formula can be applied. $V = l \times w \times h$ becomes $V = 4 \times 4 \times 4$. This simplifies to 64, so the volume of the cube is 64 cm^3. There are 64 total squares in the cube, so the volume is 64 cm^3. Notice how the volume formula takes less time than counting up each individual square.

VOLUME OF A RECTANGULAR PRISM

The volume of a rectangular prism can be found in a variety of ways. One option is to simply count every single cube within the prism. This is generally unrealistic because of the amount of time it takes. Another option is to calculate volume based on the number of **layers** within a cube. For example, consider the $5 \times 5 \times 5$ cube below. Notice how there are 5 horizontal layers, and each layer contains 25 unit cubes. There are 5 of these layers, so the total volume can be calculated as 5×25, or 5 groups of 25, which is 125. Therefore, the volume of the cube is 125 cubic units.

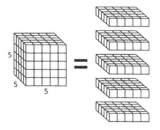

This layering strategy can be applied to cubes and rectangular prisms. For example, the prism below is constructed from 5 horizontal layers. Each layer contains 4 columns and 8 rows. This means that each layer contains 4 × 8, or 32 unit cubes. Each layer contains 32 unit cubes, and there are 5 layers. Therefore, the total number of unit cubes can be calculated as 5 × 32 = 160, or 160 cubic units.

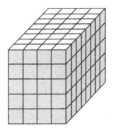

VOLUME OF PYRAMIDS

A **pyramid** is a three-dimensional shape that is formed when a base has slanted sides that meet to form a point. A rectangular pyramid has a rectangular base that is connected to a point. A triangular pyramid has a triangular base that is connected to a point. The point of a pyramid where the sides connect is called the **apex**.

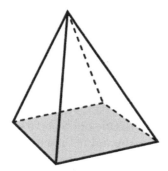
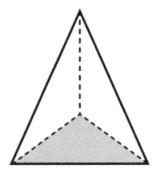

rectangular pyramid   triangular pyramid

To find the volume of a pyramid, you will multiply the area of the base of the pyramid by the height of the pyramid and then multiply the product by one third. The formula that is used to find the volume of a pyramid is $V = \frac{1}{3}Bh$.

EXAMPLE

A rectangular pyramid has a rectangular base that is connected to a point.

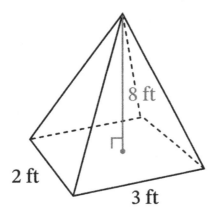

This rectangular pyramid has a rectangular base that measures 2 feet by 3 feet and has a height of 8 feet. We can find the volume by using the pyramid volume formula.

$$V = \frac{1}{3}Bh$$
$$V = \frac{1}{3}(2 \cdot 3) \cdot 8$$
$$V = \frac{1}{3}(6) \cdot 8$$
$$V = \frac{1}{3} \cdot 48$$
$$V = 48 \div 3$$
$$V = 16$$

The volume of a figure is written in cubic units, so the volume of the rectangular pyramid is 16 cubic feet, or 16 ft^3.

EXAMPLE

A triangular pyramid has a base with an area of 16.5 square centimeters, and it has a height of 10 centimeters. What is the volume of the triangular pyramid in cubic centimeters?

We are given that the base of the pyramid has an area of 16.5 square centimeters and the height of the pyramid is 10 centimeters. We can use the pyramid volume formula to solve.

$$V = \frac{1}{3}Bh$$
$$V = \frac{1}{3} \times 16.5 \times 10$$
$$V = \frac{1}{3} \times 165$$
$$V = 55$$

The volume of the triangular pyramid is 55 cubic centimeters, or 55 cm^3.

SURFACE AREA OF PRISMS AND PYRAMIDS

The **surface area** of a three-dimensional figure is the total two-dimensional area of the surface of the figure. We can find the surface area of a three-dimensional figure by adding the area of each face of the figure.

Quantitative

A **net** is an "unfolded" version of a three-dimensional figure. It is as if the figure is opened and laid flat. The net of a three-dimensional figure accurately identifies the polygon faces that make a three-dimensional figure.

EXAMPLE

The net of a rectangular prism is shown.

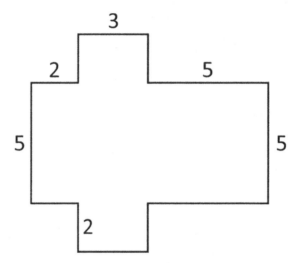

The total surface area of the rectangular prism can be found by finding the sum of the areas of each polygon in the figure. All "pieces" of the surface area of a rectangular prism are rectangles, so we can use the rectangle area formula to find the area of each rectangle.

There are many ways to divide the net of a rectangular prism into smaller rectangles. In this example, the net can be divided into one large rectangle, a small rectangle, and a square. It could also be divided into one large rectangle and two small rectangles, or it could be divided into five rectangles. The surface area is the same for every way it is divided.

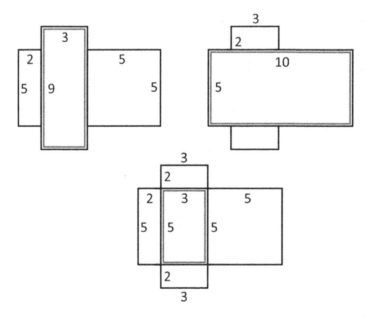

We will divide the net into one large rectangle and two small rectangles. The surface area of the rectangular prism is the sum of the areas of each rectangle. The areas of each rectangle can be found by multiplying the base and the height.

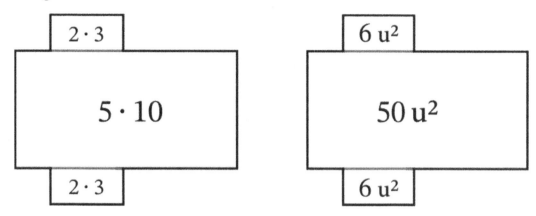

The surface area of the rectangular prism is the sum of the areas of each rectangle.

$$6 + 6 + 50 = 62$$

The surface area of the rectangular prism is 62 square units.

EXAMPLE

A square pyramid is comprised of four congruent triangular faces and a rectangular base. The net of the rectangular pyramid is shown.

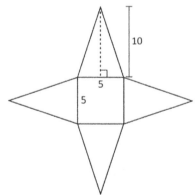

What is the surface area of the rectangular pyramid in square inches?

The surface area of the rectangular pyramid will be the sum of the areas of each shape included in the net. The net includes four triangles with a base of 5 inches and height of 10 inches.

$$A = \frac{1}{2}bh$$
$$A = \frac{1}{2} \cdot 5 \cdot 10$$
$$A = \frac{1}{2} \cdot 50$$
$$A = 25$$

The area of one triangle is 25 square inches.

Quantitative

The net also includes a rectangular base with a base of 5 inches and height of 5 inches. The area of the base can be found by using the area formula for rectangles.

$$A = bh$$
$$A = 5 \cdot 5$$
$$A = 25$$

The area of the rectangular base is 25 square inches.

There are four triangular faces and one rectangular base that form the net of the rectangular pyramid.

$$SA = (25 \cdot 4) + 25$$
$$SA = 100 + 25$$
$$SA = 125$$

The surface area of the rectangular pyramid is 125 square inches.

EXAMPLE

A triangular pyramid has a base with an area measure of 31.2 square inches. Each face has a base of 6 inches and height of 8.2 inches. What is the surface area of the triangular pyramid in square inches?

The triangular pyramid has a base with an area of 31.2 square inches, and each face has a base of 6 inches and a height of 8.2 inches.

A triangular pyramid has a triangular base and three triangular faces.

The area of one face of the pyramid can be found using the triangle area formula.

$$A = \frac{1}{2}bh$$
$$A = \frac{1}{2} \times 6 \times 8.2$$
$$A = \frac{1}{2} \times 49.2$$
$$A = 24.6$$

The area of one face is 24.6 square inches.

The area of the base of the pyramid is 31.2 square inches.

The surface area of the triangular pyramid can be found by finding the total area of the faces and base.

$$SA = (3 \times 24.6) + 31.2$$
$$SA = 73.8 + 31.2$$
$$SA = 105$$

The surface area of the triangular pyramid is 105 square inches.

LINES AND PLANES

A point is a fixed location in space. This point has no size or dimensions. Commonly, this fixed location is a dot. A collinear point is a point which is on the line. A non-collinear point is a point that is not on a line.

A line is a set of points that go forever in two opposite directions. The line has length but no width or depth. A line can be named by any two points that are on the line. A line segment is a part of a line that has definite endpoints. A ray is a part of a line that goes from a single point and goes in one direction along the line. A ray has a definite beginning but no ending.

100

Copyright © Mometrix Media. You have been licensed one copy of this document for personal use only. Any other reproduction or redistribution is strictly prohibited. All rights reserved.
This content is provided for test preparation purposes only and does not imply an endorsement by Mometrix of any particular political, scientific, or religious point of view.

A plane is a two-dimensional flat surface that has three non-collinear points. A plane goes an unending distance in all directions in those two dimensions. This plane has an unending number of points, parallel lines and segments, intersecting lines and segments. Also, a plane can have an unending number of parallel or intersecting rays. A plane will never have a three-dimensional figure or skew lines. Two given planes will be parallel, or they will intersect to form a line. A plane may intersect a circular conic surface (e.g., a cone) to make conic sections (e.g., the parabola, hyperbola, circle, or ellipse).

Perpendicular lines are lines that intersect at right angles. The symbol ⊥ stands for perpendicular lines. The shortest distance from a line to a point that is not on the line is a perpendicular segment from the point to the line.

Parallel lines are lines in the same plane that have no points in common and never meet. The lines can be in different planes, have no points in common, and never meet. However, the lines will not be parallel because they are in different planes.

A bisector is a line or line segment that divides another line segment into two equal lengths. A perpendicular bisector of a line segment has points that are equidistant (i.e., equal distances) from the endpoints of the segment.

Intersecting lines are lines that have exactly one point in common. Concurrent lines are several lines that intersect at a single point. A transversal is a line that intersects at least two other lines. The lines may or may not be parallel to one another. A transversal that intersects parallel lines is common in geometry.

COORDINATE PLANE

The **coordinate plane** is a two-dimensional plane formed from the intersection of a vertical and horizontal line. The horizontal line is referred to as the **x-axis**, and the vertical line is referred to as the **y-axis**. The x-axis and y-axis are perpendicular to each other. The x-axis and y-axis extend out from the **origin**, which is located at the point (0,0). The coordinate plane is sometimes referred to as a **coordinate plane**, and can be used to describe points, or **ordered pairs**. Ordered pairs consist of an x-coordinate and a y-coordinate. The x-coordinate indicates horizontal movement from the origin, to the right or left. The y-coordinate indicates vertical movement from the origin, up or down. In other words, the x- and y-coordinates reflect how far over and how far up an ordered pair is on the coordinate plane. For example, the point (3,2) has an x-coordinate of 3 and a y-coordinate of 2. The point (3,2) is plotted by moving 3 units to the right and 2 units up from the origin (0,0).

Quantitative

GRAPHING ORDERED PAIRS

All ordered pairs take the form (x, y), where x describes the horizontal movement, and y describes the vertical movement. For example, consider the graph below. Start at the origin (0,0). The point (3,5) indicates a movement of 3 units horizontally to the right, and 5 units vertically up. The point (3,5) can be plotted on the coordinate plane.

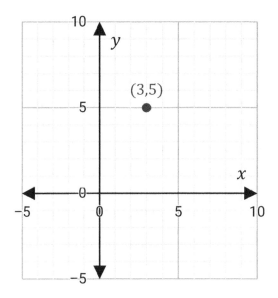

It is important not to swap the x and y locations within an ordered pair. For example, the location of (3,5) is not the same as the location of (5,3).

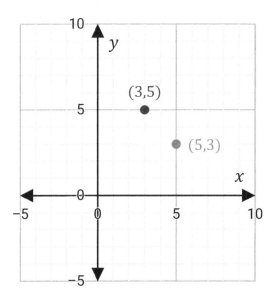

> **Review Video: Cartesian Coordinate Plane and Graphing**
> Visit mometrix.com/academy and enter code: 115173

EXAMPLE

The following points go on the coordinate plane:

A. (−4, −2) | B. (−1, 3) | C. (2, 2) | D. (3, −1)

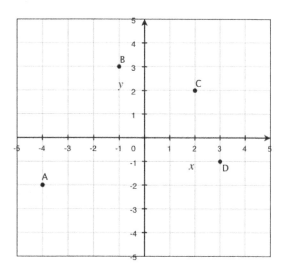

SLOPE

Before learning the different forms of equations for graphing, you need to know some definitions. A ratio of the change in the vertical distance to the change in horizontal distance is called the **slope**.

On a graph with two points, (x_1, y_1) and (x_2, y_2), the **slope** is found with the formula $m = \frac{y_2 - y_1}{x_2 - x_1}$; where $x_1 \neq x_2$ and m stands for slope. If the value of the slope is **positive**, the line has an upward direction from left to right. If the value of the slope is **negative**, the line has a downward direction from left to right.

If the y-coordinates are the same for both points, the slope is **zero**. So, the line is a horizontal line. If the x-coordinates are the same for both points, there is **no slope**. So, the line is a vertical line. Two or more lines that have equal slopes are parallel lines. Perpendicular lines have slopes that are negative reciprocals of each other. For example, $\frac{a}{b}$ and $\frac{-b}{a}$.

Quantitative

EXAMPLE

With the graph below, write an equation in slope-intercept form that describes the line.

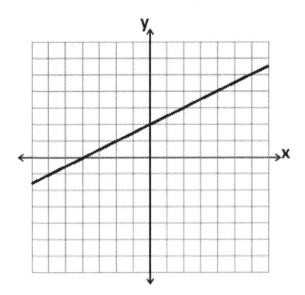

First, find several coordinates on the graph. Then, put them into a table:

x	y
-6	-1
-4	0
-2	1
0	2
2	3

Next, find a relationship between x and y. In this case, as x increases by 2, y increases by 1. This means that $m = 0.5$. The reason is that y changes by half the amount that x does. Also, you know that $b = 2$. The reason is that the graph crosses the y-axis at 2. So, the equation for this graph is $y = 0.5x + 2$.

This is a list of some forms of equations:

- Standard Form: $Ax + By = C$; the slope is $\frac{-A}{B}$ and the y-intercept is $\frac{C}{B}$
- *Slope Intercept Form*: $y = mx + b$, where m is the slope and b is the y-intercept
- Point-Slope Form: $y - y_1 = m(x - x_1)$, where m is the slope and (x_1, y_1) is a point on the line
- Two-Point Form: $\frac{y - y_1}{x - x_1} = \frac{y_2 - y_1}{x_2 - x_1}$, where (x_1, y_1) and (x_2, y_2) are two points on the given line
- *Intercept Form*: $\frac{x}{x_1} + \frac{y}{y_1} = 1$, where $(x_1, 0)$ is the point at which a line intersects the x-axis, and $(0, y_1)$ is the point at which the same line intersects the y-axis

UNIT RATE AS THE SLOPE

A new book goes on sale in book stores and online stores. In the first month, 5,000 copies of the book are sold. Over time, the book continues to grow in popularity. The data for the number of copies sold is in the table below.

# of Months on Sale	1	2	3	4	5

# of Copies Sold (In Thousands)	5	10	15	20	25

So, the number of copies that are sold and the time that the book is on sale is a proportional relationship. In this example, an equation can be used to show the data: y=5x, where x is the number of months that the book is on sale, and y is the number of copies sold. So, the slope is $\frac{rise}{run} = \frac{5}{1}$. This can be reduced to 5.

CALCULATIONS USING POINTS

Sometimes you need to do calculations by using points on a graph. With these points, you can find the midpoint and distance. If you know the equation for a line you can find the distance between the line and the point.

To find the **midpoint** of two points (x_1, y_1) and (x_2, y_2), you need the average of the x-coordinates. This average will give you the x-coordinate of the midpoint. Then, take the average of the y-coordinates. This will give you the y-coordinate of the midpoint. The formula is $\left(\frac{x_1+x_2}{2}, \frac{y_1+y_2}{2}\right) = $ midpoint.

The **distance** between two points is the same as the length of the hypotenuse of a right triangle. So, there is the length of the segment that is parallel to the x-axis. This segment is the difference between the x-coordinates of the two points. Also, there is the length of the segment parallel to the y-axis. This is the difference between the y-coordinates of the two points. Use the Pythagorean Theorem $a^2 + b^2 = c^2$ or $c = \sqrt{a^2 + b^2}$ to find the distance. The formula is $\sqrt{(x_2 - x_1)^2 + (y_2 - y_1)^2} = $ distance.

A line may be given as $Ax + By + C = 0$ where A, B, and C are coefficients. With this equation, you can use a point (x_1, y_1) not on the line and use the formula $d = \frac{|Ax_1 + By_1 + C|}{\sqrt{A^2 + B^2}}$. This formula will give the distance between the line and the point (x_1, y_1).

> **Review Video: Calculations Using Points on a Graph**
> Visit mometrix.com/academy and enter code: 883228

TRANSFORMATION

- **Rotation**: An object is rotated, or turned, between 0 and 360 degrees, around a fixed point. The size and shape of the object are unchanged.
- **Reflection**: An object is reflected, or flipped, across a line, so that the original object and reflected object are the same distance from the line of reflection. The size and shape of the object are unchanged.
- **Translation**: An object is translated, or shifted, horizontally and/or vertically to a new location. The orientation, size, and shape of the object are unchanged.

ROTATION
EXAMPLE

A line segment begins at (1, 4) and ends at (5, 4). Draw the line segment and rotate the line segment 90º about the point (3, 4).

Quantitative

The point about which the line segment is being rotated is on the line segment. This point should be on both the original and rotated line. The point (3, 4) is the center of the original line segment, and should still be the center of the rotated line segment. The dashed line is the rotated line segment.

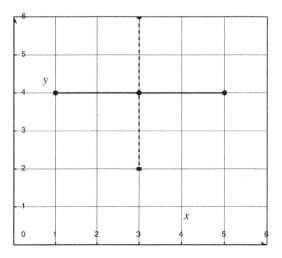

REFLECTION

To create a congruent rectangle by reflecting, first draw a line of reflection. The line can be next to or on the figure. Then draw the image reflected across this line.

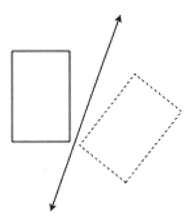

EXAMPLE

A line segment begins at (1, 5) and ends at (5, 4). Draw the line segment, then reflect the line segment across the line $y = 3$.

To reflect a segment, consider folding a piece of paper at the line of reflection. The new image should line up exactly with the old image when the paper is folded. The dashed line is the reflected line segment.

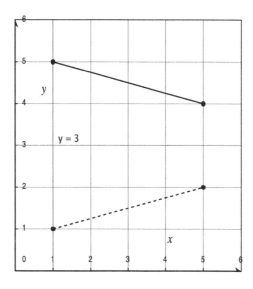

TRANSLATION

EXAMPLE

A line segment on an x-y grid starts at (3, 2) and ends at (4, 1). Draw the line segment, and translate the segment up 2 units and left 2 units.

The solid line segment is the original line segment, and the dashed line is the translated line segment. The *y*-coordinate of each point has increased by 2, because the points moved two units away from 0. The *x*-coordinate of each point has decreased by 2, because the points moved two units closer to 0.

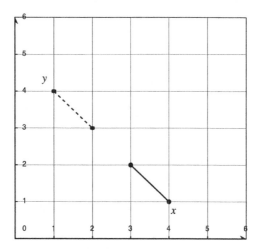

EXAMPLE

Identify a transformation that could have been performed on the solid triangle to result in the dashed triangle.

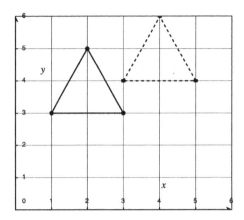

The transformed triangle has the same orientation as the original triangle. It has been shifted up one unit and two units to the right. Because the orientation of the figure has not changed, and its new position can be described using shifts up and to the right, the figure was translated.

Measurement

METRIC SYSTEM

Volume, distance, and mass can be measured using the metric system or the customary system. The **metric system** is generally preferred in math and science because values can be easily multiplied or divided by powers of 10. The metric system is convenient when working with very large or very small values. For example, there are 1,000 meters in one kilometer, so the number of meters can easily be determined if the number of kilometers are provided. For example, there are 5,000 meters in 5 kilometers. 3,000 meters in 3 kilometers. 8,000 meters in 8 kilometers. Metric conversion tables can be helpful for seeing the patterns within the metric system. The table below focuses on the base unit of meters. Notice how 1 meter is equivalent to 1,000 mm, 100 cm, and 0.001 km.

Millimeters	Centimeters	Meters	Kilometers
mm	cm	m	km
1	0.1	0.001	0.000001
10	1	0.01	0.00001
1,000	**100**	**1**	**0.001**
1,000,000	10,000	1,000	1

> **Review Video: Metric System Conversions**
> Visit mometrix.com/academy and enter code: 163709

EXAMPLE

There are 100 centimeters in 1 meter. Convert the measurements below.

a. Convert 1.4 m to cm

b. Convert 218 cm to m

Write a ratio with the conversion factor: $\frac{100\text{ cm}}{1\text{ m}}$. Use proportions to convert the given units.

a. $\frac{100\text{ cm}}{1\text{ m}} = \frac{x\text{ cm}}{1.4\text{ m}}$. Cross multiply to get $x = 140$. So, there are 1.4 m in 140 cm.

b. $\frac{100\text{ cm}}{1\text{ m}} = \frac{218\text{ cm}}{x\text{ m}}$. Cross multiply to get $100x = 218$, or $x = 2.18$. So, there are 218 cm in 2.18 m.

CUSTOMARY SYSTEM

The **customary system** is commonly used in the United States but very rarely in other regions of the world. The units of the customary system are not based on powers of ten. The conversion factors do not follow a pattern, which makes them a bit more challenging to remember. For example, study the table below. Notice how there is not one single pattern or relationship used consistently throughout the table. Each conversion factor is unique to each specific unit. This lack of a consistency is the most significant difference between the metric system and the customary system.

Length	Weight	Time	Capacity
1 foot = 12 inches	1 pound = 16 ounces	1 minute = 60 seconds	1 cup = 8 fluid ounces
1 yard = 36 inches	1 ton = 2,000 pounds	1 hour = 60 minutes	1 pint = 2 cups
1 yard = 3 feet		1 day = 24 hours	1 quart = 2 pints
1 mile = 5,280 feet		1 week = 7 days	1 quart = 4 cups
1 mile = 1,760 yards		1 year = 12 months	1 gallon = 4 quarts
		1 year = 365 days	1 gallon = 16 cups

Consider this real-world scenario for a metric conversion. Kristen walks 500 meters to work each morning, and then takes the bus home each evening. If she does this 5 days a week, for 4 weeks, how many kilometers has she walked?

Kristen walks 500 meters, 5 times a week. This means that in one week, she walks 2,500 meters. In 2 weeks she walks 5,000 meters. In 3 weeks she walks 7,500 meters. In 4 weeks she walks 10,000 meters. There are 1,000 meters in each kilometer. This means that the number of kilometers will always be 1,000 times less than the number of meters. Therefore, 10,000 meters is 10 kilometers. 10,000 divided by 1,000 is 10. Kristen has walked 10 kilometers in 4 weeks.

Consider a real-world scenario for where a customary conversion is needed. A long jump runway is 147 feet. How many yards is this?

There are 3 feet in 1 yard. This means that the number of feet will always be 3 times larger than the number of yards. Or, in this case, the number of yards will be 3 times smaller than the number of feet. Divide the number of feet by 3 to calculate the number of yards, $147 \div 3 = 49$. So, the runway is 49 yards long.

> **Review Video: Measurement Conversion**
> Visit mometrix.com/academy and enter code: 316703

EXAMPLE

There are 12 inches in 1 foot. Also, there are 3 feet in 1 yard. Convert the following measurements.

a. 42 inches to feet

b. 15 feet to yards

Write ratios with the conversion factors: $\frac{12\text{ in}}{1\text{ ft}}$ and: $\frac{3\text{ ft}}{1\text{ yd}}$. Use proportions to convert the given units.

Quantitative

109

a. $\frac{12 \text{ in}}{1 \text{ ft}} = \frac{42 \text{ in}}{x \text{ ft}}$. Cross multiply to get $12x = 42$, or $x = 3.5$. So, there are 42 inches in 3.5 feet.

b. $\frac{3 \text{ ft}}{1 \text{ yd}} = \frac{15 \text{ ft}}{x \text{ yd}}$. Cross multiply to get $3x = 15$, or $x = 5$. So, there are 15 feet in 5 yards.

Data Analysis and Probability

MEASURES OF CENTER

The **measures of center** are different methods for estimating or measuring the center of a data set. The center of a data set can be described by the most frequent value in a data set, the value appearing in the middle of a data set arranged from least to greatest, or the value that is the average of that data set. The terms used to describe the center of a data set are mode, median, and mean.

MODE

The **mode** of a data set is the number that shows up most frequently.

Let's say we are given this data set.

$$\{0, 0, 1, 1, 1, 1, 1, 1, 1, 1, 1, 1, 2, 2, 2, 2, 3, 4, 5\}$$

The mode in a data set is the number that repeats the most frequently. If we look at this list of values, we can see that 1 shows up the most often, so the mode of this data set is 1.

MEDIAN

The **median** of a data set is the literal middle value in a set of values. If you have a list of values, the median is going to be the value directly in the middle of a list of these values when the values are listed from least to greatest.

Let's say we have a set of data in a list.

$$\{3, 2, 2, 3, 0, 1, 2, 1, 1, 6, 2, 4, 2, 3, 6, 0, 0, 1, 1, 2, 4, 2, 4, 3, 1\}$$

This is a list of values, and we can determine the center, or median value in the data set by lining the values up from least to greatest and finding the middle value.

$$\{0, 0, 0, 1, 1, 1, 1, 1, 1, 2, 2, 2, 2, 2, 2, 2, 3, 3, 3, 3, 4, 4, 4, 6, 6\}$$

Now that we have our data set listed from least to greatest, the median will be the middle number in the set.

12   12

0 0 0 1 1 1 1 1 1 2 2 2 **(2)** 2 2 2 3 3 3 3 4 4 4 6 6

The center, or median value in this data set is 2, because when you list the values from least to greatest, 2 is the middle number. It is in the middle because it is the same distance from the smallest value to the greatest value and there are the same number of values, 12, on each side.

Finding the median of a data set that has even number of values requires a slightly different approach.

Let's say we are given this data set.

$$\{15, 16, 18, 20, 22, 12, 13, 14, 19, 21, 21, 11, 12, 14\}$$

First, we need to list the values from least to greatest to find the middle.

$$\{11, 12, 12, 13, 14, 14, 15, 16, 18, 19, 20, 21, 21, 22\}$$

Now, we can count to find the middle.

11 12 12 13 14 14 15|16 18 19 20 21 21 22

In this data set, there is not a middle number. Instead, the middle position lies between 15 and 16. So, to find the median value, we will have to find the mean of the two middle numbers, 15 and 16.

To find the mean of these middle values, we will add them together and divide by 2.

$$15 + 16 = 31$$
$$31 \div 2 = 15.5$$

So, the median of this data set is 15.5.

MEAN

The **mean** of a data set is often called the **average**. To find the mean of a data set, add the values in the data set together, and divide the sum by the total number of values.

In school, we are familiar with the mean of data sets because this is the way average grades are calculated. To get a final grade, often teachers will add the grade on each assignment or test together and divide by the total number of assignments or tests.

Let's say you are in a math class and your scores are listed in a data set.

$$\{76, 82, 82, 84, 87, 90, 85, 100, 94, 90\}$$

To find the mean, or average, of your scores, add the values and divide by the number of values. In this data set, if we add all the given grades together, we will get a total of 870. Now, if we divide 870 by the total number of grades, 10, we will get 87. That means that the final grade, the average grade, or the mean of the data set is 87.

> **Review Video: Mean, Median, and Mode**
> Visit mometrix.com/academy and enter code: 286207

SPREAD OF A DATA DISTRIBUTION

The **spread** of a data distribution is a way to describe the range, or how spread out or close together the data is. Data with a large spread means that there is a large variety of values, or the values are far away from each other. Data with a small spread means that there is not very much variety of values, or the values are close to each other. There are two ways we describe the spread of data. One way to describe the spread is through **range**. The range of data is the difference between the smallest value and the largest value.

Let's say you are given two sets of data.

Data Set 1

953	1,634	1,348	450	2,349	879
1,334	2,145	587	994	1,045	950
2,231	1,287	1,898	1,934	2,150	2,476

Data Set 2

3	6	1

112

2	3	2
2	0	7
4	4	3
5	2	3

Let's compare the range of these data sets. To compare the ranges, we need to identify the difference between smallest and largest values in each data set.

In data set 1, the smallest value is 450 and the largest value is 2,476. The rage in this data set is the difference between these two values, so we will use subtraction to identify the range.

$$2,476 - 450 = 2,026$$

So, the range of data set 1 is 2,026.

In data set 2, the smallest value is 0 and the largest value is 7. So, the range is the difference between these values.

$$7 - 0 = 7$$

So, the range of data set 2 is 7.

Now, we can compare. Data set 1 has a large range compared to data set 2 because 2,026 is greater than 7.

INTERQUARTILE RANGE

Another way to describe the spread is by identifying the **interquartile range**, or IQR. The interquartile range is a way to describe the middle 50% of a data set. The interquartile range is the distance between the first quartile and the third quartile.

To identify the interquartile range of a data set, you need to identify the first quartile and the third quartile. The interquartile range is the "box part" of a box plot.

Let's say you are given a list of values: 44, 41, 40, 43, 41, 45, 43, 42, 45.

To find the interquartile range, we need to identify the first and third quartiles. To find the first and third quartiles, we will start with finding the median.

The median in this data set is 43.

40   41   41   42 (43) 43   44   45   45

The next step is identifying the first quartile. The first quartile is the median of the values to the left of the median. In this case, the first quartile lies between 41 and 41, or is the mean of 41 and 41, which is 41.

40 41 41 42 (43) 43 44 45 45

↑
First Quartile

The next step is identifying the third quartile. The third quartile is the median of the values to the right of the median. In this case, the third quartile lies between 44 and 45, or is the mean of 44 and 45, which is 44.5.

40 41 41 42 (43) 43 44 45 45

↑
Third Quartile

So, now that we have identified the first quartile value, 41, and the third quartile value, 44.5, we can identify the interquartile range. The interquartile range is the distance between the first and third quartiles, so we subtract.

$$44.5 - 41 = 3.5$$

The interquartile range, or IQR, of this data set is 3.5.

EXAMPLE

A graph represents the number of paintings sold by 10 artists.

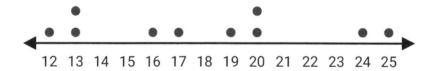

What is the interquartile range of the data set?

In this problem, we are given a dot plot that represents the number of paintings sold and we need to identify the interquartile range of the data represented by the graph.

The IQR is the difference between the first quartile and the third quartile.

The first step to solving this problem is to list the values from the graph from least to greatest.

12, 13, 13, 16, 17, 19, 20, 20, 24, 25

Once we have a list of values, we can identify the median, first quartile, third quartile, and finally the interquartile range.

Let's start with identifying the median.

12 13 13 16 17|19 20 20 24 25

114

$$17 + 19 = 36$$
$$36 \div 2 = 18$$

The median value in this data set is the mean of 17 and 19, which is 18.

Now, we can identify the first quartile by finding the median of the values to the left of the median.

12 13 ⑬ 16 17|19 20 20 24 25

The first quartile is 13.

Now, we can identify the third quartile by finding the median of the values to the right of the median.

12 13 13 16 17|19 20 ㉑ 24 25

The third quartile is 20.

To find the interquartile range, we calculate the difference between the first quartile and third quartile using subtraction.

$$20 - 13 = 7$$

The interquartile range of the data set is 7.

The correct answer is A.

BAR GRAPHS

Bar graphs display data in the form of vertical or horizontal rectangular bars, where the length of the bars indicates the measure of the data. For example, the bar graph below shows the number of pets a group of

115

people own. Notice how the tallest bar is "Cat." The bar extends vertically up to 11 people. This means 11 people own cats.

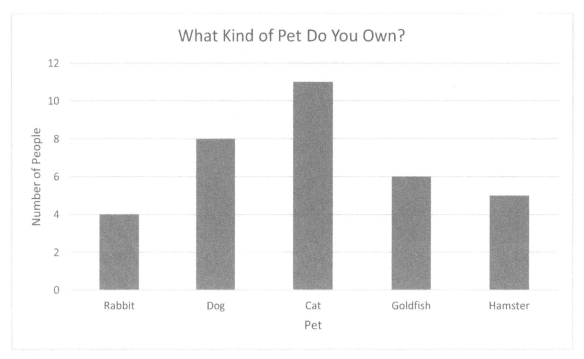

DOT PLOTS

Data can be represented graphically, or visually, in many ways. We have seen data represented using a coordinate plane. Data may also be represented through dot plots, stem-and-leaf plots, histograms, and box plots.

A **dot plot** is a type of graph where values are lined up vertically, like a number line, and dots or x's are used to show the frequency of each value, or how many times that value appears in the data. Dot plots are used to show how often something happens. Dot plots are mostly used when gathering data from multiple trials or surveys. Using a dot plot is a way to represent these types of results in an organized way.

Number of Siblings

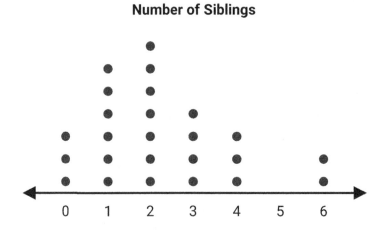

This dot plot shows the data from a survey of the 6th graders in a classroom. The survey gathered data about the number of siblings each 6th grader has in their family. The numbers along the bottom represent the

116

number of siblings and the dots represent the number of students. Each dot is equal to one student. Based on this dot plot, you can tell that 7 people said that they have 2 siblings because there are 7 dots above 2.

The data from this dot plot can also be written in list form.

6, 6, 4, 4, 4, 3, 3, 3, 3, 2, 2, 2, 2, 2, 2, 2, 1, 1, 1, 1, 1, 1, 0, 0, 0

0, 0, 0, 1, 1, 1, 1, 1, 1, 2, 2, 2, 2, 2, 2, 2, 3, 3, 3, 3, 4, 4, 4, 6, 6

3, 2, 2, 3, 0, 1, 2, 1, 1, 6, 2, 4, 2, 3, 6, 0, 0, 1, 1, 2, 4, 2, 4, 3, 1

As you can see, each value is represented on the dot plot. Regardless, there are 2 people who have 6 siblings, 0 people with 5 siblings, 3 people with 4 siblings, 4 people with 3 siblings, 7 people with 2 siblings, 6 people with 1 sibling, and 3 people with 0 siblings.

> **Review Video: Line Plot**
> Visit mometrix.com/academy and enter code: 754610

Quantitative

EXAMPLE

The dot plot shows the scores of a middle school basketball season.

Ending Basketball Scores for the Season

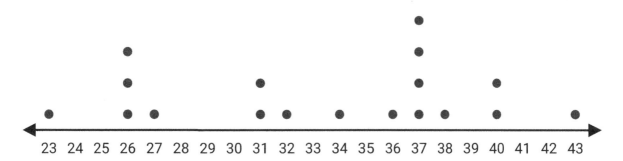

Which statement is true about the data represented by the dot plot?
   a. Less than half of the scores were between 30 and 39 points.
   b. The range of the scores is 18.
   c. There were more games that ended with a score of 31 than there were that ended with a score of 40.
   d. Half of the games ended with fewer than 35 points.

Read each answer choice and compare the statements to the data provided in the graph.

Choice A states that less than half of the scores were between 30 and 39 points. To decide if that statement is true or not, we need to compare the number of values between 30 and 39, to the total number of values.

Based on the graph, we can see that 10 scores are between 30 and 39, and there are 18 total scores. 10 is more than half of 18, since 9 is half of 18, so this statement is not true. The answer is not A.

Choice B states that the range of the scores is 18. We know that the range of a data set is the distance between the lowest value and the highest values. The lowest value on this graph is 23 and the highest value is 43. To calculate the distance between 23 and 43, we can use subtraction. $43 - 23 = 20$. So, the range of the data set is 20. The range is NOT 18, so this statement is not true. The answer is not B.

Choice C states that there were more games that ended with a score of 31 than there were that ended with a score of 40. Based on the graph, we can see that 2 games had a score of 31 and 2 games had a score of 40.

117

There were NOT more games that ended with a score of 31 than with a score of 40, there were an equal number of games that ended in these scores. This is not a true statement, so the answer is not C.

Choice D states that half of the games ended with less than 35 points. To decide if this statement is true or not, we need to identify how many games ended with fewer than 35 points and compare that value to the total number of values.

Based on the graph, we can see that 9 games ended with less than 35 points, and the total number of games was 18. We know that 9 is half of 18 because $18 \div 2 = 9$, so this statement is true.

The correct answer is D.

STEM-AND-LEAF PLOTS

A **stem-and-leaf plot** is a way to illustrate data with multi-digit values. This type of data representation is best used with a large number of data points that vary in value, say values from 0 to 100. Two common cases where stem-and-leaf plots are used are plotting the ages of a population and plotting temperature values.

In a stem-and-left plot, values are separated by place value. There is a list of numbers listed vertically along the left side; these are the stems. There is a list of numbers to the right of each stem; these are the leaves. There is a line dividing the stems from the leaves.

The stem-and-leaf plot below describes the ages of people at a family reunion.

Stem	Leaf
0	2, 2, 4, 5, 8, 8, 9
1	1, 2, 3, 3, 3, 4, 4, 5, 7, 9
2	0, 2, 8
3	2, 4, 6, 6, 7
4	3, 4, 9
5	0, 4, 5, 5, 6
6	4, 5, 5
7	0, 1
8	2
9	0, 4
10	2

Key:

$9|4 = 94$

$10|2 = 102$

You can see that there are values 0 to 9 on the left, a dividing line, and numbers to the right. The numbers on the left describe the tens place. The numbers to the right describe the ones place.

So, let's look at the second to last row, the 9's row. All these values have 9 in the tens place, and the listed value in the ones place. So, the values represented by this row are 90 and 94. This means that there are two people at the reunion in their 90s and their ages are 90 and 94.

Now let's look at the first row, the zero row. All these values have a zero in the ten's place. This means these are one-digit numbers. So, the ages represented in this row are 2, 2, 4, 5, 8, 8, 9. That means there are 7 people at the reunion under 10 years old. There are two 2-year-olds, a 4-year-old, a 5-year-old, two 8-year-olds, and a 9-year-old.

Now, sometimes your values will increase, like with our last row. We can see that 10 cannot technically be in the tens place, but this row gives the value 102. It is possible to see two digits in the stem part of the list.

Review Video: <u>Stem-and-Leaf Plots</u>
Visit mometrix.com/academy and enter code: 302339

EXAMPLE

The stem-and-leaf plot shows temperature readings in degrees Celsius.

Temperature Readings

Stem	Leaf
1	8, 9, 9, 9
2	2, 2, 3, 5, 6, 6, 6, 6, 7, 9
3	0, 1, 1, 1, 2, 3

Which statement best describes the data represented by the stem-and-leaf plot?
   a. The number of readings between 10 and 20 degrees is greater than the number of readings 30 or above.
   b. More than half of the readings were over 26 degrees Celsius.
   c. The most common temperature reading was 9 degrees Celsius.
   d. 50% of the temperature readings were in the 20s.

In this problem we are given a stem-and-leaf plot that has a series of temperatures. We need to select the statement that is true about the data represented by the plot.

To approach this type of problem, we should examine the statements and determine if they are true or not based on the data on the plot.

Choice A states that the number of readings between 10 and 20 degrees is greater than the number of readings over 30. To decide if this statement is true or not, we need to identify the number of readings that are between 10 and 20 and compare this to the number of readings over 30.

By reviewing the stem-and-leaf plot, we can see that there are 4 readings between 10 and 20: 18, 19, 19, and 19. We can also identify that there are 5 readings that are over 30: 31, 31, 31, 32, and 33. Because there are 5 readings above 30 degrees and 4 readings between 10 and 20, the number of readings between 10 and 20 is not greater than the number of readings 30 or above. This statement is not true, so A is not our answer.

Choice B states that more than half of the readings were over 26 degrees Celsius. To decide if this statement is true, we need to identify the number of readings over 26 degrees and compare this to the total number of readings.

By reviewing the stem-and-leaf plot, we can see that there are 8 readings that were over 26: 27, 29, 30, 31, 31, 31, 32, and 33. The total number of readings is 20. 8 is not more than half of 20 because half of 20 is 10, and 8 is less than 10. This statement is not true, so B is not our answer.

Choice C states that the most common temperature reading was 9 degrees Celsius. To decide if this statement is true, we need to review the data on the table. We can see that there are four 9s on the stem-and-leaf plot, but this does not mean the readings are 9 degrees. Instead, the readings with 9's are 19, 19, 19, and 29. Because there are no readings that read 9 degrees, this statement is not true, so C is not our answer.

While we have eliminated the untrue statements, we need to review the last choice to be sure.

Choice D states that 50% of the temperature readings were in the 20s. To decide if this statement is true, we need to identify the number of readings in the 20s and compare that to the total number of readings.

By reviewing the stem-and-leaf plot, we can see that there are 10 readings in the 20s: 22, 22, 23, 25, 26, 26, 26, 26, 27, and 29. We also know that the total number of readings is 20. 10 is half, or 50%, of 20, so this is a true statement.

The correct answer is D.

PROBABILITY

Probability is a branch of statistics that deals with the **likelihood** of something taking place. One classic example is a coin toss. There are only two possible results: heads or tails. The likelihood, or **probability**, that the coin will land as heads is 1 out of 2 (i.e., 1/2, 0.5, 50%). Tails has the same probability. Another common example is a 6-sided die roll. There are six possible results from rolling a single die. So, each side has an equal chance of happening. So, the probability of any number coming up is 1 out of 6.

> **Review Video: Intro to Probability**
> Visit mometrix.com/academy and enter code: 212374

TERMS RELATED TO PROBABILITY

- **Simple event**: A situation that produces results of some sort (e.g., a coin toss)
- **Compound event**: An event that involves two or more items (e.g., rolling a pair of dice and taking the sum)
- **Outcome**: A possible result in an experiment or event (e.g., heads and tails)
- **Desired outcome (or success)**: An outcome that meets a particular set of requirements (e.g., a roll of 1 or 2 when we want a number that is less than 3)
- **Independent events**: Two or more events whose outcomes do not affect one another (e.g., two coins tossed at the same time)
- **Dependent events**: Two or more events whose outcomes affect one another (e.g., drawing two specific cards right after the other from the same deck)
- **Certain outcome**: An outcome with a probability of 100% or 1
- **Impossible outcome**: An outcome with a probability of 0% or 0
- **Mutually exclusive outcomes**: Two or more outcomes whose requirements cannot all be done in a single outcome (e.g., a coin coming up heads and tails on the same toss)
- **Theoretical probability**: The likelihood of a certain outcome happening for a given event, which can be known without actually doing the event

CALCULATING THEORETICAL PROBABILITY

Theoretical probability can be calculated as:

$$P(\text{probability of success}) = \frac{(\text{Desired Outcomes})}{(\text{Total Outcomes})}$$

EXAMPLE

There are 20 marbles in a bag and 5 are red. The theoretical probability of randomly selecting a red marble is 5 out of 20, (i.e., 5/20 = 1/4, 0.25, or 25%).

When we talk about probability, we mean theoretical probability most of the time. Experimental probability, or relative frequency, is the number of times an outcome happens in an experiment or a certain number of observed events.

Theoretical probability is based on what *should* happen. Experimental probability is based on what *has* happened. Experimental probability is calculated in the same way as theoretical. However, actual desired outcomes are used instead of possible desired outcomes.

Theoretical and experimental probability do not always line up with one another. Theoretical probability says that out of 20 coin tosses 10 should be heads. However, if we were actually to toss 20 coins, we might record just 5 heads. This doesn't mean that our theoretical probability is incorrect; it just means that this particular experiment had results that were different from what was predicted.

Reading Comprehension

Comprehension Skills

MAKING PREDICTIONS

When you read a story, you should look for clues to make a prediction about what will happen. At the end of the story, you may even think about what will happen next to the main character, and use the clues in the story to make a prediction. You can also use personal experience to help make a prediction.

Suppose there is a story about a boy going swimming, and he swims too far out. Suppose the story says the boy can't get back to shore and starts to yell. Suppose the lifeguard comes and helps him. Suppose the story stops after the boy goes back in the water again. The reader might make the prediction that the boy won't swim as far out this time. This may not be true, but it is the most likely thing to happen.

EXAMPLE

Describe what prediction can be made based on the following sentences:

> When Glen is sick, his mother keeps him home from school. He stays in bed all day and takes medicine. Glen woke up this morning with a sore throat. His head was hot, and he felt achy.

The story says that Glen's mother keeps him home when he is sick and that Glen spends the day in bed when he is sick. The story says that Glen woke up this morning with a sore throat. His head was hot, and he felt achy. The reader can figure out that Glen was sick. Because Glen's mother always keeps him home when he is sick, the reader can predict that Glen will be staying home from school and spending the day in bed.

You can also use text features find information to make predictions and verify conclusions determined about different texts. Using key words as clues, looking for bold print words, looking for sentences that include captions, and words that are written in italics are a few features that can be used to help understand and make predictions about a text.

USING STRUCTURE AND GENRE TO MAKE PREDICTIONS

The structure and genre of a story can also help readers make predictions. Most stories follow the same structure. They have an exposition, rising action, a climax, falling action, and a resolution. Because most stories follow this structure, readers can predict that each of these parts will occur in the story. For example, rising action usually begins after the conflict of the story is introduced. This means that if characters have not faced any conflict, the reader can predict that something will go wrong for the characters. Likewise, stories in the same genre may contain similar events. For example, in a mystery, the characters work to solve a crime or explain a strange event. So, when reading a mystery, the reader can predict that the conflict will be a crime or event that the characters must learn more about.

MAKING CONNECTIONS TO ENHANCE COMPREHENSION

Reading involves thinking. For good comprehension, readers make text-to-self, text-to-text, and text-to-world connections. Making connections helps readers understand text better and predict what might occur next based on what they already know, such as how characters in the story feel or what happened in another text. Readers can make connections before, during, and after reading. Venn diagrams and other graphic organizers can help readers visualize connections.

TEXT-TO-SELF

Reading while looking for connections with the reader's life and experiences makes literature more personally relevant and meaningful to readers. Sentences showing text-to-self connections may begin with these examples

- This is similar to a time when…
- I understand how the character feels because…
- The setting makes me think of…
- I experienced this same thing when…

TEXT-TO-TEXT

Reading while looking for connections to other texts helps the reader learn to identify the way authors use genre, setting, characters, plot elements, literary structure and devices, and themes to create meaning. Sentences showing text-to-text connections may begin with these examples

- The character in this story reminds me of the character in…
- These two stories are alike because…
- The conflict in this story is similar to the conflict in…
- The relationship between the friends in this story is different than the relationship in…

TEXT-TO-WORLD

Reading while looking for connections to the world helps the reader begin to see literature as a reflection of real life and notice patterns in history and current events. Sentences showing text-to-world connections may begin with these examples

- The event in this story sounds like the event in history when…
- The actions of this character sound like…
- This is like what happened in real life when…
- I heard about this on the news when…

MAKING INFERENCES

An **inference** is a **conclusion** or generalization that the reader makes based on the information provided within a text. Certain facts are included to help a reader come to a specific conclusion. It is what the story may hint about, and what a reader can conclude as a result of what the author says in the passage. It is also the best guess that a reader can make based on what happened or was said or in a story. A good inference is based on or supported by details in the passage.

Readers may come to their own conclusion about a topic, or the author may state a conclusion at the end of a story. When readers are in the middle of a story, they can predict what will happen at the end of it based on the events that have occurred so far and the typical characteristics that have been presented by the author up to that point. A reader needs to consider all of the information that an author has presented, including the main point and supporting points, to make logical conclusions and inferences about the story.

For instance, if a passage says that Joan is holding her mouth and moaning, you might conclude, or **infer,** that she has a sore mouth or a toothache. You cannot be sure of this, but it is the best conclusion that you can reach using the information at hand. Inferences are considered **implicit information**. They are not found directly in a passage, but they can be supported by explicit information from the passage.

> **Review Video: Inference**
> Visit mometrix.com/academy and enter code: 379203

Reading Comprehension

123

FINDING EXPLICIT INFORMATION

Explicit information is the term for information that is **directly stated** in a story or passage. It is what **the author tells you**. It is not information that is hinted at or that you have to make a conclusion about. Explicit information can be facts or details about an event, something or someone. There is usually a lot of explicit information in a story and this information is often used to make an inference or draw a conclusion. to answer questions that ask about explicit information, simply reread the story until you find the answer. in fiction, details about characters, events, and setting are often explicit.

EXAMPLE

Read the following excerpt. Tell whether it contains explicit information or not.

> I think the most famous person in the Old West is Annie Oakley. Annie is the best rifle shot who ever lived. She almost never missed. Many men challenged her to contests of speed and accuracy. She won them all.

Most of the information in the excerpt is explicit information. The information tells the reader about Annie Oakley: that she was the best rifle shot who ever lived and that she almost never missed. It also says that many men challenged her to contests and she won them all. This information is found right in the excerpt. It is not suggested or hinted at. Everything that is said is clearly what it means. The first sentence is a personal opinion; it is also explicit because the reader does not have to guess what the author thinks of Annie Oakley.

IMPLICIT INFORMATION

Implicit information is information that is **not directly stated** in a text, but can be inferred from something that the author explicitly states. For instance, the author may say "Seth buys a new TV, laptop, and home theater system every year." from this the reader could infer several things. For instance, Seth probably likes electronics and has a lot of spending money.

EXAMPLE

Draw a conclusion based on the implicit information in the following sentence from the *Adventures of Tom Sawyer* by Mark Twain:

> He had discovered a great law of human action, without knowing it—namely, that in order to make a man or a boy covet a thing, it is only necessary to make the thing difficult to attain.

The reader can clearly see from the sentence that the character did not set out to learn something, but through an action, the character learned that people will want what is hard to attain. Although it's not explicitly stated, the reader can draw the conclusion that the character gained the experience of coveting (or desiring) something that was hard to get.

EXAMPLE

Read the passage and discuss why the conclusion that the Vikings were searching for new farmland is valid.

> The Vikings set out in their boats in summer. The number of people in Scandinavia was growing fast. They needed to grow more food. In the late 900s, Eric the Red sailed across the Atlantic to Greenland. In 985, Viking farmers settled in Greenland.

The passage says that the Viking population was growing and that they needed to be able to grow more food. It is logical to guess that they sailed in search of new farmland. There is really not another possibility. Remember, inferences are assumptions that are hinted at or suggested by the text. They are not like explicit information; they are implicit in the text based on the explicit information that is found there. They are the best guess a reader can make.

EXAMPLE

Read the following sentence and draw a conclusion based upon the information presented:

> "You know the reason Mother proposed not having any presents this Christmas was because it is going to be a hard winter for everyone; and she thinks we ought not to spend money for pleasure, when our men are suffering so in the army." (from *Little Women* by Louisa May Alcott, p. 3)

Based on the information in the sentence, the reader can conclude, or infer, that the men are away at war while the women are still at home. The pronoun 'our' gives a clue to the reader that the character is speaking about men she knows. In addition, the reader can assume that the character is speaking to a brother or sister, since the term Mother is used by the character while speaking to another person. The reader can also come to the conclusion that the characters celebrate Christmas, since it is mentioned in the context of the sentence. In the sentence, the Mother is presented as an unselfish character who is opinionated and thinks about the well-being of other people.

EXAMPLE

Draw a conclusion based on the following sentence from *The Adventures of Tom Sawyer* by Mark Twain:

> He had discovered a great law of human action, without knowing it—namely, that in order to make a man or a boy covet a thing, it is only necessary to make the thing difficult to attain.

The reader can conclude from the sentence that the character did not set out to learn something, but through an action, the character learned that people will want what is hard to attain. The character learned a fact about human nature: that a person will value something more if they have to work hard for it, than if it is simply given to them. The word *covet* means to desire, which the character learns can be manipulated by making an item or an outcome more difficult to grasp. In everyday life, this could apply toward taking a hard test and doing well. If someone studies for a hard test and does well, the person will value their score more than if the test was very easy and he or she did not study for the test.

MAIN IDEAS AND SUPPORTING DETAILS

Identifying **main ideas** helps the reader see what a text or story is mostly about. They are the **most important ideas** in a text, and everything else in the text builds around and supports them. Every piece of writing has main ideas. The **supporting details** in a story, such as the characters, events, and settings, will work together to reveal the main ideas. The details are not main ideas, themselves. They make the main ideas clear and show the reader the author's purpose for writing the text.

SYNTHESIZING A TEXT WITH EXISTING KNOWLEDGE

Synthesizing is similar to summarizing but it takes it one step further. Synthesizing involves taking the main points of a text and comparing it with existing knowledge to create a new idea, perspective, or way of thinking.

Another term for knowledge that you already have is **schema**. The plural form of this word is **schemata**. Schemata contain all the ideas you have about something. Synthesizing is all about how schemata change over time with the introduction of new information.

Reading Comprehension

125

EXAMPLE

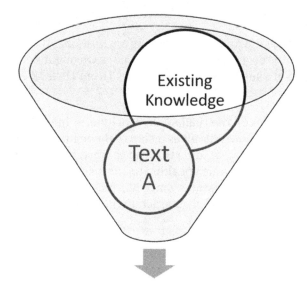

New Understanding of Topic

Using self-questioning strategies can help readers synthesize texts with their schemata to increase or change their understanding of topics. These questions include

- What do I already know about this topic?
- Is any of this new information?
- Has my perspective changed now that I've read this?
- What do I understand now that I didn't before?
- What are the main ideas of this text?
- How do the parts of the text fit together to create meaning?
- Are there any text-to-text, text-to-self, or text-to-world connections here?

SYNTHESIZING TEXTS WITHOUT EXISTING KNOWLEDGE

If the reader is completely unfamiliar with the topic, they will have no background knowledge. In this case, instead of using existing knowledge, synthesizing may instead be done by combining the ideas provided in two or three different texts. The reader must make connections between the texts, determine how the ideas fit together, and gather evidence to support the new perspective.

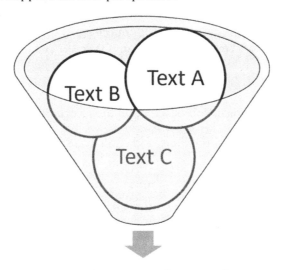

New Understanding of Topic

Using self-questioning strategies can help readers synthesize texts to increase their understanding of topics. In this case, readers are creating new schemata as they read. These questions include

- What do these texts have in common?
- What is different between these texts?
- What new information have I learned?
- What do I understand now that I didn't before?
- How do these texts relate to one another?
- If I think of these texts as parts of one whole, what meaning do they create together?
- What predictions can I make about this topic?

Response Skills

TEXT EVIDENCE

The term **text evidence** refers to information found in a text that supports a reader's claim about the text. A reader can draw conclusions or inferences based upon information found in a text. Often, the author will deliberately include information that supports the main point of the text to help the reader make conclusions and inferences that align with the author's purpose for writing the text.

DRAWING CONCLUSIONS BASED ON TEXT EVIDENCE

Readers often need to use prior experience and background information to draw an accurate conclusion about the passage they are reading. Sometimes interpreting the information in a sentence can be difficult, especially if the reader is unfamiliar with some of the words used in a sentence. Looking at the words that the reader does understand in the sentence can help. By taking a pen or pencil and underlining important information in a sentence, the reader can better understand what the author is trying to say and draw a clearer conclusion from that.

Reading Comprehension

<u>EXAMPLE</u>

Draw a conclusion based on the following sentence:

> New Orleans then was a mere huddle of buildings around Jackson Square; but with the
> purchase of the Louisiana territory from France, and the great influx of American enterprise
> that characterized the first quarter of the last century, development was working like yeast...

The sentence describes how New Orleans grew after the "purchase of the Louisiana territory" and how
"development was working like yeast". Yeast multiplies rapidly, so the reader can conclude that New Orleans
was growing rapidly.

<u>EXAMPLE</u>

Read the following sentence. Draw a conclusion based upon the information presented.

> "A rosy-faced servant-maid opened the door, and smiled as she took the letter which he
> silently offered."

The reader can conclude, based on the sentence, that the servant-maid is friendly. The words "rosy-faced" and
"smiled" lead the reader to this conclusion. People who are friendly are often described as having rosy
complexions and smiling as a common sign of pleasantness. The reader can also assume, from the sentence,
that the letter does not present any threat or unpleasantness to the servant-maid. The person presenting the
letter does not have anything to say upon offering it, so perhaps he is waiting to see how the servant-maid will
react.

When interpreting a sentence, always look for key words that describe a character. The author carefully crafts
a description of each character, to form a picture in the reader's mind about what the character is like.

PARAPHRASING AND SUMMARIZING

Paraphrasing and summarizing are two ways readers can work to understand what they read. Both involve
reading a text and recalling the main points in an accurate way, but they differ in several ways.

How to Paraphrase	How to Summarize
State the message in the text in the reader's own words, while keeping the original meaning of the text	State main points of the text clearly and to-the-point.
Take all of the original ideas and word them in a way that the reader can better understand	Take information and state it simply, in a much shorter form.
Put what the reader has read into their own words, rephrasing what the author has written	Put information in a short form that keeps the main points of the whole text.
	Do not include many details, just the main idea of the text

Paraphrasing is often done for individual ideas, while summarizing is done for an entire block of text or ideas.
Often times, a summary can be done in just one sentence, boiling down the author's words into just main idea.

> **Review Video: <u>Summarizing Text</u>**
> Visit mometrix.com/academy and enter code: 172903

PARAPHRASING THE MAIN POINT OF A SENTENCE

Paraphrase the main point of the following two sentences:

> Emmanuel went swimming in the lake by his house, where the water reached a depth of
> twenty feet in the middle. He did not venture out more than six feet into the water, however.

When paraphrasing a couple sentences or an entire paragraph, always include the main point of the text being reviewed, this is what the reader needs to know about the text. in the example, the reader needs to know that Emmanuel went swimming in the lake, but not more than six feet out. A paraphrase of the text may include: Emmanuel went swimming six feet out in the lake by his house. That is the main point that the audience needs to know.

Recall that a paraphrase is stating the author's ideas in the reader's own words. A summary typically involves including the main points of a longer text, such as a novel or full story.

EXAMPLE

Read the following paragraph and then give a one sentence summary statement:

> When choosing a pet, people need to think about what type of home they can offer the animal. For example, a small apartment might not be a good fit for a large dog, but could be a comfortable home for a kitten. A house that has a big yard would be great for a puppy, but a rabbit does not need a large yard.

In order to summarize, one has to identify the main idea and any supporting ideas in the author's work. The summary is an overview of the author's paragraph and will tell what it is about without getting into any of the details. The summary needs to be broad enough to cover all of the information in the author's paragraph. Here is a possible summary statement for the above paragraph:

> People need to consider a number of factors, particularly the available space they have, when choosing a pet.

EXAMPLE

Read the following sentences and then paraphrase the material:

> The government is debating a new health care system for our country. The Senate and the House of Representatives have both passed bills; now they need to resolve these two bills into one bill that a majority can agree on.

When paraphrasing information, one needs to read carefully and pay attention to details, then put the material away and write or tell it in their own words. One does not want to look at the material while paraphrasing to avoid plagiarizing by accident. Here is one example of a way to paraphrase the sentences:

> Our government is trying to adopt a new health care system. The Senate has passed a bill and so has the House of Representatives. Their bills are different so now they have to compromise on one bill that can be passed.

SUMMARIZING LITERATURE TO SUPPORT COMPREHENSION

When reading literature, especially demanding works, summarizing helps readers identify important information and organize it in their minds. They can also identify themes, problems, and solutions, and can sequence the story. Readers can summarize before, during, and after they read. They should use their own words, as they do when describing a personal event or giving directions. Previewing a text's organization before reading by examining the book cover, table of contents, and illustrations also aids summarizing. So does making notes of key words and ideas in a graphic organizer while reading. Graphic organizers are another useful method; readers skim the text to determine main ideas and then narrow the list with the aid of the

organizer. Unimportant details should be omitted in summaries. Summaries can include description, problem-solution, comparison-contrast, sequence, main ideas, and cause-and-effect.

Literary Elements

THEME

The **theme** of a story is a unifying idea that is used throughout the text; it can take the form of a common setting, idea, symbol, design, or recurring event. The theme of a story may vary according to place, time, and characters, but theme is often based on common human experience. A plot line is built around the theme of a story. Most themes are about life, society, or human nature. The theme is often why a passage is written. It helps give a passage unity. The theme is created through the development of the story. The events of a story help shape the kind of theme the passage. A theme is not usually stated explicitly. The reader **infers** the theme from the topic, information, or plot of a passage.

For example, a series of events in a story may be based upon people being willing to trust the actions of others. The story may be centered on why people need to trust others in order to carry out important actions. For example, a character may trust that a bus driver will stay on the road while the bus driver, in turn, trusts that the passengers stay in their seats so that they do not distract him.

The theme of a story is not the same as the topic of a story. The topic is what the story is about, but the theme is what a reader is meant to learn. When readers are discussing theme, they can determine both theme topics as well as theme statements.

> **Review Video: <u>Themes in Literature</u>**
> Visit mometrix.com/academy and enter code: 732074

CHARACTERS
CHARACTER TRAIT

The traits of a character may include how they act and physical characteristics; a character trait is a behavior or physical characteristic that is unique to a specific character. For example, a character may be outgoing, which means he or she likes to talk a lot, or they may have bright red hair. These are both character traits.

An author uses character traits to describe a character in a story and help the reader to learn more about how the character acts and what they look like. By comparing the character traits in a story, the reader can see similarities and differences between characters. The author includes character traits to help the reader understand why a character may act a certain way in the story. For example, a character who is shy may not want to talk with a lot of people in a new classroom, but a character who is outgoing may want to talk with many people.

CHARACTERS AND CONFLICT

An author typically provides many details about a character so that the reader can learn more about the character's traits, motivations, relationships, and any conflicts they may have in the story. The traits of a character may include how they act and how they look. Characters are often motivated by things that have already happened in their life or how they feel about a topic. The author will often give the reader enough information about the character so that the reader can figure out why the character responds to a situation in a certain way. The author will also often give details about the relationships between characters and points they may conflict on. For example, a character may be good friends with another character; however, the two characters may disagree on where to play outside if one character likes being near the water and the other character does not.

130

EXAMPLE

Read the following description of a character and decide, logically, whether the character is likely to go hiking outdoors:

> Jeremy lived in a high-rise in Chicago. He was studious, and not very athletic. Jeremy preferred to stay indoors and read a book, rather than enjoy outdoor weather.

Based on the description of the character's traits, preferences, and personality, he is not likely to go hiking outdoors. The description indicates that the character prefers reading, rather than enjoying outdoor weather. In addition, the character lives in a tall building in the middle of a large city, in order for him to enjoy the outdoors, he would have to travel away from where he lives. The character is not likely to change his preferences. A situation may lead the character to go hiking, but he is not likely to initiate the action on his own. A description of a character that is likely to go hiking outdoors may include a preference for outdoor activity and living near trails.

PLOT

The storyline of any text is also called a **plot**. The characters and events in the story determine what the plot will be. Readers may find a **plot line** useful as they try to put the events in the text in order and determine the relationships between events.

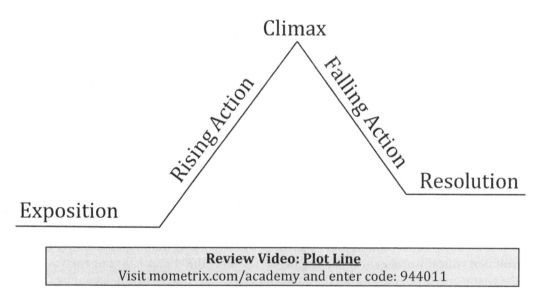

Review Video: <u>Plot Line</u>
Visit mometrix.com/academy and enter code: 944011

Every plot will begin with **exposition**, which introduces the characters and the setting of the story. The plot will continue to develop as new ideas and events centered on the main conflict in the story are revealed, which is called the **rising action**. The action in the story will rise until a **climax** is reached within the conflict. The climax can also be referred to as the turning point in the story, since the climax is where each character makes an important decision. After the climax, the action starts to wind down during the **falling action**. At this point, the characters begin to follow the paths they chose in during climax. The events of the story reach **resolution** in some way by the end of the story. Some conflicts are left open-ended, so that the reader is left to decide what really happened at the end of the story. Keep in mind that not all resolutions are happy or peaceful.

EXAMPLE

Read the following plot and analyze what event is missing from the plot sequence.

> Martin's family decided to go camping at the local park over the weekend. They packed all the camping necessities and drove to the park. Thick sheets of rain poured down all day, so they were stuck in their tent.

Martin and his family forgot to check the weather forecast before they left for their camping trip. to fill in the missing detail, the author may write: "Martin and his family checked the forecast and saw that it was going to rain, but decided to go camping anyway." the flow of the story is broken up by the sudden realization that it is raining, something that could be prevented by adding in the missing detail.

When details are missing from a plot sequence, the audience has trouble following the action in a story. By adding in additional details, the point of each step in a story can be made clearer to the audience.

CONFLICT

An important part of analyzing the plot of a passage is identifying the **main conflict**. There will likely be many smaller conflicts in the story, but there will be one main problem that influences the characters and events. to identify the main conflict, first look at who the main character is. Now ask yourself what they want. They may want to something to happen or not happen, another character to do or not do something, or to confront or avoid a problem, among other things. Once you know what they want, now ask yourself what is standing in the character's way. It may be a person, an event, or something less tangible like the passing of time. Combining what the main character wants and why they do not currently have leaves the reader with a summary of the main conflict.

EXAMPLE

Read the following sentence and explain the main conflict between the two characters:

> Joe stared angrily at Jamie's retreating back as Jamie raced away down the field with Joe's soccer ball.

The main conflict in the sentence is that Jamie has Joe's soccer ball. There may be additional conflicts between the two characters, but none are evident from the evidence shown in the sentence. in any story, a conflict may be minor and only affect part of the story, or be the main focus, taking an entire story to solve a conflict between characters. in the context of the sentence, it is not clear whether or not the entire story will revolve around Jamie taking Joe's soccer ball.

RESOLUTION

The term **resolution** usually indicates the result of a conflict in a story. Conflict between characters, within a character, or against an external element is necessary in order to have a plot for a story. without conflict, no events would occur to form the story. A conflict will come to a climax, and then conclude in some way. The resolution of a problem may be open-ended, end tragically, or end in a way that is good for everyone involved. The problem resolution typically occurs near the end of a story, after the climax has happened. A problem may be resolved by the characters involved within the conflict or by an external event; an upcoming resolution may be foreshadowed in the text, or may be completely unexpected by the reader. If the resolution is completely unexpected, it is considered to be a **twist** in the story.

FORESHADOWING

Foreshadowing is a technique authors use to give readers **hints** about events that will take place later in a story. Sometimes, foreshadowing is also used to build **suspense**. Foreshadowing most often takes place through a character's dialogue or actions. Sometimes the character will know what is going to happen and will purposefully allude to future events. For example, consider a protagonist who is about to embark on a journey through the woods. Just before the protagonist begins the trip, another character says, "Be careful, you never know what could be out in those woods!" This alerts the reader that the woods may be dangerous and prompts the reader to expect something to attack the protagonist in the woods. This is an example of foreshadowing through warning.

Alternatively, a character may unknowingly foreshadow later events. For example, consider a story where a brother and sister run through their house and knock over a vase and break it. The brother says, "Don't worry, we'll clean it up! Mom will never know!" However, the reader knows that their mother will most likely find out

what they have done, so the reader expects the siblings to later get in trouble for running, breaking the vase, and hiding it from their mother.

SETTING

The setting is where a story **takes place**. The setting of a story may stay the same for the entire story, or change as events in the story unfold. For example, an entire story may take place in one room or cross continents as the reader follows the characters along on a trail of events.

The setting of a story is described by the author in terms of what it looks like, how the character feels, and anything else that is happening at that location at the time. For example, a character may be caught on a doorstep on a cold, rainy day. The character may feel frustrated as they shiver in the doorway, waiting for the heavy rain to let up a bit.

Literary Genres

COMMON LITERARY GENRES

Literature contains many different **genres**, which are categories that texts can be divided into. Genres are used to group types of writing together for purposes of study, reading, or simple organization. Some common literary genres are

- **Realistic fiction** -A story that could actually happen and reflects life in a realistic way.
- **Adventure stories** -Short, mostly fictional stories that follow characters as they go on an adventure or quest.
- **Historical fiction** -Often strays from historical reality in order to tell a story and make a true historical event more interesting to the reader.
- **Mysteries** -Fiction stories about solving crimes or revealing secrets.
- **Humor** –Stories, mostly fictional, full of fun and excitement meant to entertain readers. Can be seen in stories from all genres.
- **Myth** -A legend or traditional narrative, often based on a historical event. The story reveals something about human behavior or the natural world, and often involves actions of gods.
- **Fantasy** -Fictional stories that contain unusual and other worldly settings and characters. The sense of "realness" in other stories is not present. The fantasy genre is known for including elements like magic and imaginary creatures like fairies, dragons, and elves.
- **Science fiction** -Fiction based on what could happen if actual, imagined, or possible scientific advances occurred. Usually set in the future, a modified past, or on other planets.

POETRY

POET VERSUS SPEAKER

The author of a poem is called a **poet**. Many poems are written in first person, which means the **stanzas** (groups of lines) include words like "I" and "me." However, the poet is not always the **speaker** of the poem. In a novel, the author can create characters with different points of view. The characters can argue or have different roles to play in telling the story. Similarly, a poet may write a poem from a different point of view or even include more than one voice. The speaker is the voice of the poem, and is not always the same person as the poet him or herself. The reader or listener should know that the person telling the story is a character, and not always a real person.

For example, this excerpt from a poem by Dr. Seuss reads:

> When you think things are bad,
> when you feel sour and blue,
> when you start to get mad...

133

Reading Comprehension

you should do what I do!
Just tell yourself, Duckie,
you're really quite lucky!
Some people are much more...
oh, ever so much more...
oh, muchly much-much more
unlucky than you!

Even though one line has the word "I" in it, the poem is not from the perspective of Dr. Seuss. He is the author of the poem, but not the speaker. The person saying "I" is a character, just like in a story.

METER, RHYME, AND REPETITION IN POETRY

The **meter** of a poem refers to the number of syllables per line as well as the pattern of emphasis on those syllables. The use of meter gives a poem a rhythmic context and contributes to the poem's flow. Certain types of meter can also make a poem more appealing to the reader or represent natural speech rhythms.

Rhymes repeat the ending sound of words: "So very soon/We will fly to the moon." Here the "oo" sound is repeated in the words *soon* and *moon*. Rhymes are frequently used in poetry, mostly older forms of poetry rather than modern poems.

Another type of repetition is **alliteration**. Alliteration repeats beginning sounds, usually consonants: "Rah, rah, rah," the crowd cried, "rah, rah, rah." It is often used in poetry as well as in spoken forms of writing.

RHYME SCHEME

When determining what a poem's rhyme scheme is, readers should look at the last word of each line to see which words rhyme with each other. Words that rhyme are assigned a letter of the alphabet, beginning with "a." The next time words rhyme, if the rhyme is different than the last one, they assigned a new letter, going forward in order of the alphabet until the poem is over or there are no more rhymes. This sounds complicated, but it's easy with practice.

Let's take a look at an excerpt from Dylan Thomas' poem "Do not go gentle into that good night":

Do not go gentle into that good night,
Old age should burn and rave at close of day;
Rage, rage against the dying of the light.

Though wise men at their end know dark is right,
Because their words had forked no lightning they
Do not go gentle into that good night.

The words at the end of the lines are *night, day, light, right, they,* and *night.*

We know that the first rhyme is assigned the letter "a," and can clearly see that *night, light,* and *right* all rhyme, so we can mark the poem like this

Do not go gentle into that good night,	a
Old age should burn and rave at close of day;	
Rage, rage against the dying of the light.	a
Though wise men at their end know dark is right,	a
Because their words had forked no lightning they	
Do not go gentle into that good night.	a

134

Now, we'll look at the only other rhyme in the poem, which is made up of the words *day* and *they*. This rhyme does not rhyme with the first set of words, so it gets a new letter, "b."

Do not go gentle into that good night,	a
Old age should burn and rave at close of day;	b
Rage, rage against the dying of the light.	a
Though wise men at their end know dark is right,	a
Because their words had forked no lightning they	b
Do not go gentle into that good night.	a

After looking at all six lines and determining how they rhyme, we can confidently say that the rhyme scheme for this excerpt is a, b, a, a, b, a.

Rhymes are used at the discretion of the poet and are not always mandatory. Many modern poems—actually, most of them—use a blank verse, where there are no rhyme schemes. However, there are many formal poetic types, such as the sonnet, that have a specific rhyme scheme that poets must follow to achieve that kind of poetic form.

EXAMPLE

Explain the rhyme scheme of the following excerpt from a poem entitled "Alone" by Edgar Allan Poe.

> From childhood's hour I have not been
> As others were; I have not seen
> As others saw; I could not bring
> My passions from a common spring.
> From the same source I have not taken
> My sorrow; I could not awaken
> My heart to joy at the same tone;
> And all I loved, I loved alone.

The rhyme scheme that Edgar Allan Poe uses in this excerpt from his poem "Alone" is: a, a, b, b, c, c, d, d, e, e. Every two lines rhyme, but the rhyme is not repeated in the other lines. This is a rather unusual rhyme scheme; many others have lines that repeat the rhyme scheme, but not in a consecutive order, such as a, b, a, b or a, b, c a, b, c.

GRAPHICAL ELEMENTS IN POETRY

Graphic elements in a poem such as capitalization, line length, and word position can call special attention to words or phrases. **Capitalization** can signal the beginning of a sentence, or all caps may be used to provide emphasis. **Line length** can be used to help create a shape, like in concrete poems, or to create a bold statement, like a one-word line. A poet can create tension by using line length and punctuation independently of one another. **Word position** can be used to contribute to a feeling, or it can also be used to help create a shape, so poets are often careful where they end lines.

LINE BREAKS

Line breaks are used to end a line of poetry. Poets use **line breaks** to control the **length** of **each line**. The length of lines in a poem can impact the poem's meaning and the **speed** at which the poem is read. **Long** lines are usually read more **quickly**, while **short** lines cause the reader to briefly pause and look to the next line, so their reading is **slowed**. These effects often contribute to the reader's experience when reading the poem, so poets aim to make the effects match the tone of their message in the poem.

Reading Comprehension

PUNCTUATION

The punctuation in each line of a poem causes the reader to **pause** after certain words. This lets the poet **emphasize** specific **ideas** or **images**. Similar to the effects of line length, punctuation at the end of a line can guide the **speed** at which the reader reads each line. Lines with a punctuation mark at the end cause readers to pause, while lines that do not end with a punctuation mark carry a sentence to the next line. This creates an effect that is like the effect of long lines.

CAPITALIZATION

Poets also use capitalization to **highlight** certain words in their poetry. Authors will often capitalize words that are not proper nouns so that the reader pays more attention to them. While this is not grammatically correct, it is used in poetry to create a certain effect and guide the reader as they read and form their understanding of the poem.

INFORMATIONAL TEXT

CONTROLLING IDEA

The controlling idea, also called the main idea or thesis, of a passage is usually located in the first paragraph or two of text. Having the controlling idea near the beginning of the passage allows the author to grab the reader's attention and let them know what the rest of the passage will discuss.

To find the controlling idea in a passage, there are questions the reader can ask while reading: What is this passage about? What does the author want the reader to know about the topic? The supporting details will provide evidence that the controlling idea is correct and are found in the body of a passage. The supporting details often provide examples of the controlling idea.

For example, a passage may contain the controlling idea: "Ellis Island was an entry-point to America for many immigrants during the Industrial Revolution." A supporting detail for the controlling idea may be "Immigrants were examined for contagious diseases at Ellis Island before being granted entry to America."

> **Review Video: Thesis Statements**
> Visit mometrix.com/academy and enter code: 691033

EXAMPLE

Determine the controlling idea the following sentence tells the reader and indicate what details support the controlling idea:

> Her breath billowed out in clouds of white and disappeared into the quiet air.

The controlling idea is what the author wants the reader to understand about the text. Details help to explain or support that controlling idea. A controlling idea usually states the point of an entire essay, article, or book, but can be simply stated in one sentence. The controlling idea in the sentence above is that a girl is outside in the cold. Details to support this statement include the word 'her,' showing that the character is a girl, and 'clouds of white,' which indicate that the air is cold. in order to conclude that the girl is out in the cold, the reader needs to understand that breath can be seen when the air is cold.

SUPPORTING DETAILS

Authors use supporting details to provide evidence and backing for the main point. All texts contain details, but they are only classified as supporting details when they serve to reinforce some larger point. Supporting details are most commonly found in informative and persuasive texts. in some cases, they will be clearly indicated with words like **for example** or **for instance**, or they will begin with words like **first**, **second**, and **last**. However, these special words are not a requirement. As a reader, it is important to consider whether the author's supporting details really back up his or her main point. Supporting details can be factual and correct but still not relevant to the author's point. Sometimes, supporting details can seem important but they might not support the controlling idea in the story well because they are based on opinion that cannot be proven.

EXAMPLE

Decide whether the following sentence is the main point or a supporting point of a text, and state where the information would be placed in an outline:

> One type of horseback riding, bareback horseback riding, involves sitting on a moving horse without a saddle and grasping the horse's mane.

This sentence is a supporting point, with the main point of the entire text likely about horseback riding in general. As a supporting point, this sentence would go further down in an outline, next to any numeral after numeral I. This sentence can be followed by additional sub-points that further explain the concept of bareback horseback riding. When a supporting point is used to clarify a main point or topic, the supporting point helps to break the topic down into smaller pieces.

STRUCTURAL FEATURES OF INFORMATIONAL TEXT

Texts which intend to inform the reader about a topic are often accompanied by visual aids or graphics. Some common examples are listed below.

- **Forewords** appear before the actual text. Usually, forewords are not written by the author of the text. They are written by a different person who is well-respected in a related field of work or study. The author of the foreword usually provides some information about the texts and explains why they support the text.
- **Prefaces** are written to provide the reader with supporting information that was not included in the text. This information may help the reader better understand the text or may show the reader why the topic of the text is important or interesting to the author.
- **Introductions** usually appear as the first paragraph in a text. An introduction is used to catch the reader's attention and let the audience know what the text is about and how the topic will be covered by the text.
- **Insets and sidebars** show additional information related to the text in boxes or on the sides of the page. Insets can contain pictures or text, and sometimes have different colored backgrounds or font types to make them stand out from the text.
- **Visual aids** include features like diagrams, graphs, and charts. These can help the user think about information in a different way. They do this by visually presenting the relationship between the information in the text.
- **Bullet points** list items separately, making facts and ideas easier to see and understand.
- **Numbers** can also be used to list separate items. Usually, numbers are used to show that the items are part of a sequence. For example, in a list of instructions, each instruction may be numbered to show the reader the order in which each instruction should be completed.
- **References** are the sources of the information the author included in the text. In most works, the references will all be listed after the last page of the main text. These may be included on a page titled "Bibliography," "Works Cited," or, simply, "References." Reviewing the author's sources and reviewing their credibility can show the reader whether the work itself is credible, unbiased, and accurate.
- **Acknowledgements** appear near the end of books, after the main text and any resources that the author has included for the reader. The acknowledgements section is used by authors to thank the people that helped them create the work. People who encouraged the author, assisted the author with writing and editing, or made it possible for the work to be published are usually named in the acknowledgements section.

Reading Comprehension

ORGANIZATIONAL PATTERNS

When writing there are a variety of ways that an author can choose to organize their text. It is important for them to choose the pattern that best presents their information, as not all patterns will work for every piece of writing. Some examples are

ADVANTAGE/DISADVANTAGE

The author chooses a topic or concept and addresses both the advantages and disadvantages (or pros and cons) of the subject. In this type of text the author is not trying to persuade their audience to choose a side, but rather, to inform the reader of all the possible positive and negative effects.

CAUSE AND EFFECT

The author will write about relationship between two events that occur, where the second event occurs as a result of the first.

For example, a text may discuss a school policy stating that when a student is late to school too many times, they receive a detention. Later in the text, we might see a student repeatedly arriving late to school, after which he is given a detention. In this example, the **cause** is the student being late to school, and the **effect** is the student receiving a detention.

CLASSIFICATION

The author chooses a topic and divides it into smaller parts or groups in order to discuss them individually. These types of texts address how parts work within a whole, or what characteristics can be used to classify a given subject or concept.

CHRONOLOGICAL ORDER

The author organizes the progression of events based upon when they occurred and what was included in each step of the story. By organizing the text in this way the author presents all necessary information about the six questions readers can ask to help themselves understand the text: who, what, when, where, why, and how.

COMPARE AND CONTRAST

The author will show similarities and differences between items or events.

For example, the author may write about cats and dogs. They might start by giving a brief description of the two. Then they will want to point out all the similarities, such as; they both have tails, and both are kept as pets. Next, they will explain the differences, such as; dogs are canines, while cats are felines. They will try to provide as much detail as possible about both the similarities and the differences.

DEFINITION

Authors introduce a concept or word and then explain or describe it. This type of text often included examples that will help the reader gain understanding of what is presumably a new concept for them.

INDUCTIVE / DEDUCTIVE

Authors organize ideas from general to specific or specific to general. If ideas are organized **inductively**, they are arranged from specific facts to general conclusions. If ideas are organized from general conclusions to specific facts, they are organized **deductively**. A reader can make a logical assumption about a topic based on the facts that are presented in the text.

For example, in these two sentences the ideas are organized deductively, from general to specific.

> Many canoers use the lake in the summer. Jeff learned how to canoe last summer, and is on his way to the lake now.

138

The idea that "Many canoers use the lake in the summer" is a general idea. The facts that Jeff already knows how to canoe and is headed to the lake are specific to him as a character.

<u>ORDER OF IMPORTANCE</u>

The author puts the information in the text in order of what is most important. **Order of importance** can be either increasing or decreasing, depending on how the writer wants to structure the work.

<u>PROPOSITION AND SUPPORT</u>

The author states a proposition that they believe to be true, and then provides support for that proposition in the paper. The topics that use this type of structure are generally things that reader might feel uncertain about or might not already have an opinion about. The support that the author gives for the proposition should include facts, statistics, logic, and reasoning. The more hard evidence an author can give the reader, the better it will help convince them to see things from the author's point of view.

IDENTIFYING ORGANIZATIONAL STRATEGIES
EXAMPLE

Explain which organization pattern would be the best choice for this writer and why.

> Sara is writing a report on sea turtles. She has researched the various dangers that they face: their predators, the difficulties they encounter in their life cycle starting with their birth, their migration to the ocean, and the dangers that await them as they mature. She is unsure of how to organize her report.

A cause and effect order would seem to be the best idea for Sara because she would be able to identify the causes and effects of the dangers that sea turtles encounter. She could organize the report so that each paragraph deals with a different threat, using headings to identify what would be in each section. A chart would also be useful because it puts the same information in a clear format so that readers would be able to refer to it. She might also consider using a video showing baby turtles migrating towards the open sea, which would give her audience an even greater understanding of the turtles' plight.

EXAMPLE

Identify the text structure that is used in the following sentences:

> Madison and her brother Jake used to live on a wind-torn island in the Chesapeake Bay. Last year they moved to Baltimore, a city in Maryland. Next summer they plan to visit the island where they grew up.

Chronological order is used as a text structure in the example sentences, as they are organized according to the passage of time. Note that each sentence refers to a point in time. The first sentence refers to where the siblings lived in the past. The second sentence refers to the siblings' move to Baltimore last year. The final sentence refers to what the siblings plan to do in the future. By referring to a specific place in time, the reader can see what occurred in the story during that time period. An author will often use flashback to indicate what happened in the past, and foreshadowing to give the reader a glimpse of what may occur in the future.

EXAMPLE

Identify the text structure that is used in the following sentences:

> Three cousins lived in the same small town. One day the cousins decided to journey together to enter a singing contest across the country. The cousins won the contest and made their hometown fans proud.

The information in the story can be organized according to the passage of time, called chronological order. The story will start based in the cousins' hometown, to give some background on where the cousins come from.

139

Subsequent events in the story will occur over time based on the cousins' motivations due to their background. The story will end by referring back to how far the cousins have come from their small-town roots.

EXAMPLE

Read the following thesis statement and discuss the organizational pattern that the author will use:

> Throughout his life, Thomas Edison used his questioning and creative mind to become one of America's greatest inventors.

Based on the thesis statement, the reader can assume that the author is going to use chronological order to organize the information in the rest of the essay. The words "throughout his life" clue the reader in to the chronological organizational structure, which presents information in the order than it occurred. The author will probably discuss Edison's childhood and initial inventions first and then move on to his later queries and inventions. Chronological order is often used as the organizational structure in biographies as a way to logically present the important events in a person's life.

ARGUMENTATIVE TEXTS

IDENTIFYING THE CLAIM

In a persuasive or argumentative text, the author is writing in order to make and support a claim. A claim is similar to the main idea of an informational text. However, a claim can be argued, which means that some readers may not agree with it. The author of the text will need to use the body of the text to support the claim and show readers why they should agree with it. To identify the claim of a text, first identify the topic. Then, read the introduction text to see what the author writes about the topic.

The claim should be clearly stated in the introduction. However, if the claim is still not clear, read the body to see what kind of evidence the author uses to support the claim. The way that the author gives and applies evidence may also show what the claim of the text is.

CALL TO ACTION

Another strategy is to look for a call to action in the text. A call to action is a statement that instructs the reader to do something after reading the text. Often, the call to action will tell the reader to do something that shows that he or she agrees with the author's claim. For example, if an author's claim is that reading is better than watching a movie, the author may include a call to action that says "Turn off the TV and dig in to a new book today!" By including this statement, the author is telling the readers to show their agreement by choosing to read rather than watch a movie.

IDENTIFYING HOW THE AUTHOR SUPPORTS A CLAIM

In a persuasive or argumentative text, the author must use information to support his or her claim. This information is called evidence. Below are common types of evidence an author may use to support a claim:

- **Facts:** Authors may use facts that show that their claim is true. For example, a claim that fish are better pets than dogs can be supported by the fact that fish cannot make a mess inside a house.
- **Personal Anecdotes:** A personal anecdote is a story from a person's own experience. Authors can use personal anecdotes to tell stories that show why their claim is true. For example, an author can support the claim that people should wear elbow pads when riding a bike can be supported by sharing a story about their experience of scraping their elbow after falling off of a bicycle.
- **Statistics:** Statistics are observations that are based on a collection of data. Statistics can show trends or preferences among members of a group. An author can use statistics to support a claim by sharing the statistic says is likely to happen or be true for many people.

- **Examples:** Authors may give examples of events or experiences that suggest that their claim is true. For example, an author may claim that people should exercise because it will make them healthier. The author could give an example of how exercise can improve a person's health in order to support this claim.
- **Quotes:** An author can support a claim by using quotes from other people or texts. If the person or text makes a statement that shows that the author's claim is true, the author can include that quote in his or her text. When authors include quotes in their work, they must always tell the reader where the quote came from.

The author must use enough evidence to support the claim. If the evidence does not fully support the claim in the text, then the author must continue working to find evidence for the claim. The evidence used to support a claim must also be believable and come from a reliable source.

COUNTERARGUMENTS

A counterargument is a claim that seeks to disprove another claim. Sometimes, an author of a persuasive or argumentative text will include a **counterargument** to their own claim in a text. Doing this allows the author to show why someone may disagree with his or her claim and then show why the counterargument is wrong. Authors include counterarguments in order to strengthen their own argument and show the reader why claims that oppose their own are incorrect.

IDENTIFYING THE INTENDED AUDIENCE

Authors of persuasive and argumentative texts want to convince others to agree with a claim or take a certain action. Because of this, they will often write to a specific audience. Often, the target audience will include people who disagree with the author's claim. The author's desire is to give these people information that will lead them to change their minds or actions.

STRATEGIES FOR IDENTIFYING THE INTENDED AUDIENCE

One way to identify the intended audience of a persuasive or argumentative text is to first identify the author's claim. Then, consider who would disagree with the author's claim. This group of people is likely the group that the author wants to persuade.

Another way to identify the audience is to look for clues in the text. Sometimes, authors will clearly state which people are included in the intended audience. For example, imagine that an author includes the statement, "Teachers should reward their students every time they make a good grade on a test." This shows that the text is written to persuade teachers who do not already reward their students for good test grades. Similarly, a call to action may show who the target audience is by instructing the members of the audience to take a certain action.

Author's Purpose and Craft

AUTHOR'S PURPOSE

The purpose of a text is the author's main reason for writing the text. As the reader reads a text, they should always try to figure out the author's purpose for writing as this will help them to better understand the message that the author is trying to convey.

INFORMATIONAL TEXTS

- Inform the reader on a topic that they previously knew nothing about, such as many non-fiction texts.
- The author will usually include sources of information for an informative piece.
- For example, an informative paper on early Native American Indian tribes would detail where Native American Indians lived, what types of foods they ate, how they bartered for goods, and other aspects of their culture.

PERSUASIVE TEXTS

- Influence the reader to think a certain way about a topic, calling them to action or pointing them toward resources that would help them to learn more about the topic.
- A **proposition and support** paper would be an example of this, where an author gives their opinion and then tries to convince the reader to see something from their point of view.
- An author will often use positive expert testimonials when trying to persuade the reader to accept a given point-of-view.
- For example, an author may try to persuade the reader that technology is negatively affecting social interaction, and that limits should be set on how much people can use their technological devices.

EXPRESSIVE TEXTS

- Express the author or speaker's opinion or emotions about a topic. Generally, expressive texts include descriptive words to clearly show the reader how the author or speaker feels.
- For example, the author may think that history is important for all people to study, and express the opinion that education without history class would be incomplete.

ENTERTAINING TEXTS

- Entertain the reader, such as in most fictional texts.
- For example, Lois Lowry, the author of *The Giver,* entertains his readers with the story of a young boy named Jonas who is learning how to navigate his unexpected life assignment.
- Entertaining texts can be either fiction or non-fiction, but are usually stories such as a fairy tale or fictional piece of writing. Entertaining texts usually follow a chronological order.

Authors usually write to entertain, to inform, or to persuade their readers. The organization structure or pattern they use is related to what the author's purpose is. It is important to choose the pattern that best presents the information, as not all patterns will work for every piece of writing.

DETERMINING THE PURPOSE OF A TEXT

When reading, the reader should always determine the purpose of a text. to do so, ask yourself what effect the writing has on you. Does the text try to explain or persuade you of something? Perhaps the text is making an appeal to your emotions. The signs that a text is attempting to persuade you include an author offering an opinion and explaining why she thinks this way. On the other hand, if a text is simply informative, it will have many facts that will give details about an event, person, or idea without trying to persuade you of anything. Manuals that come with equipment are clearly not persuasive, simply instructive.

> **Review Video: Understanding the Author's Intent**
> Visit mometrix.com/academy and enter code: 511819

PRINT AND GRAPHIC FEATURES

An author may show information in a chart, a graph, in paragraph format, or as a list. Information may also be shown in a picture or a diagram. The way an author chooses to show information is often based on the purpose of the text and the audience that the text is meant to reach.

A reader may be asked to answer questions based on the graphic by itself, how the graphic relates to the text, or how the text would best be shown in a graphic form. Some common examples of graphics are cause and effect organizers, circle graphs, bar graphs, illustrations, and diagrams.

IMAGERY

Imagery is the use of **descriptive language** to add life or feeling to a work of literature. Many authors add literary and sound devices to create vivid pictures in the minds of their readers. Most of the time, imagery is thought to be one of the best ways to help readers fully understand and remember a work.

The most common forms of imagery are those that appeal to the sense of sight and sound. Imagery that appeals to the sense of sight, or **visual imagery**, helps the reader picture an event in their mind, usually by including specific details in the text that are not strictly necessary for the purpose of the story, but allow the reader to more easily "see" the scene. Some common forms of figurative language can help create visual imagery.

Review Video: Sensory Language
Visit mometrix.com/academy and enter code: 177314

LITERAL AND FIGURATIVE LANGUAGE

Many types of text use both **literal language**, which means just what it says, and **figurative language**, which allows the writer to expand the way in which he or she uses language. When an author uses figurative language, she connects things in an exaggerated and non-literal way in order to create a memorable image, which helps to describe a situation in a new way for the reader.

Review Video: Figurative Language
Visit mometrix.com/academy and enter code: 584902

SIMILE

- Shows similarity between two ideas or objects, using the words "**like**" or "**as**"
- For example, an author might write "The princess is as beautiful as a rose" to compare the appearance of a woman to a beautiful flower.

METAPHOR

- Puts one idea in place of another to draw a parallel between the two ideas.
- For example, an author might write "Her room was a pigsty," to compare a person's bedroom to a dirty spot where pigs sleep.

SYMBOLISM

- Using one object to stand for something else.
- For example, an author may include a flag flying high throughout a story to show pride in the characters' country and to represent the idea of patriotism.

HYPERBOLE

- An extreme exaggeration of an idea.
- For example, a character might say "I'm starving to death!" to show that they are really hungry. Most of the time a character who says this is not literally going to die from hunger, they are just ready for a snack.

IRONY

- Uses sarcasm or humor (usually with an emphasis on the opposite) to show difference from literal meaning.
- For example, if a character says "Well today must be my lucky day!" after they left their homework on the kitchen table, they are being ironic. The irony used here helps show that it is definitely *not* the character's lucky day.

PERSONIFICATION

- Gives life or human characteristics to an inanimate object
- For example, if an author writes "The trees whispered to each other across the wide blue sky," they are using personification to help the reader imagine the scene. Trees are not human beings, so they do not whisper, but the image created in the reader stands out more than a literal description would.

143

EXAMPLE

Based on current knowledge, identify whether metaphor, simile, or hyperbole is used in this sentence:

> The chiming bell was a beacon of hope for the downtrodden villagers.

A **metaphor** is used in this sentence to draw a parallel between "the chiming bell" and "a beacon of hope." The bell is being compared to something else in the sentence, which indicates the use of metaphor or simile, but the reader knows that the sentence does not contain a simile, because the words **like** and **as** are not used to show the comparison. The sentence also does not contain an exaggeration of facts, so the reader can see that hyperbole is not used.

EXAMPLE

Read the excerpt from a poem by William Blake and describe what form of figurative language it uses.

> The wild winds weep,
> And the night is a-cold;
> Come hither, sleep,
> And my griefs unfold.

This poem contains several examples of **personification**. In the poem, the speaker says "The wild winds weep," thereby giving the winds the human characteristic of weeping. Later it says "Come hither, sleep," which is another use of personification asking that sleep to go somewhere as though it were a person. The poem gives the winds and sleep human characteristics. This is the definition of personification. It is not an example of simile because there is no comparison using the words "as" or "like." It is not a metaphor because there is no comparison between two things sharing a similar quality. And it is not an example of hyperbole because there is no exaggeration. The poem does contain some alliteration, however; the repetition of the letter "w" in "wild winds weep" qualifies as alliteration, which is another literary technique.

POINT OF VIEW

Authors choose which character tells the story they are writing. This is called **point of view**. The point of view affects the story in many ways. There are three general types of point of view:

FIRST PERSON

- Tells a story through the eyes of one character.
- Uses the pronouns 'I,' 'me,' 'we,' and 'my.'
- The reader gets only one side of the story, without any other angles on what may have happened in the text

SECOND PERSON

- Tells a story using the pronoun 'you.'
- The least common point of view.

THIRD PERSON

- Tells a story about a character or group of characters from an outside viewpoint.
- Uses the words 'her', 'his,' 'they,' or a name to talk about a character or characters.
- A common way to show action in a story which allows the author to easily and realistically tell a story from more than one person's viewpoint.
- Gives readers a more complete view of a story as it is told from many different perspectives.

DIFFERENT FORMS OF THIRD PERSON

When an author writes in third-person point of view, there are a few options to choose from:

- **Third person omniscient** - There is an all-knowing narrator telling the story as well as interpreting events, and relating thoughts of the characters.
- **Third person limited (or closed)** - The author writes in the third person, but does so from only one character's point of view. There are two different variations of this type of narration: the narrator can either stay with the same character throughout or cycle through different characters over the course of the story.

SUBJECTIVE AND OBJECTIVE POINT OF VIEW

The point of view of a character or narrator can either be **subjective** or **objective**. When a character or narrator is describing a person, object, or idea using phrases that are based on opinions or motivated by feelings, their point of view is subjective. When they use phrases based on facts or something that can be proven, their point of view is objective. For example, if a character describes a person walking toward them and they say "Her shirt was a beautiful shade of yellow, which made her blonde hair shine even brighter" they are speaking in subjective point of view. The yellow color they think is beautiful could be someone else's least favorite color. If the same character described the situation objectively, they might say "As she walked by, I noticed her shirt was yellow and her hair was blonde." The narrator doesn't comment on his opinion of the color, just that it is factually yellow.

STYLE, VOICE, TONE, AND MOOD

Style, tone, and mood all play an important role in the development of a story. The reader's impression of a story can vary based on the style, tone, and mood established by the author.

- **Style** refers to the way an author uses words, phrases, and sentence structure. The style of the text can change depending on whether the author uses short, choppy sentences, long, elaborate sentences, formal language, or informal language.
- **Voice** refers to the characteristics of a text that show the author's personality and distinguish the author from other writers. An author's voice may be recognized through the way they use words or the way they organize and present their thoughts. Voice is specific to each writer, and it can be as specific and unique as personality.
- **Tone** refers to the attitude of the writer toward the subject matter. The tone can change throughout the text or stay the same. There are many ways to describe the tone of the text, such as light, playful, questioning, humorous, serious, solemn, or tense. The reader can identify the tone by paying attention to the author's word choice.
- **Mood** refers to the overall feeling conveyed by a setting. For example, a story may be dark in terms of setting, characters, and events that occur. If a story is presented in a picturesque countryside location where the characters are content and the style of speaking is elaborate, the reader will have a different impression of the story than if the setting is in a rundown house with a pale, unhappy caretaker that rarely speaks.

> **Review Video: Style, Tone, and Mood**
> Visit mometrix.com/academy and enter code: 416961

RHETORICAL DEVICES VS LOGICAL FALLACIES

Writers of persuasive and argumentative texts will often use strategies that may help them persuade the reader to agree with their claims. These strategies may be used to convince the reader on a logical or emotional level. The writer may also use them to prove his or her own credibility, or reliability. These strategies are called **rhetorical devices**. However, writers make statements that seem like rhetorical devices, but are not actually logical. They may sound persuasive, but they are unreasonable and may leave out part of the truth or try to prove a weak argument. These are called **logical fallacies**.

Reading Comprehension

145

COMMON RHETORICAL DEVICES

- **Direct Address**: Direct address is a strategy that authors can use to create a call to action or lead their audience to make a personal connection to the author's claim. When making a direct address, the author will make a statement or claim as if they mean to say it to each audience member, personally.
- **Analogy:** An analogy is a comparison of relationships. For example, saying that a hen is to a chick as a mare is to a colt. Both pairs include a mother animal and a baby animal, and the analogy shows a similarity between hens and mares and a similarity between colts and chicks. Authors may use analogies to explain their claims. Analogies allow authors to show how their claim is similar to a concept that the reader is more familiar with or already approves.
- **Juxtaposition:** Juxtaposition is when two contrasting ideas are presented together. Authors can use juxtaposition to make the differences between the two ideas more obvious to the reader. This may also help the author lead the reader to pay attention or prefer one idea over the other.
- **Rhetorical Question:** A rhetorical question is a question that does not need to be answered. Authors may use rhetorical questions to encourage a reader to think more deeply about an idea or apply it to their own lives. Authors may also use rhetorical questions to influence the way a reader thinks about an idea.

COMMON LOGICAL FALLACIES

- **Bandwagon Appeals:** Bandwagon appeals claim that everybody else agrees with the author's argument, so readers to should conform and agree, also.
- **Circular Reasoning:** When authors use circular reasoning, they use the idea they want to prove as part of their proof for the idea. People using circular arguments are actually "talking in circles." For example, someone argues, "X is illegal. Because it is illegal, one should not do it. Because one shouldn't do it, the government should prevent people from doing it. This is why it is illegal."
- **Sweeping Generalizations:** When an author makes a statement as if it is true for everyone, the author is making a sweeping generalization. For example, the statement, "Everyone loves chocolate," is a sweeping generalization. While most people do enjoy chocolate, the statement is still not true because there are people who do not like chocolate. Authors may use sweeping generalizations as evidence because they will expect the reader to ignore the fact that they are not true. Readers must be careful to consider whether statements that apply to many people are actually true.
- **Loaded Language:** An author uses loaded language when he or she makes claims that include words or phrases that lead the audience to react emotionally. While making an emotional appeal can be an effective strategy, loaded language is often used only to draw on emotions. Authors use loaded language in order to lead the audience to agree based on how the author's words have made them feel, rather than whether or not the author's words are logical and supported by evidence. Loaded language may rely on the sympathy, anger, or fear of the audience.

Vocabulary

DICTIONARY

A print or digital dictionary can be used to find out many things about a word. A dictionary will show the correct pronunciation of a word, provide its meaning, and identify what part of speech the word is. It will also tell how the word was derived—that is, what words it came from originally. A dictionary will have a **pronunciation guide** for each word that shows how to sound it out and where its syllables start and end. It will use symbols to indicate sounds, and will also use sample sounds (the "a" in "bad," for instance). A dictionary lists all of the meanings of a word and the parts of speech the word can be used as.

EXAMPLE

Philippe used his dictionary to check the various meanings of the word *eliminate*. He found this entry:

eliminate \ i-'li-mə-ˌnāt \ verb

146

> 1. to put an end to or get rid of
> 2. to expel from the living body
> 3. to cause to disappear by combining two or more equations

Identify which definition of *eliminate* is used in the following sentence:

> Harold couldn't wait to *eliminate* the other team from the playoffs by winning the first two games.

The correct answer is meaning 1: "to put an end to or get rid of." If you substitute that definition for the word, the sentence makes sense. Meanings 2 and 3 do not fit with the context of the sentence. When considering which meaning is being used, always check for context clues in the sentence or in the sentences before or after the sentence in which the word is used. Dictionaries also tell you how to pronounce words and often the derivation of the word, although that is not given here.

THESAURUS

A thesaurus is a reference book that gives **synonyms** of words. It is different from a dictionary because a thesaurus does not give definitions. A thesaurus can be helpful in finding the meaning of an unfamiliar word when reading. If the meaning of a synonym is known, then the meaning of the unfamiliar word will be known. Another time in which a thesaurus can be helpful is when writing. Using a thesaurus helps authors to vary their word choice.

GLOSSARY

A glossary is a **list of terms and their definitions** that can be found **at the back** of certain types of books, such as textbooks or reference books. A glossary does not have the definitions of all words, like a dictionary, but instead gives the definitions of the important terms within that particular book which are either uncommon or newly introduced. One may use a glossary when reading a book about economics or a chapter in a science textbook, for example, to define some of the technical terms within the text.

DENOTATIVE AND CONNOTATIVE MEANINGS

The **denotative meaning** of a word is the exact dictionary definition of the word. The **connotative meaning** of a word is the emotion conveyed by the use of the word in context. The word may have associated meaning in addition to its dictionary definition. A good way to remember the difference between denotative and connotative is to think "direct" or "dictionary" in relation to denotative.

An example of a denotative meaning for the adjective *ablaze* would be "burning", as in the logs burning in a fireplace. A connotative meaning for the adjective *ablaze*, based on the context of the word, may indicate a level of comfort while sitting in front of a fireplace. For instance, in the context: "A logs were *ablaze* in the fireplace, radiating heat out into the corners of the snow-enclosed room", the word *ablaze* implies comfort and coziness within the space described. The connotative meaning of a word can often have an emotional association for the reader.

EXAMPLE

Define the denotative and connotative meaning of the word *palace* in the following sentence:

> The golden *palace* gates opened slowly to reveal an expansive garden that was well-tended by precise gardeners all wearing the king's insignia.

In the example, the denotative meaning of the word is that a *palace* is literally a place where royalty lives. A *palace* implies, or connotes, a place of riches and is usually associated with wealth. The words "golden",

147

"expansive garden", and "king's insignia" all give clues that the *palace* can be viewed as a place of importance, one that is well taken care of.

When looking for the denotative meaning of a word, remember to think "direct", or the literal meaning of the word. The connotative meaning of the word is implied and not directly stated; the connotative meaning is often associated with emotion and feeling about the typical context of the word.

USING CONTEXT TO DETERMINE THE MEANINGS OF WORDS

Readers of all levels will encounter words that they have either never seen or that they have seen before but still don't know what it means. The best way to define a word in **context** is to look for nearby words that can assist in learning the meaning of the word.

CONTEXT CLUES

Context clues are hints about the meaning of a word. They are the words or phrases in the sentence or sentences before and after a new or unfamiliar word. Context clues give the reader an idea about what a word means. A context clue may also contain words that help define the new word or an example of what the new word means. A context clue in the form of an example may contain the words including 'such as', a dash, or a colon before stated information.

Using context clues to figure out meaning can be helpful when learning a new set of vocabulary words or reading a difficult text. The dictionary definition of a word can always be looked up to double-check intended meaning.

> **Review Video: Reading Comprehension: Using Context Clues**
> Visit mometrix.com/academy and enter code: 613660

EXAMPLE

Using context clues, determine the meaning of *gregarious* in the following excerpt.

> Beverly is the most *gregarious* person I have ever known. She loves people and spends a lot of her time talking to her friends and arranging get-togethers. She doesn't mind spending hours cooking as long as she knows that her house will be filled with people.

This excerpt says Beverly loves people and spends a lot of her time talking with friends and arranging get-togethers. It also says that she likes her house filled with people. These clues in the sentence help the reader determine that *gregarious* means Beverly is someone who likes to talk with other people, so she is "sociable."

EXAMPLE

Read the sentence and explain the meaning of *sense of foreboding*:

> All day long Ron kept thinking about Sue. For some unknown reason he was worried about her. He had a strong *sense of foreboding* that something was about to go wrong in Sue's city. Then he heard about the earthquake there. Luckily Sue was not injured.

To figure out the meaning of the phrase *sense of foreboding*, the reader needs to look for context clues in just the same way the reader would do to figure out the meaning of a single word. The excerpt says that Ron was "worried" about Sue for "some unknown reason." It also says that he felt that "something was going to go wrong in Sue's city." Ron also heard about an earthquake taking place in Sue's city. A "sense of foreboding" must mean that Ron had an idea that something bad was going to happen. The context clues help the reader figure out the meaning of the phrase.

SUBSTITUTION TO FIND MEANING

One way to find out if you have figured out the correct meaning of a new word is to **substitute** the meaning for the word. Using the example for *basin*, if the reader substituted in "depression in the earth," the sentence would read:

> The "depression in the earth" had filled with water over the summer months, so that the rocky bottom was no longer visible to the casual hiker.

This is a way for the reader to confirm that they have used the context clues in the sentence correctly.

SYNONYMS AND ANTONYMS

When you understand how words relate to each other, you will discover more in a passage. This is explained by understanding **synonyms**, which are words that mean the same thing, and **antonyms**, which are words that mean the opposite of one another. As an example, *dry* and *arid* are synonyms, and *dry* and *wet* are antonyms.

> **Review Video: Synonyms and Antonyms**
> Visit mometrix.com/academy and enter code: 105612

DEFINITION WITHIN A TEXT

An author may **define** a word in the text. For example, an author may write, "The company did not have sufficient capital, that is, available money, to continue operating." The author defined "capital" as "available money." Authors will use words and phrases, such as "that is," "or," "meaning," and "which is," to let the reader know that they are defining the word.

ANALOGY

Analogies are used to **compare relationships**. For example, the analogy "restaurant is to eating as store is to shopping." A restaurant is a place where you eat, and a store is a place where you shop. The analogy compares locations and the things people do at those locations. **Analogies** can also be used to show the meaning of unfamiliar words. For example, consider the analogy "author is to writing as artisan is to crafting." *Artisan* may be an unfamiliar word to some. However, this analogy begins with "author is to writing." An author writes to create books, articles, and poems. The first part of the analogy pairs a person's job title with the action that their job requires. Based on this, a reader can conclude that an artisan is someone who crafts things.

EXAMPLES THAT CLARIFY MEANING

An author may use a word and then give examples that reveal its meaning. Consider this text: "Those who do not know sign language can communicate with people who are deaf or hard of hearing by using gestures. These may include pointing their fingers to indicate which direction to look or go or holding up a hand to indicate stopping." The author of this text has used the word *gestures* and then followed it with examples. This shows a reader who is unfamiliar with the word that gestures are hand motions. Readers can find examples by looking for signal words like "for example," "for instance," "like," and "such as."

CONTRAST

Readers can use these **contrasting** words and **opposites** as context clues to help them understand unfamiliar words. For example, an author may write, "Our conversation was not cheery. We sat and talked very solemnly about the events." Because the author says the conversation was "not cheery," a reader who is not familiar with the word "solemnly" can see that "solemn" means the opposite of cheery. This shows that *solemn* must mean serious or sad.

CAUSE AND EFFECT

A text that discusses a **cause and effect** can also show the meaning of an unfamiliar word. Consider the following sentence: "The student was mortified after she learned that she accidentally sang the wrong song at the talent show." *Mortified* may be an unfamiliar word. However, this sentence shows that the student became

149

Reading Comprehension

mortified as a result of her mistake. The reader can understand that making a mistake in front of many people is the cause. Usually, this would have the effect of making someone very embarrassed. *Mortified* means "extremely embarrassed," which is supported by the event in the sentence.

MULTIPLE-MEANING WORDS

A multiple-meaning word has different definitions, depending on the contextual use of the word. A multiple-meaning word is also called a **homonym**. A homonym is defined as a word that has more than one meaning, but is spelled and pronounced the same for all of them. For example, look at the word *leaves* in the following two sentences:

1. Michelle *leaves* the building at 5 o'clock every day.
2. The *leaves* fell off the oak tree in September.

In the first sentence, *leaves* means exits. In the second sentence, *leaves* refers to parts of a tree. By looking at the rest of each sentence, the reader can understand which definition of the multiple-meaning word the author is referring to.

SIMILAR WORDS

Homophones are words that are pronounced the same, but may be spelled differently. An example of two homophones would be *heir* (someone due to inherit an estate) and *air* (the invisible substance people breathe).

Homographs are words that are spelled the same, but may be pronounced differently. An example of a homograph is the word *row*, which is pronounced one way when used to mean a horizontal grouping and is pronounced another way when used to mean an argument.

Verbal

The Verbal test of the SSAT consists of a total of 60 questions (30 Synonyms and 30 Analogies).

Synonyms

Synonyms are words that have the same definition or similar meanings. For example, *wise* and *intelligent* can be used to describe someone who is good at solving problems. However, *wise* is used for good judgment. *Intelligent* is closer to good thinking. Since these words have meanings that are very similar, they are synonyms, even though their definitions are not exactly the same.

Even though words with unidentical definitions can be synonyms, words cannot be called synonyms when their definitions are very different. For example, *hot* and *warm* are not synonyms because their meanings are too different. They are both used to describe something that has heat. However, *warm* is used to describe a medium amount of heat while *hot* is used to describe a large amount of heat. How do you know when two words are synonyms? First, try to replace one word with the other word. Then decide whether or not the meaning of the sentence has changed. Replacing *warm* with *hot* in a sentence gives the sentence a different meaning.

> **Review Video: <u>What Are Synonyms and Antonyms?</u>**
> Visit mometrix.com/academy and enter code: 105612
>
> **Review Video: <u>Synonyms</u>**
> Visit mometrix.com/academy and enter code: 355036

Below, each example includes one word and four answer choices. For each example, choose the answer choice that is a synonym for the word at the top. Before you look at the answer choices, try to think of a few words that could be a synonym for the word at the top. Then, check the choices and see if one of the words you thought of is present. If not, decide which answer choice is a synonym for the given word. Remember to read all of the answer choices and choose the one that has the most similar meaning to the given word.

EXAMPLE 1
Tranquil:

- a. Agitated
- b. Nervous
- c. Stable
- d. Thrive
- e. Violent

EXAMPLE 2
Agile:

- a. Cultivated
- b. Dispirited
- c. Frustrate
- d. Rapid
- e. Sluggish

EXAMPLE 3

Obstruction:

   a. Assistance
   b. Barrier
   c. Displace
   d. Exhibition
   e. Promotion

ANSWERS

Example 1: C, Stable

Example 2: A, Rapid

Example 3: D, Barrier

Analogies

Analogies are used to **compare relationships**. For example, consider the analogy "restaurant is to eating as store is to shopping." A restaurant is a place where you eat, and a store is a place where you shop. The analogy compares types of places and the things people do at those places.

DETERMINE THE RELATIONSHIP

When completing analogies, it is important to understand the connection, or relationship, between the words in the analogy. To understand the relationship, you can start by creating a sentence that describes how the first two pieces of the analogy are connected. For example, consider an analogy that begins, "Duck is to quack." The two pieces are *duck* and *quack*. The simple sentences "*Quack* is the sound a duck makes" or "A duck makes a quacking noise" describe the relationship between these pieces of the analogy. This means that another pair of terms used to complete the analogy must have the same relationship.

Once you have a simple sentence, go through each answer choice and replace the pieces of your sentence with the pieces from each answer choice. Depending on the question, you may need to make changes to your sentence to make it more specific.

EXAMPLE

Wood is to fire as

Sentence: Wood feeds a fire.

Wood is to fire as

   a. Farmer is to cow
   b. Gasoline is to engine

Using the sentence, you would state "Farmer feeds a cow" which is correct. Yet, the next answer choice "Gasoline feeds an engine" is also true. So, which is the correct answer? The sentence used to describe this relationship needs to be more specific.

Specific Sentences: "Wood feeds a fire and is used up." / "Wood is burned in a fire."

Replace the pieces in the specific sentences with the pieces from the answer choices. Consider the sentences using the pieces from choice A:

"Farmer feeds a cow and is used up."

"Farmer is burned in a cow."

152

Neither of these sentences are correct. Look at the sentences using the pieces from choice B:

"Gasoline feeds an engine and is used up."

"Gasoline is burned in an engine."

These sentences are correct. This shows that choice B is the correct answer. If your sentence seems correct with more than one answer choice, then keep making changes until only one answer choice makes sense.

ELIMINATING SIMILARITIES

Sometimes, the relationship between two pieces of an analogy may not be clear. When this happens, look over the answer choices and see what clues they provide. If any of the answer choices show the exact same type of relationship, then those answer choices must be incorrect.

EXAMPLE

Tough is to rugged as
   a. Soft is to hard
   b. Clear is to foggy
   c. Inhale is to exhale
   d. Throw is to catch
   e. Rigid is to taut

Tough and *rugged* are synonyms. The first four answer choices contain pairs of antonyms. You may not realize that *taut* and *rigid* are synonyms. However, because the first four answer choices show the exact same kind of relationship, the last answer choice must be correct.

WORD TYPES

EXAMPLE

Gardener is to hedge as
   a. Wind is to rock
   b. Woodcarver is to stick

In this example, you could start with the sentence "Gardener cuts away at hedges." Now, both answer choices seem correct when inserted in this sentence. For choice A, you can say that "Wind cuts away at rocks" due to erosion. For choice B, you can say that a "Woodcarver cuts away at sticks." The difference is that the wind is a thing, but a woodcarver is a person. Because a gardener is a person, answer choice B is the correct option.

READ CAREFULLY

To understand the analogies, you need to read the terms and answer choices carefully. You can miss the question because you misread the terms. Each question here has only a few words, so you can spend time reading them carefully. Yet, you cannot forget your time limit of the section. So, don't spend too much time on one question. Just focus on reading carefully and be sure to read all of the choices. You may find an answer choice that seems correct. Yet, when you finish reading over the choices, you may find a better choice.

Verbal

Practice Test #1

Want to take this practice test in an online interactive format?
Check out the bonus page, which includes interactive practice questions and much more: **mometrix.com/bonus948/ssatmiddle**

Writing

Instructions: Read the following prompt, taking a few moments to plan a response. Then, write your response in essay form.

Prompt: *NSA wiretapping and spying policies have been a topic of interest lately with much discussion taking place over the need for security as it relates to the right to individual privacy.*

Do you agree or disagree with this statement? Use examples from history, literature, or your own personal experience to support your point of view.

Quantitative

1. Janice makes x phone calls. Elaina makes 23 more phone calls than Janice. June makes 14 more phone calls than Janice. In terms of x, what is the sum of their phone calls minus 25 calls?

    a. $3x + 37$
    b. $3x + 12$
    c. $x + 12$
    d. $3x - 25$
    e. $9x - 25$

2. Olga drew the regular figure shown here. She painted part of the figure a light color and part of it a darker color. She left the rest of the figure white.

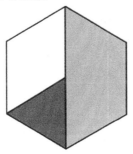

Which of the following equations best models the part of the figure Olga left white?

    a. $1 - \frac{1}{3} - \frac{1}{3} = \frac{1}{3}$
    b. $1 - \frac{1}{6} - \frac{1}{6} = \frac{2}{3}$
    c. $1 - \frac{1}{6} - \frac{1}{2} = \frac{1}{3}$
    d. $1 - \frac{1}{2} - \frac{1}{3} = \frac{2}{3}$
    e. $1 - \frac{1}{2} - \frac{1}{6} = \frac{2}{3}$

3. On a floor plan drawn at a scale of 1:100, the area of a rectangular room is 30 cm². What is the actual area of the room?

    a. 30 m^2
    b. 300 cm^2
    c. 300 m^2
    d. $3{,}000 \text{ m}^2$
    e. $30{,}000 \text{ cm}^2$

4. Restaurant customers tip their server only 8 percent for poor service. If their tip was $4, how much was their bill?

    a. $40
    b. $42
    c. $46
    d. $48
    e. $50

5. The number of flights a flight attendant made per month is represented by the line graph below.

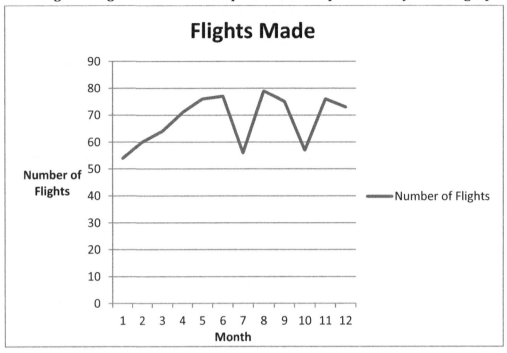

What is the range in the number of flights the flight attendant made?

    a.   20
    b.   22
    c.   25
    d.   29
    e.   32

6. In Figure 1 (pictured below), the distance from A to D is 48. The distance from A to B is equal to the distance from B to C. If the distance from C to D is twice the distance of A to B, how far apart are B and D?

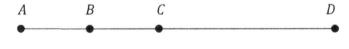

Figure 1

    a.   12
    b.   16
    c.   19
    d.   24
    e.   36

156

7. John buys 100 shares of stock at $100 per share. The price goes up by 10%, and he sells 50 shares. Then, prices drop by 10%, and he sells his remaining 50 shares. How much did he get for the last 50 shares?

    a. $4,900
    b. $4,950
    c. $5,000
    d. $5,050
    e. $5,500

8. A long-distance runner does a first lap around a track in exactly 50 seconds. As she tires, each subsequent lap takes 20% longer than the previous one. How long does she take to run 3 laps?

    a. 72 seconds
    b. 150 seconds
    c. 160 seconds
    d. 188 seconds
    e. 182 seconds

9. Hannah draws two supplementary angles. One angle measures 34°. What is the measure of the other angle?

    a. 56°
    b. 66°
    c. 146°
    d. 168°
    e. 326°

10. Jeremy put a heavy chalk mark on the tire of his bicycle. His bike tire is 27 inches in diameter. When he rolled the bike, the chalk left marks on the sidewalk. Which expression can be used to best determine the distance, in inches, the bike rolled from the first mark to the fourth mark?

    a. $3(27\pi)$
    b. $4\pi(27)$
    c. $(27 \div 3)\pi$
    d. $(27 \div 4)\pi$
    e. $4\pi(27 \div 3)$

11. A data set has five values: 5, 10, 12, 13, and one unknown value. The average of the data set is 9.6. What is the unknown value?

    a. 4.6
    b. 5
    c. 6
    d. 7.2
    e. 8

12. A hat contains 6 red dice, 4 green dice, and 2 blue dice. What is the probability that Sarah pulls out a blue die, replaces it, and then pulls out a green die?

    a. $\frac{1}{18}$
    b. $\frac{1}{16}$
    c. $\frac{2}{12}$
    d. $\frac{1}{3}$
    e. $\frac{1}{2}$

13. If $a - 16 = 8b + 6$, what does $a + 3$ equal?

    a. $b + 3$
    b. $8b + 19$
    c. $8b + 22$
    d. $8b + 25$
    e. $b + 6$

14. A bag of coffee costs \$9.85 and contains 16 ounces of coffee. Which of the following best represents the cost per ounce?

    a.   \$0.62
    b.   \$0.64
    c.   \$0.65
    d.   \$0.67
    e.   \$0.70

15. What is the slope of the line shown in the graph?

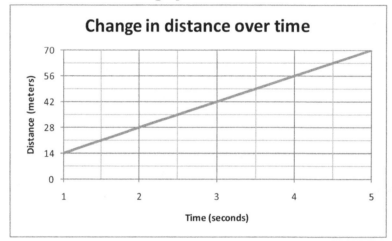

    a.   7
    b.   14
    c.   16
    d.   21
    e.   28

16. Adam builds a bridge that is 12 feet long. If 1 foot equals 0.3048 meters, which of the following best represents the length of the bridge, in meters?

    a.   1.83 meters
    b.   3.66 meters
    c.   4.96 meters
    d.   5.7 meters
    e.   39.37 meters

17. Amy saves \$450 every 3 months. How much does she save after 3 years?

    a.   \$4,800
    b.   \$5,200
    c.   \$5,400
    d.   \$5,800
    e.   \$6,000

18. The figure below shows a square. If side $\overline{AD} = 10$ and if $\overline{AE} = \overline{EB}$ and $\overline{BF} = \overline{FC}$, what is the area of the shaded region?

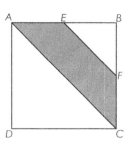

a. 16.5
b. 24
c. 28
d. 37.5
e. 42.5

19. Simplify the following expression: $4(6 - 3)^2 - (-2)$

a. 34
b. 36
c. 38
d. 42
e. 48

20. If $\sqrt{x} - 2 = 8$, determine the value of x.

a. 64
b. 66
c. 100
d. 110
e. 144

21. Which of the following transformations has been applied to $\triangle ABC$?

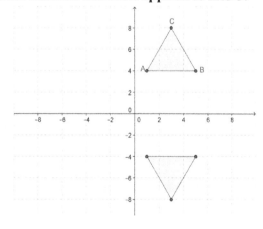

a. translation
b. rotation of 90 degrees
c. reflection
d. dilation
e. rotation of 180 degrees

22. The distance between two towns is 275 miles. A truck driver must leave one town and arrive at the other at 9:30 p.m. If the trucker drives at an average rate of 55 miles per hour, at what time should the trucker depart?

a. 4:00 p.m.
b. 4:30 p.m.
c. 5:00 p.m.
d. 4:00 a.m.
e. 4:30 a.m.

23. The chart below shows the annual number of visitors to the Augusta Planetarium. Which year shows the greatest increase in visitors over the prior year?

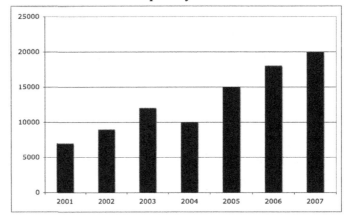

a. 2001
b. 2002
c. 2003
d. 2004
e. 2005

24. What is the simplest way to write the following expression?

$$5x - 2y + 4x + y$$

a. $9x - y$
b. $9x - 3y$
c. $9x + 3y$
d. $x - y$
e. $9x + y$

25. A wall clock has the numbers 1 through 12 written on it. If you spin the second hand, what is the probability of landing on an even number?

a. 10%
b. 20%
c. 30%
d. 40%
e. 50%

Reading Comprehension

<u>Global Warming</u>

Global warming and the depletion of natural resources are constant threats to the future of our planet. All people have a responsibility to be proactive participants in the fight to save Earth by working now to conserve resources for later. Participation begins with our everyday choices. From what you buy to what you do to how much you use, your decisions affect the planet and everyone around you. Now is the time to take action.

When choosing what to buy, look for sustainable products made from renewable or recycled resources. The packaging of the products you buy is just as important as the products themselves. Is the item minimally packaged in a recycled container? How did the product reach the store? Locally grown food and other products manufactured within your community are the best choices. The fewer miles a product traveled to reach you, the fewer resources it required.

You can continue to make a difference for the planet in how you use what you bought and the resources you have available. Remember the locally grown food you purchased? Don't pile it on your plate at dinner. Food that remains on your plate is a wasted resource, and you can always go back for seconds. You should try to be aware of your consumption of water and energy. Turn off the water when you brush your teeth, and limit your showers to five minutes. Turn off the lights, and don't leave appliances or chargers plugged in when not in use.

Together, we can use less, waste less, recycle more, and make the right choices. It may be the only chance we have.

1. What is the author's primary purpose in writing this article?
   a.   The author's purpose is to scare people.
   b.   The author's purpose is to warn people.
   c.   The author's purpose is to inspire people.
   d.   The author's purpose is to inform people.
   e.   The author's purpose is to scold people.

2. How does the author make a connection between the second and third paragraphs (lines 7-19)?
   a.   The author indicates he will now make suggestions for how to use what you bought.
   b.   The author indicates he will continue to give more examples of what you should buy.
   c.   The author indicates he will make suggestions for how to keep from buying more items.
   d.   The author indicates he will make suggestions for how to tell other people what to buy.
   e.   The author indicates he will continue to encourage people to be aware of their energy consumption.

3. What is the main idea of this article?
   a.   People should use less water and energy.
   b.   People should make responsible choices in what they purchase and how they use their available resources.
   c.   People are quickly destroying the earth, and there is no way to stop the destruction.
   d.   People should organize everyone they know to join the fight to save the environment.
   e.   A few people need to keep the majority encouraged to save the planet's resources.

4. Which organizational pattern did the author use?
   a.   Comparison and contrast
   b.   Chronological order
   c.   Cause and effect
   d.   Problem/solution
   e.   None of the above

5. What does the author say is the place to begin saving our planet?

    a.   The place to begin is with getting rid of products that are not earth friendly.

    b.   The place to begin is with using less water when we take a shower.

    c.   The place to begin is with a commitment to fight for the improvement of Earth.

    d.   The place to begin is with buying locally-grown food.

    e.   The place to begin is with the choices we make every day.

6. What does the author imply will happen if people do not follow his suggestions?

    a.   The author implies we will run out of resources in the next 10 years.

    b.   The author implies water and energy prices will rise sharply in the near future.

    c.   The author implies global warming and the depletion of natural resources will continue.

    d.   The author implies local farmers will lose their farms.

    e.   The author implies that we will other opportunities to save the planet.

The Educational Market Town

Aberystwyth is a market town on the West Coast of Wales within the United Kingdom. A market town refers to European areas that have the right to have markets, which differentiates it from a city or village. The town is located where two rivers meet, the River Ystwyth and River Rheidol and is best known as an educational center, housing an established university since 1872.

The town is situated between North Wales and South Wales, and is a large vacation destination as well as a tourist attraction. Constitution Hill is a hill on the north end of Aberystwyth, which provides excellent views of Cardigan Bay and which is supported by the Aberystwyth Electric Cliff Railway. Although Aberystwyth is known as a modern Welsh town, it is home to several historic buildings, such as the remnants of a castle.

Although there are several grocery, clothing, sporting goods, and various other miscellaneous shops, Aberystwyth is best known for its educational services. Aberystwyth University, formerly known as University College Wales, as well as the National Library of Wales, which is the legal deposit library for Wales and which houses all Welsh publications, are both located within Aberystwyth. The two main languages traditionally spoken in Aberystwyth are English and Welsh. With local live music, arts center, and educational opportunities in gorgeous scenery, Aberystwyth is a hidden luxury within the United Kingdom.

7. Where is Aberystwyth located?

    a.   England

    b.   Ireland

    c.   Scotland

    d.   Wales

    e.   Isle of Man

8. What is the purpose of this essay?

    a.   To explain that the university was established in 1872

    b.   To explain the legal deposit library in Wales

    c.   To provide a portrait of a town

    d.   To explain the views in Aberystwyth

    e.   To help tourists

163

9. What does the word *situated* mean in paragraph 2?

  a. located
  b. fighting
  c. luxurious
  d. hidden
  e. indefinite

10. Which of the following statements is an opinion?

  a. Although Aberystwyth is known as a modern Welsh town, it is home to several historic buildings, such as the remnants of a castle
  b. With local live music, arts center, and educational opportunities in gorgeous scenery, Aberystwyth is a hidden luxury within the United Kingdom
  c. The two main languages traditionally spoken in Aberystwyth are English and Welsh
  d. Aberystwyth is a market town on the West Coast of Wales within the United Kingdom
  e. Aberystwyth is best known for its educational services

11. How many languages are traditionally spoken in Aberystwyth?

  a. One
  b. Two
  c. Three
  d. Four
  e. More than four

12. What makes Aberystwyth a market town?

  a. It is a city
  b. It is a village
  c. It has the right to have a market
  d. There are markets in town every day
  e. The local live music, arts center, and educational opportunities

13. What is Constitution Hill supported by?

  a. Cardigan Bay
  b. The ocean
  c. North Wales
  d. Aberystwyth Electric Cliff Railway
  e. Tourism

14. What is Aberystwyth best known as?

  a. An educational center
  b. A market town
  c. A music center
  d. A hiking center
  e. A large vacation destination

An Excerpt from <u>The Fifty-First Dragon</u> by Heywood Broun

Of all the pupils at the knight school Gawaine le Cœur-Hardy was among the least promising. He was tall and sturdy, but his instructors soon discovered that he lacked spirit. He would hide in the woods when the jousting class was called, although his companions and members of the faculty sought to appeal to his better nature by shouting to him to come out and break his neck like a man. Even when they told him that the lances were padded, the horses no more than ponies and the field unusually soft for late autumn, Gawaine refused to grow enthusiastic. The Headmaster and the Assistant Professor of Pleasaunce were discussing the case one spring afternoon and the Assistant Professor could see no remedy but expulsion.

"No," said the Headmaster, as he looked out at the purple hills which ringed the school, "I think I'll train him to slay dragons."

"He might be killed," objected the Assistant Professor.

"So he might," replied the Headmaster brightly, but he added, more soberly, "we must consider the greater good. We are responsible for the formation of this lad's character."

"Are the dragons particularly bad this year?" interrupted the Assistant Professor. This was characteristic. He always seemed restive when the head of the school began to talk ethics and the ideals of the institution.

"I've never known them worse," replied the Headmaster. "Up in the hills to the south last week they killed a number of peasants, two cows and a prize pig. And if this dry spell holds there's no telling when they may start a forest fire simply by breathing around indiscriminately."

"Would any refund on the tuition fee be necessary in case of an accident to young Cœur-Hardy?"

"No," the principal answered, judicially, "that's all covered in the contract. But as a matter of fact he won't be killed. Before I send him up in the hills I'm going to give him a magic word."

"That's a good idea," said the Professor. "Sometimes they work wonders."

15. What is this passage about?
a. The problems that may arise from fighting dragons
b. How the educators would change Gawaine's course of study
c. The way the Professor and the Headmaster taught about dragons
d. Giving Gawaine a magic word to help him fight dragons
e. A shy boy's troubles in a new school environment

16. What can be inferred about Gawaine le Couer-Hardy from the first paragraph (lines 1-9)?
a. Gawaine does not want to be a knight
b. Gawaine is not as strong as the other pupils at the knight school
c. Gawaine's family history is made of unremarkable knights
d. Gawaine enjoys playing in the forest
e. Gawaine has no friends at the school

17. What is the best way to describe Gawaine's character?
a. Fearless and excitable
b. Careless and frigid
c. Spiritual and careful
d. Cowardly and apathetic
e. Rebellious and misunderstood

18. What is the meaning of "his better nature"?
a. An increased sense of honesty
b. Gawaine's love interest
c. A desire for ownership
d. A man's nobler instincts
e. His knowledge of the forests

19. Why does the Headmaster mention some "peasants, two cows, and a prize pig"?
   a.   To help the professor understand dragon behavior
   b.   To show that Gawaine would be perfect for fighting dragons
   c.   To illustrate how much trouble dragons are this year
   d.   To explain why Gawaine's talents were needed
   e.   To remind the professor of the painful event

20. How does the Headmaster put the professor at ease about Gawaine?
   a.   He tells him that Gawaine will only fight small dragons.
   b.   He assures him that Gawaine's contract has not expired.
   c.   He talks to him about the animals that have been killed by the dragons.
   d.   He reminds him of their responsibility for the boy's character.
   e.   He mentions that Gawaine will be given a magic word.

<u>Charles Darwin on the Galapagos Islands</u>

During the 1800s, Charles Darwin became known for his studies of plants and animals on the Galapagos Islands. He is often referred to as "the father of evolution," because he was first to describe a mechanism by which organisms change over time.

The Galapagos Islands are situated off the coast of South America. Much of Darwin's work on the islands focused on the birds. He noticed that island birds looked similar to finches on the South American continent and resembled a type of modified finch. The only differences in the finches Darwin saw were in their beaks and the kind of food they ate. Finches on the mainland were seed-eating birds, but the island finches ate insects, seeds, plant matter, egg yolks, and blood.

Darwin theorized that the island finches were offspring of one type of mainland finch. The population of finches was changing over time due to their environment. He believed the finches' eating habits changed because of the island's limited food supply. As the finches began to eat differently, the way their beaks worked and looked changed as well. For instance, insect-eating finches needed longer beaks for digging in the ground. Seed-eating and nut-eating finches required thicker beaks to crack the seed shells.

The process by which the finches changed happened over many generations. Among the population of beetle-eating finches, those finches born with longer, sharper beaks naturally had access to more beetles than those finches with shorter beaks. As a result, the sharp-beaked, insect-eating finches thrived and produced many offspring, while the short-beaked insect-eating finches gradually died out. The sharp beak was in effect selected by nature to thrive. The same thing happened in each finch population until finches within the same population began to look similar to each other and different from finches of other populations. These observations eventually led Darwin to develop the theory of natural selection.

21. Why is Charles Darwin called "the father of evolution"?
   a.   because he coined the term "evolution"
   b.   because he was the first scientist to study species on the Galapagos Islands
   c.   because he was the first to describe how organisms changed over time
   d.   because he was the first to suggest that birds adapted to their environment
   e.   because he was the first to develop the theory of natural selection

22. What is the main point of this passage?
   a.   to inform
   b.   to entertain
   c.   to critique
   d.   to persuade
   e.   to shock

166

23. According to the passage, why did finches with sharp, long beaks thrive while other finches died off?

    a.   They were able to reproduce faster than other types of finches on the island.

    b.   They were more numerous and eventually outlived the other finches on the island.

    c.   They were randomly selected by nature to reproduce over other types of finches on the island.

    d.   They had a diet that improved their fitness for their environment.

    e.   They had better access to insects than other types of finches on the island.

24. Based on Darwin's studies on the islands, what could also be inferred about how geography affects the diversity of species?

    a.   Geographical barriers decrease diversity of a species.

    b.   Geographical barriers increase diversity of a species.

    c.   Geographical barriers have an insignificant impact on the diversity of a species.

    d.   Geographical barriers left the finches open to predators.

    e.   There is no relationship between geographical barriers and the diversity of a species.

25. Which of the following statements correctly compares the finches Darwin observed in the Galapagos Islands with the finches found on the mainland?

    a.   The island finches were very similar with no visible differences.

    b.   The island finches differed only in the shape of their beaks.

    c.   The island finches differed only in size.

    d.   The island finches differed in the shape of their beaks and their diet.

    e.   The island finches produced fewer offspring.

New Zealand Inhabitants

The islands of New Zealand are among the most remote of all the Pacific islands. New Zealand is an archipelago, with two large islands and a number of smaller ones. Its climate is far cooler than the rest of Polynesia. According to Maori legends, it was colonized in the early fifteenth century by a wave of Polynesian voyagers who traveled southward in their canoes and settled on North Island. At this time, New Zealand was already known to the Polynesians, who had probably first landed there some 400 years earlier.

The Polynesian southward migration was limited by the availability of food. Traditional Polynesian tropical crops such as taro and yams will grow on North Island, but the climate of the South Island is too cold for them. Coconuts will not grow on either island. The first settlers were forced to rely on hunting and gathering, and, of course, fishing. Especially on the South Island, most settlements remained close to the sea. At the time of the Polynesian influx, enormous flocks of moa birds had their rookeries on the island shores. These flightless birds were easy prey for the settlers, and within a few centuries had been hunted to extinction. Fish, shellfish and the roots of the fern were other important sources of food, but even these began to diminish in quantity as the human population increased. The Maori had few other sources of meat: dogs, smaller birds, and rats. Archaeological evidence shows that human flesh was also eaten, and that tribal warfare increased markedly after the moa disappeared.

By far the most important farmed crop in prehistoric New Zealand was the sweet potato. This tuber is hearty enough to grow throughout the islands, and could be stored to provide food during the winter months, when other food-gathering activities were difficult. The availability of the sweet potato made possible a significant increase in the human population. Maori tribes often lived in encampments called *pa*, which were fortified with earthen embankments and usually located near the best sweet potato farmlands.

167

26. A definition for the word *archipelago* is

    a.   A country

    b.   A place in the southern hemisphere

    c.   A group of islands

    d.   A roosting place for birds

    e.   A place with few visitors

27. This article is primarily about what?

    a.   The geology of New Zealand

    b.   New Zealand's early history

    c.   New Zealand's prehistory

    d.   Food sources used by New Zealand's first colonists

    e.   The differences between the North Island and the South Island

28. Why did early settlements remain close to the sea?

    a.   The people liked to swim

    b.   The people didn't want to get far from the boats they had come in

    c.   Taro and yams grow only close to the beaches

    d.   They were dependent upon sea creatures for their food

    e.   They would be able to leave the island quickly if they were attacked

29. Why do you suppose tribal warfare increased after the moa disappeared?

    a.   Increased competition for food led the people to fight

    b.   Some groups blamed others for the moa's extinction

    c.   They had more time on their hands since they couldn't hunt the moa, so they fought

    d.   One group was trying to consolidate political control over the entire country

    e.   None of the above

30. How did the colder weather of New Zealand make it difficult for the Polynesians to live there?

    a.   The Polynesians weren't used to making warm clothes

    b.   Cold water fish are harder to catch

    c.   Some of them froze

    d.   Some of their traditional crops would not grow there

    e.   They had to use too many resources to make their shelters

31. Why was it important that sweet potatoes could be stored?

    a.   They could be eaten in winter, when other foods were scarce

    b.   They could be traded for fish and other goods

    c.   They could be taken along by groups of warriors going to war

    d.   They tasted better after a few weeks of storage

    e.   It allowed farmers to use more space for other foods

<u>"The Road Not Taken" by Robert Frost</u>

Two roads diverged in a yellow wood,

And sorry I could not travel both

And be one traveler, long I stood

And looked down one as far as I could

To where it bent in the undergrowth;

Then took the other, as just as fair,

And having perhaps the better claim,

Because it was grassy and wanted wear;

Though as for that the passing there

Had worn them really about the same,

And both that morning equally lay

In leaves no step had trodden black.

Oh, I kept the first for another day!

Yet knowing how way leads on to way,

I doubted if I should ever come back.

I shall be telling this with a sigh

Somewhere ages and ages hence:

Two roads diverged in a wood, and I—

I took the one less traveled by,

And that has made all the difference.

32. In the second stanza, is there a big difference between one road and the other?
   a. Yes, because one path is more dangerous than the other.
   b. Yes, because one road is much less traveled than the other.
   c. No, because one road is only a little less traveled than the other.
   d. No, because both roads lead to the same place in the end.
   e. There is not enough information given to the reader to make a decision.

33. Why does the narrator of the poem say that he will tell the story of the two roads "With a sigh/ Somewhere ages and ages hence"?
   a. The narrator is regretting the choice he has made.
   b. The narrator is sad that he had to walk alone.
   c. The narrator is looking back on a fond memory.
   d. The narrator does not remember what happened.
   e. The narrator knows that the two roads were removed many years ago.

34. Why is the path in the middle of the woods, rather than a road through the city?
   a. There are no signs to point out which road is faster.
   b. There are no distractions from the decision that the narrator has to make.
   c. There are no other people who can give the narrator advice.
   d. All of the above
   e. None of the above

35. Why does the narrator of the poem take so long to make a decision?

a. He is not sure where the roads will lead him.
b. He is trying to guess which road will be best for exploring.
c. He is trying to remember if he has walked this way before.
d. He is sure that one of the choices will be a wrong turn.
e. He thinks the choice he makes represents who he is.

36. What does it say about the narrator that he wants to take the road less traveled?

a. He wants to explore a place that no one has ever been to before.
b. He wants to feel unique by making a less popular journey.
c. He wants to take a shortcut through the woods.
d. He wants to avoid other people.
e. He wants to show off his bravery to other people.

The Inventions of Technology

Stories have been a part of the world since the beginning of recorded time. For centuries before the invention of the printing press, stories of the world were passed down to generations through oral tradition. With the invention of the printing press, which made written material available to wide ranges of audiences, books were mass-produced and introduced into greater society.

For the last several centuries, books have been at the forefront of education and entertainment. With the invention of the Internet, reliance on books for information quickly changed. Soon, almost everything that anyone needed to know could be accessed through the Internet. Large, printed volumes of encyclopedias became unnecessary as all of the information was easily available on the Internet.

Despite the progression of the Internet, printed media was still very popular in the forms of both fiction and non-fiction books. While waiting for an appointment, enduring a several-hour flight, or relaxing before sleep, books have been a reliable and convenient source of entertainment, and one that society has not been willing to give up.

With the progression and extreme convenience of technology, printed books are going to soon become a thing of the past. Inventions such as the iPad from Macintosh and the Kindle have made the need for any kind of printed media unnecessary. With a rechargeable battery, a large screen, and the ability to have several books saved on file, electronic options will soon take over and society will no longer see printed books.

Although some people may say that the act of reading is not complete without turning a page, sliding a finger across the screen or pressing a button to read more onto the next page is just as satisfying to the reader. The iPad and Kindle are devices that have qualities similar to a computer and can be used for so much more than just reading. These devices are therefore better than books because they have multiple uses.

In a cultural society that is part of the world and due to a longstanding tradition, stories will always be an important way to communicate ideas and provide information and entertainment. Centuries ago, stories could only be remembered and retold through speech. Printed media changed the way the world communicated and was connected, and now, as we move forward with technology, it is only a matter of time before we must say goodbye to the printed past and welcome the digital and electronic future.

37. What is the main argument of this essay?

a. iPad and Kindles are easier to read than books
b. The printing press was a great invention
c. The Internet is how people receive information
d. Technology will soon replace printed material
e. People need frequent changes in how they receive stories

38. What is the main purpose of paragraph 1?
   a. To explain oral tradition
   b. To explain the importance of the printing press
   c. To explain the progression of stories within society
   d. To introduce the essay
   e. To show why iPads and Kindles are necessary today

39. According to the essay, what was the first way that stories were communicated and passed down?
   a. Oral tradition
   b. Printed books
   c. Technology
   d. Hand writing
   e. Cave drawings

40. Which of the following statements is an opinion?
   a. Despite the progression of the Internet, printed media was still very popular in the forms of both fiction and non-fiction books.
   b. The iPad and Kindle are devices that have qualities similar to a computer and can be used for so much more than just reading.
   c. With the invention of the Internet, reliance on books for information quickly changed.
   d. Stories have been a part of the world since the beginning of recorded time.
   e. Although some people may say that the act of reading is not complete without turning a page, sliding a finger across the screen or pressing a button to read more onto the next page is just as satisfying to the reader.

Verbal

Synonyms

Directions: Select the one word whose meaning is closest to the word in capital letters.

1. ABROAD
   a. harsh
   b. overseas
   c. selfish
   d. truthful
   e. reception

2. RUMINATE
   a. concern
   b. decision
   c. hesitation
   d. reflect
   e. neglect

3. CONCISE
   a. brief
   b. difficult
   c. lengthy
   d. reasonable
   e. repetitive

4. MOURN
   a. cry
   b. direction
   c. approve
   d. help
   e. praise

5. RESIDENCE
   a. home
   b. area
   c. office
   d. resist
   e. warehouse

6. LEVITY
   a. attended
   b. delivered
   c. happiness
   d. prepared
   e. serious

7. RASH

 a. wise
 b. careless
 c. plan
 d. shy
 e. event

8. BANISH

 a. experiences
 b. pleasures
 c. remove
 d. solutions
 e. welcome

9. OPPORTUNITY

 a. direction
 b. chance
 c. conclusion
 d. caution
 e. sequence

10. DISABLE

 a. improve
 b. lecture
 c. rebuke
 d. replace
 e. damage

11. FRAGILE

 a. reliable
 b. firm
 c. constant
 d. delicate
 e. healthy

12. LOYAL

 a. cover
 b. proof
 c. calm
 d. faithful
 e. healthy

13. PRINCIPLE

 a. end
 b. overall
 c. punctual
 d. standard
 e. uncertain

14. ASSESS

    a. anger
    b. ignore
    c. determine
    d. loneliness
    e. guess

15. MORAL

    a. arrive
    b. fake
    c. honest
    d. portion
    e. unfair

16. SUPERIOR

    a. short
    b. similar
    c. better
    d. weak
    e. usual

17. REMARK

    a. rebuke
    b. comment
    c. lecture
    d. replace
    e. question

18. SPECIFY

    a. confuse
    b. indicate
    c. solid
    d. sturdy
    e. unsettle

19. COMMENCE

    a. begin
    b. progress
    c. finish
    d. comment
    e. exhaust

20. SWIFTLY

    a. surely
    b. quickly
    c. slowly
    d. lightly
    e. lazy

21. WILY

a. clever
b. dainty
c. open
d. trustworthy
e. direct

22. HUMANE

a. cold
b. fed
c. friendly
d. hunted
e. selfish

23. ASSERT

a. deny
b. argue
c. hesitate
d. perform
e. surrender

24. PERILOUS

a. normal
b. secure
c. emblem
d. guarded
e. hazardous

25. DONATE

a. interrupt
b. excessive
c. contribute
d. petition
e. reserve

26. FINITE

a. described
b. intended
c. limited
d. wanted
e. endless

27. DOCILE

a. disagree
b. obedient
c. relate
d. state
e. determined

28. TAINT
   a. built
   b. clean
   c. damage
   d. improve
   e. unite

29. FALTER
   a. criticism
   b. delivery
   c. statement
   d. stumble
   e. steady

30. ABRUPTLY
   a. commonly
   b. homely
   c. slowly
   d. suddenly
   e. gradually

Analogies

Directions: For each of the following questions, you will find terms and five answer choices designated a, b, c, d, and e. Select the one answer choice that best completes the analogy.

31. Historian is to perspective as
   a. explorer is to questionable
   b. victim is to autopsy
   c. native is to insight
   d. fact is to opinion
   e. director is to spirit

32. Geography is to mountains as history is to
   a. preserved
   b. events
   c. roots
   d. future
   e. behavior

33. Exhale is to inhale as
   a. annual is to yearly
   b. reckless is to brave
   c. spontaneous is to chaos
   d. invert is to reverse
   e. consent is to prohibit

34. Fiction is to myth as nonfiction is to

a. drama
b. poem
c. legend
d. biography
e. hero

35. Astronomer is to encounter as

a. vendor is to protect
b. commander is to resign
c. prophet is to inform
d. academic is to camouflage
e. architect is to disorient

36. Dual is to duel as

a. docile is to fossil
b. seam is to seem
c. factor is to feature
d. finite is to ample
e. twice is to double

37. Nausea is to illness as

a. bacteria is to infection
b. surgery is to fracture
c. frail is to vulnerable
d. disease is to potent
e. pollen is to flower

38. Evidence is to condemn

a. generator is to restore
b. gauge is to dignity
c. antidote is to tension
d. destruction is to chariot
e. preamble is to threat

39. Liberty is to freedom as faithful is to

a. triumph
b. nimble
c. sincere
d. advantage
e. inspect

40. Masculine is to feminine as

a. paternal is to dad
b. invincible is to undefeatable
c. community is to individual
d. defiant is to resistant
e. concise is to summary

177

41. Artist is to imagination as advisor is to

    a. despair

    b. clarity

    c. oppress

    d. regal

    e. renew

42. Temple is to sacred as

    a. furnace is to basement

    b. auditorium is to musical

    c. church is to member

    d. sanctuary is to lofty

    e. cocoon is to violent

43. Gourmet is to critic as

    a. menu is to diverse

    b. meager is to portion

    c. cuisine is to exotic

    d. brick is to mason

    e. spice is to ingredient

44. Summit is to mountain as king is to

    a. battlefield

    b. powerful

    c. monarchy

    d. liberator

    e. parliament

45. Tactics is to marine

    a. data is to researcher

    b. navigate is to inspector

    c. forecast is to conductor

    d. distract is to editor

    e. incompetent is to trader

46. Chamber is to contain as

    a. throne is to cower

    b. agenda is to organize

    c. nook is to comfort

    d. chronicle is to story

    e. banjo is to instrument

47. Altar is to alter as

    a. loom is to whom

    b. shrine is to change

    c. denial is to veto

    d. rain is to reign

    e. align is to adjust

48. Nutrition is to physician as

    a. refugee is to nomad
    b. wildlife is to guide
    c. pottery is to navigator
    d. pitfall is to colonist
    e. tyranny is to tourist

49. Bravery is to cowardice as comedy is to

    a. glee
    b. grief
    c. celebrate
    d. relief
    e. inspire

50. Child is to naive as

    a. novice is to wisdom
    b. medal is to exhibit
    c. mother is to censor
    d. baptism is to custom
    e. soldier is to disciplined

51. Colonel is to kernel as

    a. agile is to fragile
    b. serial is to cereal
    c. mantle is to dismantle
    d. concept is to sonnet
    e. imply is to ally

52. Proton is to electron as

    a. productive is to efficient
    b. wept is to mourn
    c. renewable is to energy
    d. potent is to ineffective
    e. chromosome is to neutron

53. Documentary is to protestor as

    a. persist is to director
    b. banished is to renegade
    c. unpopular is to resident
    d. rotor is to mechanic
    e. fashion is to patriot

54. Tear is to tier as air is to

    a. breath
    b. ozone
    c. heir
    d. dare
    e. spare

55. Epidemic is to plague as vigor is to

a. pneumonia
b. endurance
c. incompetence
d. apathy
e. postseason

56. Eternal is to momentary as

a. frequent is to periodic
b. express is to rash
c. hinder is to interfere
d. exotic is to ordinary
e. termination is to decline

57. Meadow is to tranquility as

a. tributary is to consoling
b. suburbs is to danger
c. prairie is to campfire
d. traffic is to boring
e. exercise is to rural

58. Verses is to versus as

a. autobiography is to competition
b. lane is to cane
c. receive is to recieve
d. carat is to carrot
e. poetry is to confront

59. Aviator is to destination as sculptor is to

a. originals
b. restore
c. unrest
d. cathedral
e. strategy

60. Constellation is to star as

a. president is to campaign
b. child is to prank
c. sprout is to bloom
d. movement is to locomotive
e. orchestra is to instrument

Quantitative

1. How many one-fourths are contained in $8\frac{1}{2}$?

    a. 17
    b. 34
    c. 36
    d. 42
    e. 64

2. Given the sequence represented in the table below, where n represents the position of the term and a_n represents the value of the term, which of the following describes the relationship between the position number and the value of the term?

n	1	2	3	4	5	6
a_n	5	2	−1	−4	−7	−10

    a. Multiply n by 2 and subtract 4
    b. Multiply n by 2 and subtract 3
    c. Multiply n by −3 and add 8
    d. Multiply n by −4 and add 1
    e. Multiply n by −3 and subtract 8

3. A triangle has the following angle measures: 98°, 47°, and 35°. What type of triangle is it?

    a. equidistant
    b. right
    c. equiangular
    d. acute
    e. obtuse

4. The TV weatherman warned of a snowstorm approaching the area. If the snow is supposed to fall at a rate of 2 inches per hour, which of the following equations represents the total snowfall (t) after it has been snowing for h hours?

    a. $t = \frac{2}{h}$
    b. $t = h + 2$
    c. $t = h - 2$
    d. $t = 2h$
    e. $t = 2 - h$

5. Student scores on Mrs. Thompson's last math test are shown below. Which of the following is the best representation of class performance?

    76, 39, 87, 85, 91, 93, 86, 90, 77, 89, 74, 82, 68, 86, 79

    a. mean
    b. median
    c. mode
    d. range
    e. None of the above

6. In the figure below, find the value of x:

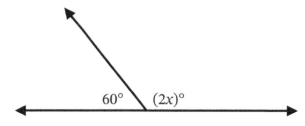

a. $x = 30$
b. $x = 60$
c. $x = 80$
d. $x = 100$
e. $x = 120$

7. If number x is subtracted from 27, the result is -5. What is number x?

a. 19
b. 22
c. 23
d. 25
e. 32

8. Which of the following is equivalent to $4^3 + 12 \div 4 + 8^2 \times 3$?

a. 211
b. 249
c. 259
d. 278
e. 393

9. The original price of a jacket is \$36.95. The jacket is discounted by 25%. Before tax, which of the following best represents the cost of the jacket?

a. \$27.34
b. \$27.71
c. \$28.11
d. \$28.82
e. \$29.56

10. The number 123 is the 11th term in a sequence with a constant rate of change. Which of the following sequences has this number as its 11th term?

a. $5, 17, 29, 41, \ldots$
b. $3, 15, 27, 39, \ldots$
c. $-1, 11, 23, 35, \ldots$
d. $1, 13, 25, 37, \ldots$
e. $3, 17, 23, 40, \ldots$

11. What is the product of four squared and six?

a. 22
b. 28
c. 55
d. 96
e. 104

12. A rectangular prism has a length of 14.3 cm, a width of 8.9 cm, and a height of 11.7 cm. Which of the following is the best estimate for the volume of the rectangular prism?

a. 1,287 cm^3
b. 1,386 cm^3
c. 1,512 cm^3
d. 1,573 cm^3
e. 1,620 cm^3

13. Each month, Aisha invests twice the amount invested the previous month. If she invested $26.25 during the first month, how much did she invest during the sixth month?

a. $157.50
b. $420.00
c. $768.50
d. $840.00
e. $900.00

14. Find the value of x in the figure below:

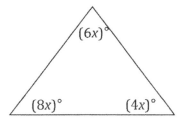

a. 10
b. 16
c. 18
d. 40
e. 60

15. Elijah drove 45 miles to his job in an hour and ten minutes in the morning. On the way home, however, traffic was much heavier, and the same trip took an hour and a half. What was his average speed in miles per hour for the round trip?

a. 30 mph
b. 32.5 mph
c. 33.75 mph
d. 35 mph
e. 45 mph

16. Chan receives a bonus from his job. He pays 30% in taxes, gives 30% to charity, and uses another 25% to pay off an old debt. He has $600 left. What was the total amount of Chan's bonus?

a. $3,000
b. $3,200
c. $3,600
d. $4,000
e. $4,200

17. If $3x + 5 = 11$, then $x = ?$

    a. 1
    b. 2
    c. 3
    d. 4
    e. 6

18. Which of the following fractions is halfway between 2/5 and 4/9?

    a. 2/3
    b. 2/20
    c. 17/40
    d. 19/45
    e. 7/10

19. Solve for y in the following equation if $x = -3$

$$y = x + 5$$

    a. $y = -2$
    b. $y = 2$
    c. $y = 3$
    d. $y = 6$
    e. $y = 8$

20. Which of the following is the symbol that represents the negative square root of 100?

    a. $\sqrt{-100}$
    b. $\sqrt{100}$
    c. $\sqrt{10}$
    d. $-\sqrt{10}$
    e. $-\sqrt{100}$

21. Anna wants to buy a new bicycle that costs \$125, but she currently only has \$40. If Anna can earn \$5 each week for doing chores around the house, how many weeks will it take for Anna have enough money to buy the bicycle?

    a. 3 weeks
    b. 8 weeks
    c. 17 weeks
    d. 20 weeks
    e. 25 weeks

22. A sequence is formed from the equation, $y = 6x + 2$, where x represents the term number and y represents the value of the term. What is the value of the 18th term in the sequence?

    a. 98
    b. 104
    c. 110
    d. 116
    e. 120

23. Simplify $\frac{5}{9} \times \frac{3}{4}$.

   a. $\frac{5}{12}$

   b. $\frac{8}{13}$

   c. $\frac{20}{27}$

   d. $\frac{47}{36}$

   e. $\frac{52}{26}$

24. Rachel spent $24.15 on vegetables. She bought 2 pounds of onions, 3 pounds of carrots, and $1\frac{1}{2}$ pounds of mushrooms. If the onions cost $3.69 per pound and the carrots cost $4.29 per pound, what is the price per pound of mushrooms?

   a. $2.25
   b. $2.60
   c. $2.75
   d. $2.80
   e. $3.10

25. At a picnic, cans of soda are put into a cooler. In the cooler, there are 12 colas, 6 diet colas, 9 lemon-limes, 2 root beers, 4 ginger ales, and 3 orange sodas. What would be the probability of reaching into the cooler without looking and pulling out a ginger ale?

   a. $\frac{1}{9}$

   b. $\frac{1}{8}$

   c. $\frac{1}{6}$

   d. $\frac{1}{5}$

   e. $\frac{1}{3}$

Answer Key and Explanations for Test #1

Quantitative

1. B: Translate this word problem into a mathematical equation. Let the number of Janice's phone calls $= x$. Let the number of Elaina's phone calls $= x + 23$. Let the number June's calls $= x + 14$. Add their calls together and subtract 25 calls:

$$= x + x + 23 + x + 14 - 25$$
$$= 3x + 37 - 25$$
$$= 3x + 12$$

2. C: To answer this question, notice that this figure is a regular hexagon, having 6 equal sides and angles. The part painted darker can be represented by $\frac{1}{6}$. The part painted lighter is clearly $\frac{1}{2}$, which is equivalent to $\frac{3}{6}$. The whole figure is represented by the number 1. So, 1 minus $\frac{1}{6}$ minus $\frac{3}{6}$ equals $\frac{2}{6}$ which is equivalent to $\frac{1}{3}$. Therefore, the equation, $1 - \frac{1}{6} - \frac{1}{2} = \frac{1}{3}$ best models the part of the figure Olga left white.

3. A: Since there are 100 cm in a meter, on a 1:100 scale drawing, each centimeter represents one meter. Therefore, an area of one square centimeter on the drawing represents one square meter in actuality. Since the area of the room in the scale drawing is 30 cm², the room's actual area is 30 m².

Another way to determine the area of the room is to write and solve an equation, such as this one: $\frac{l}{100} \times \frac{w}{100} = 30$ cm² , where l and w are the dimensions of the actual room

$$\frac{lw}{10,000} = 30 \text{ cm}^2$$

$$\text{Area} = 300,000 \text{ cm}^2$$

Since this is not one of the answer choices, convert cm² to m²:

$$300,000 \text{ cm}^2 \times \frac{1 \text{ m}}{100 \text{ cm}} \times \frac{1 \text{ m}}{100 \text{ cm}} = 30 \text{ m}^2.$$

4. E: The total amount of the bill is: $\frac{4}{x} = \frac{8}{100}$; $400 = 8x$; $x = \$50$.

5. C: The line graph shows the largest number of flights made during a month as 79 with the smallest number of flights made during a month as 54. The range is equal to the difference between the largest number of flights and smallest number of flights, i.e., $79 - 54 = 25$. Therefore, the range is equal to 25.

6. E: Segment $\overline{AD} = 48$. Because the length of $\overline{CD}$ is 2 times the length of $\overline{AB}$, let $\overline{AB} = x$ and let $\overline{CD} = 2x$. Since $\overline{AB} = \overline{BC}$, let $\overline{BC} = x$ also. Thus:

$$\overline{AD} = \overline{AB} + \overline{BC} + \overline{CD}$$
$$= x + x + 2x$$
$$= 4x$$

Since $\overline{AD} = 48$, $x = 12$ and therefore $\overline{BC} + \overline{CD} = x + 2x = 3x = 3 \times 12 = 36$.

186

7. C: The stock first increased by 10%, that is, by $10 (10% of $100) to $110 per share. Then, the price decreased by $11 (10% of $110) so that the sale price was $110 − $11 = $99 per share, and the sale price for 50 shares was 99 × $50 = $4950.

8. E: If the first lap takes 50 seconds, the second one takes 20% more, or $T_2 = 1.2 \times T_1 = 1.2 \times 50 = 60$ seconds, where T_1 and T_2 are the times required for the first and second laps, respectively. Similarly, $T_3 = 1.2 \times T_2 = 1.2 \times 60 = 72$ seconds, the time required for the third lap. To find the total time, add the times for the three laps together: $50 + 60 + 72 = 182$ seconds.

9. C: Supplementary angles add to 180 degrees. Therefore, the other angle is equal to the difference between 180 degrees and 34 degrees: $180 − 34 = 146$. Thus, the other angle measures 146°.

10. A: The distance given from the top to the bottom of the tire through the center is the diameter. Finding the distance the bike traveled in one complete roll of the tire is the same as finding the circumference. Using the formula, $C = \pi d$, we multiply 27 by π. From the first mark to the fourth, the tire rolls three times. Then, you would multiply by 3, and the equation would be $3(27\pi)$.

11. E: First: Add the known values together: $5 + 10 + 12 + 13 = 40$. Now, set up an equation with the sum of the known values in the divisor. Then, put the number of values in the dividend.

For this question, you have 5 values. So, you would write the equation as $\frac{40+?}{5} = 9.6$. Now, multiply both sides by 5: $5 \times \frac{40+?}{5} = 9.6 \times 5$. You are left with $40+? = 48$. Now, subtract 40 from both sides: $40 − 40+? = 48 − 40$. Now, you know that the missing value is 8.

12. A: The events are independent since Sarah replaces the first die. The probability of two independent events can be found using the formula $P(A \text{ and } B) = P(A) \times P(B)$. The probability of pulling out a blue die is $\frac{2}{12}$. The probability of pulling out a green die is $\frac{4}{12}$. The probability of pulling out a blue die and a green die is $\frac{2}{12} \times \frac{4}{12}$, which simplifies to $\frac{1}{18}$.

13. D: Start by isolating a on one side of the equation.

$$a − 16 = 8b + 6$$
$$a = 8b + 6 + 16$$
$$a = 8b + 22$$

Next, add 3 to both side of the equation.

$$a + 3 = 8b + 22 + 3$$
$$a + 3 = 8b + 25$$

14. A: The cost per ounce can be calculated by dividing the cost of the bag by the number of ounces the bag contains. Thus, the cost per ounce can be calculated by writing $9.85 ÷ 16, which equals approximately $0.62 per ounce.

15. B: The slope of a line describes the change in the dependent variable divided by the change in the independent variable, i.e. the change in y over the change in x. To calculate the slope, consider any two points on the line. Let the first point be (1, 14), and let the second point be (2, 28).

16. B: Since 1 foot equals 0.3048 meters, The proportion can be written as: $\frac{1}{0.3048} = \frac{12}{x}$. Solving for x gives $x =$ 3.6576, which rounds to 3.66. Thus, the length of the bridge is approximately 3.66 meters.

17. C: There are 36 months in 3 years. The following proportion may be written: $\frac{450}{3} = \frac{x}{36}$. The equation $3x =$ 16,200, may be solved for x. Dividing both sides of the equation by 3 gives $x = 5,400$.

18. D: The area of the shaded region must be equal to the area of the square minus the areas of the two triangular areas ΔACD and ΔBEF. The area of a triangle is given by $A = \frac{1}{2}bh$, where b is the base and h is the height. Since ΔACD and ΔBEF are both right triangles, one of the orthogonal sides is the base and the other is the height. Further, since $\overline{AE} = \overline{EB}$ and $\overline{BF} = \overline{FC}$, it follows that $\overline{EB} = \overline{BF} = 5$, this being one half the side $\overline{AB}$. Thus, $A_{ADC} = \frac{1}{2}(10 \times 10) = 50$, and $A_{BEF} = \frac{1}{2}(5 \times 5) = 12.5$. The area of the square is the product of its two sides, or $10 \times 10 = 100$. Therefore, for the shaded region, $A = 100 - 50 - 12.5 = 37.5$.

19. C: Remember to use the order of operations when simplifying this expression. The acronym *PEMDAS* will help you remember the correct order: Parenthesis, Exponentiation, Multiplication/Division, Addition/Subtraction.

$$\begin{aligned}
4(6-3)^2 - (-2) &= 4 \times 3^2 - (-2) \\
&= 4 \times 9 - (-2) \\
&= 36 - (-2) \\
&= 36 - (-2) \\
&= 38
\end{aligned}$$

20. C: Isolate the variable on one side of the equal sign by adding 2 to both sides of the equation. This yields $\sqrt{x} = 8 + 2 = 10$. Now, solve the equation by squaring both sides: $x = 10^2 = 100$.

21. C: The original triangle was reflected across the x-axis. When reflecting across the x-axis, the x-values of each point remain the same, but the y-values of the points will be opposites.

$$(1,4) \rightarrow (1,-4), (5,4) \rightarrow (5,-4), (3,8) \rightarrow (3,-8)$$

22. B: To solve this problem, you need to find the time needed to drive 275 miles at a speed of 55 miles per hour. If $rate \times time = distance$, then $time = distance \div rate$:

$$275 \text{ miles} \div 55 \frac{\text{miles}}{\text{hour}} = 5 \text{ hours}$$

The truck driver needs to arrive at 9:30 p.m., so subtract 5 hours from 9:30. The truck driver needs to leave at 4:30 p.m. to arrive on time.

23. E: Attendance in 2004 decreased from about 12,000 to 10,000 visitors. In 2005 it rebounded to 15,000 visitors, an increase of 5,000. This is the greatest year-to-year increase shown on the chart.

24. A: Add the coefficients of the 'x-terms' together as follows: $5x + 4x = 9x$
Add the coefficients of the 'y-terms' as follows: $-2y + y = -y$
Put the x- and y-terms back into the same equation: $9x - y$.

25. E: Out of the twelve numbers, half are even. That means there is a 50% chance that the spinner will land on an even number.

Reading Comprehension

1. D: Various parts of the article are intended to scare (choice A), warn (choice B), and inspire (choice C) people, but the primary purpose of the article is to offer practical advice about what products people should buy and how to use their available resources to make responsible decisions for the future of our planet.

2. A: The author begins the third paragraph with, "You can continue to make a difference for the planet in how you use what you bought and the resources you have available." This sentence makes the connection between the second paragraph which deals with what people should buy and the third paragraph which makes suggestions for how to use what they have.

3. B: The author does suggest that people should use less water and energy (choice A), but these are only two suggestions among many and not the main idea of the article. The article does not say that people are destroying the earth (choice C) or make a suggestion that people organize their acquaintances (choice D).

4. D: The author presents the problems of global warming and the rapid depletion of the planet's natural resources and offers several practical suggestions for how to stop global warming and use remaining resources judiciously.

5. E: The author makes suggestions to use less water (choice B) and buy locally grown food (choice D), but they are not suggested as the place to begin saving the planet. The author does not suggest getting rid of products that are not earth friendly (choice A). The author states: "Participation begins with our everyday choices."

6. C: The author does not mention running out of resources in a specific time period (choice A), the cost of water and energy (choice B), or the possibility of hardship for local farmers (choice D).

7. D: Paragraph 1 states that Aberystwyth is located on the West Coast of Wales.

8. C: The essay provides information on various aspects of the town of Aberystwyth, providing a portrait of the town as a whole.

9. A: Situated means to be located in a certain place.

10. B: In an essay that is factual, proclaiming that the scenery is "gorgeous" or that a town is a "hidden luxury" is an opinion.

11. B: Paragraph 3 states that two main languages are traditionally spoken in Aberystwyth.

12. C: Paragraph 1 states, "A market town refers to European areas that have the right to have markets, which differentiates it from a city or village."

13. D: Paragraph 2 states, "Constitution Hill is a hill on the north end of Aberystwyth, which provides excellent views of Cardigan Bay and which is supported by the Aberystwyth Electric Cliff Railway."

14. A: Paragraph 1 explains that Aberystwyth is best known as an education center, and this is repeated in paragraph 3, which states that Aberystwyth is best known for its educational services.

15. B: While some of the other choices are mentioned in the selection, they do not adequately explain what the entire selection is about.

16. A: From the first paragraph, you can determine that Gawaine has little or no interest in becoming a knight.

17. D: Gawaine is said to be tall and sturdy, but he would run away and hide at the smallest sign of trouble.

18. D: "His better nature" is one way of talking about a person's deeper character.

19. C: This forms part of the answer to the professor's question, "Are the dragons particularly bad this year?"

20. D: Choice A is not mentioned in the text, and the other choices do not directly answer the question.

21. C: The passage states that he was given this title since he was the first to explain how organisms change over time.

22. A: The tone and purpose of this passage is to inform the reader.

23. E: The passage explains that finches with longer, sharper beaks were able to reach insects more easily than finches with shorter beaks, giving them an advantage over the other finches on the island.

24. B: The island finches were different from the mainland finches, so geographical separation over time increased the diversity of finches.

25. D: The passage states that the island finches differed from the mainland finches by the shape of their beaks and in their diet.

26. C: An archipelago is a large group or chain of islands.

27. D: The article deals primarily with the ways the colonists fed themselves: their crops and the foods they hunted. While the history and agriculture discussed are part of the Māori culture, that is not the focus of the passage.

28. D: The passage states that the first settlers were forced to rely on fishing for their food.

29. A: When an increased population had driven a major food source to extinction, they began to fight for control over the remaining food supply.

30. D: The article tells us that coconuts did not grow in New Zealand, and that some of the other crops would grow only on North Island.

31. A: The sweet potato provided a winter food source through storage, allowing the population to increase.

32. C: Both roads in the woods are more or less equally covered in leaves. One is only a little more traveled than the other, but this is enough for the narrator to choose the less-traveled path.

33. C: Looking back on the memory, the narrator is proud that he "chose the [road] less traveled by," and he will make sure that other people know that, too.

34. D: The poem is based on the narrator having to decide upon a path based only on his own personality and how well traveled the road is. It is a decision that he must make alone.

35. E: The narrator thinks that whatever road he chooses will say something about his character. He waits a long time because he wants to be sure of his choice.

36. B: The narrator wants to be as unique as he can, and so takes the road less traveled. However, he cannot be truly unique, as he is not the first person to have walked that road.

37. D: The main argument is stated in paragraph 4: "With the progression and extreme convenience of technology, printed books are going to soon become a thing of the past."

38. C: Paragraph 1 explains how stories have progressed, beginning with oral tradition and past the invention of the printing press. In context with the rest of the essay, this paragraph is important in explaining how stories progress and are provided within society.

39. A: In paragraph 1, it is stated that oral tradition was the main medium for storytelling before the invention of the printing press.

40. E: It is not a fact that "sliding a finger across the screen or pressing a button to move onto the next page is just as satisfying to the reader." Satisfaction is not something universal that can be proven for every reader. This statement is an opinion.

Verbal

1. B: When someone is abroad, it usually means that they are away, overseas, or in a foreign country.

2. D: When someone ruminates, it means that they are reflecting, thinking, or brainstorming about something or someone.

3. A: When something is described as concise, it usually means that it is brief or compact.

4. A: When someone mourns, it means that they are crying or filled with regret.

5. A: Residence is a place where a person lives. So, a home is the best answer choice.

6. C: Levity means happiness or silliness.

7. B: When something is described as rash, it usually means that it is careless or bold.

8. C: When it is said that someone has been banished, it means that they have been removed or dismissed from a place.

9. B: When you are extended an opportunity, you are being offered a chance to try something.

10. E: To disable means that something is damaged or harmed.

11. D: An object that is fragile is something that can be broken very easily. So, one could say that the object is delicate.

12. D: A loyal person is someone who is committed and faithful.

13. D: The principle is something that is the standard or source. This should be confused with principal who may the head of a school or an organization.

14. C: To assess something is to evaluate or determine something.

15. C: If somebody is moral, it means that they are honest or good and correct in their behavior.

16. C: Something that is superior is understood to be preferable or better.

17. B: A remark is a statement or comment.

18. B: Specify is when you indicate or name something to give a clear understanding to others. For example, there are several trees in a yard, and you are talking about one tree. So, you would need to be clear or specify which tree that you meant.

19. A: To commence something is to begin or start something.

20. B: Something that is moving swiftly is something that is moving at a high speed or quickly.

21. A: Someone that is wily is clever or mischievous. For example, a child who avoids something that he or she doesn't want to do will be creative with excuses or deceptive about their plans.

22. C: Humane is another word for friendly. Saying someone is humane is the same as saying that they are very helpful and generous.

23. B: When someone is asserting something, they are insisting or arguing that something is the case.

24. E: A situation that is perilous is one that is risky or hazardous.

25. C: To donate means to offer a service or gift something as a contribution.

26. C: When something is finite, we mean that it is limited or fixed. Saying that there is a finite amount of gold in the world has the same meaning as saying that there is a limited amount of gold in the world.

27. B: When somebody is docile, it means that they are obedient or easily led. A student who respects and obeys their teachers will be a docile student.

28. C: To taint has a similar meaning to harm or damage. If you say that a shirt is tainted, for example, you are saying that the shirt is ruined or damaged.

29. D: When a person falters, we mean that they stumbled or hesitated. For example, a good character in a story has to make a difficult decision, and he or she struggles to make the decision in time. So, we could say that the character faltered to make a decision.

30. D: Something that is done suddenly means that it is done unexpectedly or without warning. For example, saying that the car stopped suddenly and saying it stopped unexpectedly convey the same meaning.

31. C: The analogy focuses on a characteristic of historians who need to consider an event with the surrounding context of time before and after an event. The best choice is the comparison to a native who has insight about his or her village or country and provide context to events of their area.

32. B: This analogy is about the use of geography and how one thing that it studies is mountains. Among the choices, one use of history is the study of events and how they have made an important influence.

33. E: This comparison is about the antonyms exhale and inhale. The other answer choices are synonyms, and choice E has the antonyms of consent and prohibit.

34. D: This comparison is about the synonyms of fiction and myth. The other answer choices are antonyms or something that is incompatible with nonfiction. So, the correct choice that remains is biography.

35. C: A simple sentence for this analogy could be "An astronomer's task is to encounter new things." The other users in the answer choices do not match with this sentence, and their "tasks" are not typical jobs for them. Answer choice C could be written as "A prophet's task is to inform about new things."

36. B: This analogy is about the homonyms *dual* and *duel* which sound similar but have different meanings. The only answer choice that makes sense is choice B which has the homonyms of *seam* and *seem*.

37. A: This analogy of degree focuses on a symptom that is part of an illness. The best answer is choice A which starts with a bacteria that develops into an infection.

38. A: Evidence that is used in a court of law can be condemning for someone by bringing a punishment on him or her. The best comparison for this question is choice A where the use of a generator is to restore energy or electricity to something.

39. C: *Liberty* and *freedom* are close synonyms, and *sincere* is a close synonym of *faithful*.

192

40. C: This comparison is about the antonyms *masculine* and *feminine*. The other answer choices are synonyms. So, the best answer is choice C which has the antonyms *community* and *individual*.

41. B: An artist brings imagination to complete their tasks and help others. In a similar way, an advisor uses clarity to complete their tasks and help others.

42. D: This comparison shows that one characteristic of a temple is that it is sacred. The best answer choice is the comparison of a sanctuary to its loftiness or grandness and beauty.

43. E: A gourmet is a person who is very familiar with food, and this person would fall under the category of a critic. With the topic of food in mind, a spice is an item that provides flavor to meals and can come under the category of ingredient.

44. C: As a part to whole analogy, a summit is the highest point of a mountain. Now, you need to judge how a king is a part of a whole. The best answer is choice C as a member of a monarchy government.

45. A: The analogy highlights a product to producer relationship. The tactics of a mission are made and developed by marines. In a similar way, data is developed by a researcher.

46. B: A chamber is needed to contain or hold items. Choice A is nearly a product to producer as some rulers on thrones can be intimidating to the point that people bow or cower before the throne. Choice C is a characteristic analogy. Answer choice D is a synonym. Answer choice E is a category analogy. So, the best choice is B as an agenda is used to organize the use of time.

47. D: This analogy is about the homonyms *altar* and *alter*. The correct answer choice D has the homonyms *rain* and *reign*.

48. B: To help more patients, a physician would study the nutritional value of certain items and harm from other items. So, this analogy focuses on a user. The other answer choices do not focus on the relationship of an item or field of study and a user, or they make incorrect connections. Thus, the best answer choice is choice B because wildlife would be studied by a guide for future tours.

49. B: The terms *bravery* and *cowardice* are antonyms in this analogy. So, the best answer choice is the one that is an antonym for *comedy*, and the best choice is choice B for *grief*.

50. E: When we say that a child is *naïve*, we are naming one of their characteristics. The correct answer choice is choice E which has *disciplined* as a characteristic of a *soldier*.

51. B: This analogy focuses on the homonyms of *colonel* and *kernel*. So, the correct answer choice is the homonyms *serial* and *cereal*.

52. D: You may recall from science classes that protons and electrons are parts of an atom. A proton has a positive charge, and an electron has a negative charge. So, the comparison focuses on these as opposites or antonyms. Therefore, the best answer choice is choice D which compares *potent* and *ineffective* as antonyms.

53. D: A documentary can be used by a protestor to bring more attention to his or her cause. So, this analogy highlights the comparison of someone who uses something. The best answer choice is choice D which has a *rotor* being used by a *mechanic*.

54. C: Again, we have a homonym analogy with the terms *tear* and *tier*. You are provided with the term *air*, and the best choice available is choice C which has *heir*.

55. B: An *epidemic* is a disease that is far reaching. The same definition applies to *plague*. So, you know that we are working with a comparison of synonyms. You are supplied with the term *vigor* which means high energy and strength. So, the best available synonym is *endurance*.

193

56. D: You may recognize that *eternal* means that something continues without an end. *Momentary* means that something is brief or short-lived. So, the best answer choice is choice D which has the antonyms of *exotic* (i.e., unusual or mysterious) and *ordinary* (i.e., plain or familiar).

57. A: Often, an open field of a meadow is described as a peaceful and restful place to rest. So, one could say that a meadow has the characteristic of being tranquil. The best match for this analogy would be choice A as a *tributary* (i.e., river or stream) can be a *consoling* or restful place to visit.

58. D: This analogy highlights another homonym relationship. The other answer choices are terms that rhyme or have no understandable relationship. So, the best answer choice is choice D of *carat* and *carrot*.

59. A: An *aviator* is a person who flies an aircraft. So, this relationship can be understood as an *aviator* is responsible for flying an aircraft to a certain *destination*. In a similar way, choice A can be understood as a *sculptor* or artist is responsible for creating *original* works of art.

60. E: A *constellation* is a group of stars that form an outline of a person, animal, or object. So, this analogy can be understood as a whole moving to a part. The *constellation* is the whole, and a *star* is a part of the whole. Now, the best answer choice would be choice E as an *orchestra* is a group of musicians playing music with their respective *instruments*. Thus, an *instrument* would a part of the whole *orchestra*.

Quantitative

1. B: The number of one-fourths contained in $8\frac{1}{2}$ can be determined by dividing $8\frac{1}{2}$ by $\frac{1}{4}$. In order to find the quotient, $8\frac{1}{2}$ can be multiplied by the reciprocal of $\frac{1}{4}$, or 4. Thus, the quotient can be found by writing $\frac{17}{2} \times 4$, which equals 34.

2. C: The equation that represents the relationship between the position number, n, and the value of the term, a_n, is $a_n = -3n + 8$. Notice each n is multiplied by –3, with 8 added to that value. Substituting position number 1 for n gives $a_n = -3(1) + 8$, which equals 5. Substitution of the remaining position numbers does not provide a counterexample to this procedure.

3. E: A triangle with an obtuse angle (an angle greater than 90°) is called an obtuse triangle.

4. D: Since the snow will fall at a constant rate, the snowfall follows a directly proportional relationship. Then, Total Snowfall = (Snowfall rate) × (Number of hours of snowfall), $t = 2h$. In Answer A, the values were set up as an inversely proportional relationship. In Answer B, the snowfall rate was incorrectly added to the number of hours of snowfall. In Answer C, the snowfall rate was incorrectly subtracted from the number of hours of snowfall.

5. B: Whenever the data includes an extreme outlier, such as 39, the median is the best representation of the data. The mean would include that score and heavily skew the data.

6. B: Angles that form a straight line add up to 180 degrees. Such angles are sometimes referred to as being supplementary.

$$60 + 2x = 180$$
$$2x = 120$$
$$x = 60$$

7. E: In this problem, if you do not know how to solve, try filling in the answer choices to see which one checks out. Many math problems may be solved by a guess and check method when you have a selection of answer choices.

$$27 - x = -5$$
$$x = 32$$

8. C: The order of operations states that numbers with exponents must be evaluated first. Thus, the expression can be rewritten as $64 + 12 \div 4 + 64 \times 3$. Next, multiplication and division must be computed as they appear from left to right in the expression. Thus, the expression can be further simplified as $64 + 3 + 192$, which equals 259.

9. B: The discounted price is 25% less than the original price. Therefore, the discounted price can be written as $36.95 - ((0.25)(36.95))$, which equals approximately 27.71. Thus, the discounted price of the jacket is $27.71.

10. B: All given sequences have a constant difference of 12. Subtraction of 12 from the starting term, given for Choice B, gives a y-intercept of −9. The equation $123 = 12x - 9$ can thus be written. Solving for x gives $x = 11$; therefore, 123 is indeed the 11th term of this sequence. Manual computation of the 11th term by adding the constant difference of 12 also reveals 123 as the value of the 11th term of this sequence.

11. D: Turn the word problem into an equation. Remember that product means multiplication:

$$4^2 \times 6 = 96$$

12. C: The dimensions of the rectangular prism can be rounded to 14 cm, 9 cm, and 12 cm. The volume of a rectangular prism can be determined by finding the product of the length, width, and height. Therefore, the volume is approximately equal to $14 \times 9 \times 12$, or 1,512 cm^3.

13. D: The amount Aisha invests doubles each month. Thus, the invested amounts for months $1 - 6$ are as follows: $26.25, $52.50, $105, $210, $420, and $840. She invests $840 during the sixth month.

14. A: The sum of the measures of the angles in a triangle equals 180°. Use the numbers given in the figure to make the following equation:

$$6x + 8x + 4x = 180$$
$$18x = 180$$
$$x = 10$$

15. C: To determine this, first determine the total distance of the round trip. This is twice the 45 miles of the one-way trip to work in the morning, or 90 miles. Then, to determine the total amount of time Elijah spent on the round trip, first convert his travel times into minutes. One hour and ten minutes is the same as 70 minutes, and an hour and a half is 90 minutes. So, Elijah's total travel time was $70 + 90 = 160$ minutes. Elijah's average speed can now be determined in miles per minute:

$$\text{Average Speed} = \frac{90 \text{ miles}}{160 \text{ min}} = 0.5625 \text{ miles per minute}$$

Finally, to convert this average speed to miles per hour, multiply by 60, since there are 60 minutes in an hour: Average speed (mph) $= 60 \times 0.5625 = 33.75$. Therefore, his average speed for the round trip was 33.75 mph.

16. D: Besides the $600 he has remaining; Chan has paid out a total of 85% (30% + 30% + 25%) of his bonus for the expenses described in the question. Therefore, the $600 represents the remaining 15%. Remember that 15% can be written as 15/100. To determine his total bonus, solve

$$\frac{15}{100}x = \$600$$
$$x = \frac{100}{15} \times \$600$$
$$x = \$4,000$$

17. B: Since 11 – 5 = 6, then $3x = 6$, and $x = \frac{6}{3} = 2$.

18. D: Find the common denominator for the two fractions so that you can compare them. You can use the common denominator of 45, as follows:

$$\frac{2}{5} = \frac{18}{45}$$
$$\frac{4}{9} = \frac{20}{45}$$

Look at the numerators: 18 and 20. The number halfway between them is 19, so the answer is $\frac{19}{45}$

19. B: $y = x + 5$, and you were told that $x = -3$. Fill in the missing information for x, then solve.

$$y = (-3) + 5$$
$$y = 2$$

20. E: You would write the negative square root of 100 as follows: $-\sqrt{100}$

21. C: The equation to determine how Anna can earn the \$125 is set up as:

$$Weekly\ Pay \times Number\ of\ Weeks + Money\ Anna\ Already\ Has = \$125$$

If w = number of weeks, substitute for the remaining values to get the equation: $\$5w + \$40 = \$125$. To solve that equation, start by subtracting \$40 from both sides: $\$5w = \$85$. Then, divide both sides by 5 to get $h = 17$. In Answer A, the equation was incorrectly set up as $(\$5 + \$40)w = \$125$. In Answer B, the equation was incorrectly set up as $\$5w = \$40$. In Answer D, the equation was incorrectly set up as $\$5w = \$125$.

22. C: The value of the 18th term can be found by substituting 18 for the variable, x, in the equation, $y = 6x + 2$. Doing so gives: $y = 6(18) + 2$, or $y = 110$. Therefore, the value of the 18th term is 110.

23. A: When multiplying fractions, multiply the terms straight across the fraction: $\frac{5}{9} \times \frac{3}{4} = \frac{15}{36}$. Then, simplify the fraction. Since 15 and 36 are both multiples of 3, divide each term by 3 to reach the final result: $\frac{5}{12}$.

24. B: To answer this question, we first determine the total cost of the onions and carrots, since these prices are given. This will equal $2 \times \$3.69 + 3 \times \$4.29 = \$20.25$. Next, this sum is subtracted from the total cost of the vegetables to determine the cost of the mushrooms: $\$24.15 - \$20.25 = \$3.90$. Finally, the cost of the mushrooms is divided by the quantity in lbs to determine the cost per lb:

$$Cost\ per\ lb = \frac{\$3.90}{1.5} = \$2.60$$

Therefore, the mushrooms cost \$2.60 per pound.

25. A: There are 36 total cans in the cooler. Four of the cans are Ginger Ale. Therefore, there is a $\frac{4}{36} = \frac{1}{9}$ probability of pulling a Ginger Ale out of the cooler.

Practice Test #2

Writing

25 Minutes

Instructions: Read the following prompt, taking a few moments to plan a response. Then, write your response in essay form.

Prompt: *Fast food restaurants should be held legally responsible for the current rise in obesity in children.*

Do you agree or disagree with this statement? Use examples from history, literature, or your own personal experience to support your point of view.

Quantitative

Read each question, perform the appropriate calculations, and determine the correct answer.

1. Harold learned that 6 out of 10 students at his school live within two miles of the school. If 240 students attend Grade 6 at his school, about how many of these students should Harold expect to live within two miles of the school?

    a.   24
    b.   40
    c.   144
    d.   180

2. Given the counters shown below, where ◯ represents negative 1 and ⬤ represents positive 1, what is the sum?

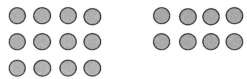

    a.   −20
    b.   4
    c.   20
    d.   −4

3. Akita is thinking of a number. The number is the opposite of 7. What must be true about Akita's number?

        I.   The number is 7
        II.   The number is −7
        III.   The number has an absolute value of 7
        IV.   The number has an absolute value of −7

    a.   II and III
    b.   I and III
    c.   II and IV
    d.   I and IV

4. Given the sequence represented in the table below, where n represents the position of the term and a_n represents the value of the term, which of the following describes the relationship between the position number and the value of the term?

n	1	2	3	4	5	6
a_n	5	2	−1	−4	−7	−10

    a.   Multiply n by 2 and subtract 4
    b.   Multiply n by 2 and subtract 3
    c.   Multiply n by −3 and add 8
    d.   Multiply n by −4 and add 1

5. A trash company charges a fee of $80 to haul off a load of trash. There is also a charge of $0.05 per mile the load must be hauled. Which equation can be used to find c, the cost for hauling a load of trash m miles?

  a. $80(m + 0.05)$
  b. $0.05(m + 80)$
  c. $80m + 0.05$
  d. $0.05m + 80$

6. A clothing company is reviewing their quarterly report. Last quarter, 36% of their customers purchased sweatshirts. Which fraction is equivalent to the percentage of customers who purchased sweatshirts last quarter?

  a. $\frac{36}{50}$
  b. $\frac{9}{25}$
  c. $\frac{1}{36}$
  d. $\frac{13}{50}$

7. Which of the following scenarios can be represented by the equation $14 + x = 52$?

  a. Stella has $14 in her wallet. How much money does she have if she adds the $52 she earned babysitting last night?
  b. Marcus earns $52 mowing yards. How much money does he save if he buys his brother a birthday present that costs $14 and saves the rest?
  c. Troy earns $52 working for a neighbor. How much money does he have if he earns an additional $14 working for his aunt?
  d. Izzy has $14 of money in her piggy bank. How much money does she have if she adds the $52 she receives for her birthday?

8. Which situation best represents the inequality $12.5x \geq 375$?

  a. Dustin can ride his bike 12.5 miles per hour and rides 375 miles in x hours.
  b. Darla needs to drive at least 375 minutes to get her driver's permit and has driven 12.5 minutes so far and has x number of minutes remaining.
  c. Desiree makes $12.5 per hour and made more than $375 over x hours.
  d. Desmond has a goal of making at least 375 bracelets and makes 12.5 bracelets each day for x days.

9. A tree casts a shadow that is 4 feet long. At the same time, a 5-foot girl standing next to the tree casts a shadow that is 2.5 feet long. Which of the following proportions can be used to determine the height of the tree?

  a. $\frac{x}{4} = \frac{5}{2.5}$
  b. $\frac{x}{4} = \frac{2.5}{5}$
  c. $\frac{x}{2.5} = \frac{4}{2.5}$
  d. $\frac{x}{4} = \frac{2.5}{5}$

10. According to the order of operations, which of the following steps should be completed immediately following the evaluation of the squared number when evaluating the expression

$$9 - 18^2 \times 2 + 12 \div 4$$

  a. Subtract 18^2 from 9
  b. Multiply the squared value by 2
  c. Divide 12 by 4
  d. Add 2 and 12

11. Tomas needs $100 to buy a telescope he wants. He received $40 as a gift and spent $10 on a book about telescopes. He earned $35 doing small jobs for his family. The steps Tomas can use to find the amount he still needs to save to buy the telescope are shown here in incorrect order.

Step R: Subtract 65 from 100.
Step S: Subtract 10 from 40.
Step T: Add 35 to 30.

Which sequence shows the steps in the correct order?

a. T, S, R
b. T, R, S
c. S, T, R
d. R, S, T

12. Caroline put 3 drops of blue food coloring in 2 cups of water. Devon put 5 drops of blue food coloring in 4 cups of water. If more blue food coloring makes a darker shade of blue, what is true about Caroline 's and Devon's water?

a. Caroline's water is a darker blue than Devon's because 3 : 2 is greater than 5 : 4.
b. Devon's water is a darker blue than Caroline's because 5 drops is greater than 3 drops.
c. The water is the same shade of blue because 3 : 2 is equivalent to 5 : 4.
d. Devon's water is a darker blue than Caroline's because 5 : 4 is greater than 3 : 2.

13. A figure is depicted below. Use the ruler to measure the figure to the nearest $\frac{1}{2}$ inch.

$3\frac{1}{2}$ in. 4 in.

$12\frac{1}{2}$ in.

What is the area of the parallelogram in square inches?

a. 32 in^2
b. $43\frac{3}{4}$ in^2
c. $36\frac{1}{4}$ in^2
d. 50 in^2

14. Which of the following statements is NOT true about this figure?

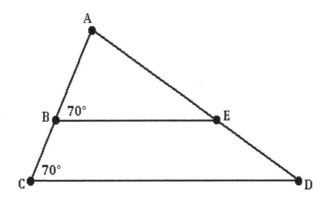

a. $\triangle ABE$ is similar to $\triangle ACD$
b. $BE = CD$
c. $\angle B \cong \angle C$
d. $\dfrac{AB}{AC} = \dfrac{AE}{AD}$

15. Which situation best represents the inequality $\frac{n}{4} > 36$?

a. Theresa packaged more than 36 packages when she packaged n cupcakes into packages of 4.
b. Tyler has more than 36 pages to read and reads 4 pages each day for n days.
c. Tamar practiced for n hours on the piano. She practiced the piano for more than 36 hours each day for 4 days.
d. Tamika ran n miles over 4 days, which is less than 36 miles.

16. Xi wrote an expression that is equivalent to $9z + (z - 3)$. Which expression could be the one Xi wrote?

a. $9z \cdot z - 27z$
b. $(z - 3) + 9z$
c. $10z + 3$
d. $(z - 3) - 9z$

17. Ana has completed approximately $\frac{2}{7}$ of her research paper. Which of the following best represents the percentage of the paper she has completed?

a. 24%
b. 26%
c. 27%
d. 29%

18. A display at the bottom of the laptop computer Erica was using showed that the battery had a 70% charge. Which decimal is equivalent to 70%?

a. 0.07
b. 70.0
c. 7.0
d. 0.7

19. Which number line represents the solution to $17 - x \geq 9$?

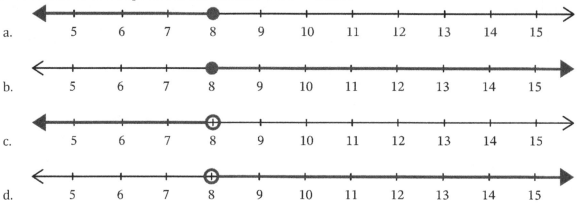

a.

b.

c.

d.

20. Nova is redecorating her bedroom and spent $\frac{7}{25}$ of her time painting. What percentage of her time did Nova spend painting?

    a.   28%
    b.   7%
    c.   25%
    d.   48%

21. Which statement is true about the product of 5 and $\frac{1}{2}$?

    a.   The product is less than 5.
    b.   The product is greater than 5.
    c.   The product is less than 1.
    d.   The product is less than $\frac{1}{2}$.

22. Which expression is equivalent to $81 \div 9 + 36$?

    a. $3^2 + 6^2$
    b. $3 \cdot 3 + 3 \cdot 3 \cdot 3$
    c. $\frac{9^2}{3^3} + (12 \cdot 3)$
    d. $(9 \cdot 9) \div (3 \cdot 3 \cdot 5)$

23. Which of the following correctly represents the solution to the following inequality on a number line?

$$-2x + 5 > 13$$

a.

b.

c.

d.

24. The volume of a cylinder is equal to the product of the area of one base and the height. Which of the following represents the area of one of the bases?

  a. πr
  b. πd
  c. πd^2
  d. πr^2

25. The total number of views on a new video increased by a scale factor of 13 each day. What does that mean about the number of views on the video?

  a. The number of views increased by adding 13 to the total each day.
  b. Each day the number of views increased by 13,000.
  c. Each day the number of views increased by multiplying the number of days by 13.
  d. The number of views increased by multiplying the previous day's total by 13.

Reading Comprehension

Read each passage closely and answer the associated questions. Be sure to choose the answer that BEST answers the question being asked.

Questions 1-4 refer to the following passage:

It is most likely that you have never had diphtheria. You probably don't even know anyone who has suffered from this disease. In fact, you may not even know what diphtheria is. Similarly, diseases like whooping cough, measles, mumps, and rubella may all be unfamiliar to you. In the nineteenth and early twentieth centuries, these illnesses struck hundreds of thousands of people in the United States each year, mostly children, and tens of thousands of people died. The names of these diseases were frightening household words. Today, they are all but forgotten. That change happened largely because of vaccines.

You probably have been vaccinated against diphtheria. You may even have been exposed to the bacterium that causes it, but the vaccine prepared your body to fight off the disease so quickly that you were unaware of the infection. Vaccines take advantage of your body's natural ability to learn how to combat many disease-causing germs, or microbes. What's more, your body remembers how to protect itself from the microbes it has encountered before. Collectively, the parts of your body that remember and repel microbes are called the immune system. Without the proper functioning of the immune system, the simplest illness—even the common cold—could quickly turn deadly.

On average, your immune system needs more than a week to learn how to fight off an unfamiliar microbe. Sometimes, that isn't enough time. Strong microbes can spread through your body faster than the immune system can fend them off. Your body often gains the upper hand after a few weeks, but in the meantime you are sick. Certain microbes are so virulent that they can overwhelm or escape your natural defenses. In those situations, vaccines can make all the difference.

Traditional vaccines contain either parts of microbes or whole microbes that have been altered so that they don't cause disease. When your immune system confronts these harmless versions of the germs, it quickly clears them from your body. In other words, vaccines trick your immune system in order to teach your body important lessons about how to defeat its opponents.

1. What is the main idea of the passage?

    a.   The nineteenth and early twentieth centuries were a dark period for medicine.
    b.   You have probably never had diphtheria.
    c.   Traditional vaccines contain altered microbes.
    d.   Vaccines help the immune system function properly.

2. Which statement is not a detail from the passage?

    a.   Vaccines contain microbe parts or altered microbes.
    b.   The immune system typically needs a week to learn how to fight a new disease.
    c.   The symptoms of disease do not emerge until the body has learned how to fight the microbe.
    d.   A hundred years ago, children were at the greatest risk of dying from now-treatable diseases.

3. What is the meaning of the word virulent as it is used in the third paragraph?

a. tiny
b. malicious
c. contagious
d. annoying

4. What is the author's primary purpose in writing the essay?

a. to entertain
b. to persuade
c. to inform
d. to analyze

Questions 5-8 refer to the following passage:

Foodborne illnesses are contracted by eating food or drinking beverages contaminated with bacteria, parasites, or viruses. Harmful chemicals can also cause foodborne illnesses if they have contaminated food during harvesting or processing. Foodborne illnesses can cause symptoms ranging from upset stomach to diarrhea, fever, vomiting, abdominal cramps, and dehydration. Most foodborne infections are undiagnosed and unreported, though the Centers for Disease Control and Prevention estimates that every year about 76 million people in the United States become ill from pathogens in food. About 5,000 of these people die.

Harmful bacteria are the most common cause of foodborne illness. Some bacteria may be present at the point of purchase. Raw foods are the most common source of foodborne illnesses because they are not sterile; examples include raw meat and poultry contaminated during slaughter. Seafood may become contaminated during harvest or processing. One in 10,000 eggs may be contaminated with Salmonella inside the shell. Produce, such as spinach, lettuce, tomatoes, sprouts, and melons, can become contaminated with Salmonella, Shigella, or Escherichia coli (E. coli). Contamination can occur during growing, harvesting, processing, storing, shipping, or final preparation. Sources of produce contamination vary, as these foods are grown in soil and can become contaminated during growth, processing, or distribution. Contamination may also occur during food preparation in a restaurant or a home kitchen. The most common form of contamination from handled foods is the calicivirus, also called the Norwalk-like virus.

When food is cooked and left out for more than two hours at room temperature, bacteria can multiply quickly. Most bacteria don't produce an odor or change in color or texture, so they can be impossible to detect. Freezing food slows or stops bacteria's growth but does not destroy the bacteria. The microbes can become reactivated when the food is thawed. Refrigeration also can slow the growth of some bacteria. Thorough cooking is required to destroy the bacteria.

5. What is the subject of the passage?

a. foodborne illnesses
b. the dangers of uncooked food
c. bacteria
d. proper food preparation

6. Which statement is not a detail from the passage?

a. Every year, more than 70 million Americans contract some form of foodborne illness.
b. Once food is cooked, it cannot cause illness.
c. Refrigeration can slow the growth of some bacteria.
d. The most common form of contamination in handled foods is calicivirus.

Practice Test #2

7. What is the meaning of the word pathogens as it is used in the first paragraph?

   a. diseases

   b. vaccines

   c. disease-causing substances

   d. foods

8. What is the meaning of the word sterile as it is used in the second paragraph?

   a. free of bacteria

   b. healthy

   c. delicious

   d. impotent

Questions 9-12 refer to the following passage:

There are a number of health problems related to bleeding in the esophagus and stomach. Stomach acid can cause inflammation and bleeding at the lower end of the esophagus. This condition, usually associated with the symptom of heartburn, is called esophagitis, or inflammation of the esophagus. Sometimes a muscle between the esophagus and stomach fails to close properly and allows the return of food and stomach juices into the esophagus, which can lead to esophagitis. In another unrelated condition, enlarged veins (varices) at the lower end of the esophagus rupture and bleed massively. Cirrhosis of the liver is the most common cause of esophageal varices. Esophageal bleeding can be caused by a tear in the lining of the esophagus (Mallory-Weiss syndrome). Mallory-Weiss syndrome usually results from vomiting but may also be caused by increased pressure in the abdomen from coughing, hiatal hernia, or childbirth. Esophageal cancer can cause bleeding.

The stomach is a frequent site of bleeding. Infections with Helicobacter pylori (H. pylori), alcohol, aspirin, aspirin-containing medicines, and various other medicines (such as nonsteroidal anti-inflammatory drugs [NSAIDs]—particularly those used for arthritis) can cause stomach ulcers or inflammation (gastritis). The stomach is often the site of ulcer disease. Acute or chronic ulcers may enlarge and erode through a blood vessel, causing bleeding. Also, patients suffering from burns, shock, head injuries, cancer, or those who have undergone extensive surgery may develop stress ulcers. Bleeding can also occur from benign tumors or cancer of the stomach, although these disorders usually do not cause massive bleeding.

9. What is the main idea of the passage?

   a. The digestive system is complex.

   b. Of all the digestive organs, the stomach is the most prone to bleeding.

   c. Both the esophagus and the stomach are subject to bleeding problems.

   d. Esophagitis afflicts the young and old alike.

10. Which statement is not a detail from the passage?

   a. Alcohol can cause stomach bleeding.

   b. Ulcer disease rarely occurs in the stomach.

   c. Benign tumors rarely result in massive bleeding.

   d. Childbirth is one cause of Mallory-Weiss syndrome.

11. What is the meaning of the word rupture as it is used in the first paragraph?

   a. tear

   b. collapse

   c. implode

   d. detach

12. What is the meaning of the word erode as it is used in the second paragraph?

a. avoid

b. divorce

c. contain

d. wear away

Questions 13-16 refer to the following passage:

We met Kathy Blake while she was taking a stroll in the park . . . by herself. What's so striking about this is that Kathy is completely blind, and she has been for more than 30 years.

The diagnosis from her doctor was retinitis pigmentosa, or RP. It's an incurable genetic disease that leads to progressive visual loss. Photoreceptive cells in the retina slowly start to die, leaving the patient visually impaired.

"Life was great the year before I was diagnosed," Kathy said. "I had just started a new job; I just bought my first new car. I had just started dating my now-husband. Life was good. The doctor had told me that there was some good news and some bad news. 'The bad news is you are going to lose your vision; the good news is we don't think you are going to go totally blind.' Unfortunately, I did lose all my vision within about 15 years."

Two years ago, Kathy got a glimmer of hope. She heard about an artificial retina being developed in Los Angeles. It was experimental, but Kathy was the perfect candidate.

Dr. Mark Humayun is a retinal surgeon and biomedical engineer. "A good candidate for the artificial retina device is a person who is blind because of retinal blindness," he said. "They've lost the rods and cones, the light-sensing cells of the eye, but the rest of the circuitry is relatively intact. In the simplest rendition, this device basically takes a blind person and hooks them up to a camera."

It may sound like the stuff of science fiction . . . and just a few years ago it was. A camera is built into a pair of glasses, sending radio signals to a tiny chip in the back of the retina. The chip, small enough to fit on a fingertip, is implanted surgically and stimulates the nerves that lead to the vision center of the brain. Kathy is one of twenty patients who have undergone surgery and use the device.

It has been about two years since the surgery, and Kathy still comes in for weekly testing at the University of Southern California's medical campus. She scans back and forth with specially made, camera-equipped glasses until she senses objects on a screen and then touches the objects. The low-resolution image from the camera is still enough to make out the black stripes on the screen. Impulses are sent from the camera to the 60 receptors that are on the chip in her retina. So, what is Kathy seeing?

"I see flashes of light that indicate a contrast from light to dark—very similar to a camera flash, probably not quite as bright because it's not hurting my eye at all," she replied.

Humayun underscored what a breakthrough this is and how a patient adjusts. "If you've been blind for 30 or 50 years, (and) all of a sudden you get this device, there is a period of learning," he said. "Your brain needs to learn. And it's literally like seeing a baby crawl—to a child walk— to an adult run."

While hardly perfect, the device works best in bright light or where there is a lot of contrast. Kathy takes the device home. The software that runs the device can be upgraded. So, as the software is upgraded, her vision improves. Recently, she was outside with her husband on a moonlit night and saw something she hadn't seen for a long time.

"I scanned up in the sky (and) I got a big flash, right where the moon was, and pointed it out. I can't even remember how many years ago it's been that I would have ever been able to do that."

This technology has a bright future. The current chip has a resolution of 60 pixels. Humayun says that number could be increased to more than a thousand in the next version.

"I think it will be extremely exciting if they can recognize their loved ones' faces and be able to see what their wife or husband or their grandchildren look like, which they haven't seen," said Humayun.

Kathy dreams of a day when blindness like hers will be a distant memory. "My eye disease is hereditary," she said. "My three daughters happen to be fine, but I want to know that if my grandchildren ever have a problem, they will have something to give them some vision."

13. What is the primary subject of the passage?
a. a new artificial retina
b. Kathy Blake
c. hereditary disease
d. Dr. Mark Humayun

14. What is the meaning of the word progressive as it is used in the second paragraph?
a. selective
b. gradually increasing
c. diminishing
d. disabling

15. Which statement is not a detail from the passage?
a. The use of an artificial retina requires a special pair of glasses.
b. Retinal blindness is the inability to perceive light.
c. Retinitis pigmentosa is curable.
d. The artificial retina performs best in bright light.

16. What is the author's intention in writing the essay?
a. to persuade
b. to entertain
c. to analyze
d. to inform

Questions 17-21 refer to the following passage:

Usher syndrome is the most common condition that affects both hearing and vision. The major signs of Usher syndrome are hearing loss and an eye disorder called retinitis pigmentosa, or RP. Retinitis pigmentosa causes night blindness and a loss of peripheral vision (side vision) through the progressive degeneration of the retina. The retina, which is crucial for vision, is a light-sensitive tissue at the back of the eye. As RP progresses, the field of vision narrows, until only central vision (the ability to see straight ahead) remains. Many people with Usher syndrome also have severe balance problems.

There are three clinical types of Usher syndrome. In the United States, types 1 and 2 are the most common. Together, they account for approximately 90 to 95 percent of all cases of juvenile Usher syndrome. Approximately three to six percent of all deaf and hearing-disabled children have Usher syndrome. In developed countries, such as the United States, about four in every 100,000 newborns have Usher syndrome.

Usher syndrome is inherited as an autosomal recessive trait. The term autosomal means that the mutated gene is not located on either of the chromosomes that determine sex; in other words, both males and females can have the disorder and can pass it along to a child. The word recessive means that in order to have Usher syndrome, an individual must receive a mutated form of the Usher syndrome gene from each parent. If a child has a mutation in one Usher syndrome gene but the other gene is normal, he or she should have normal vision and hearing. Individuals with a mutation in a gene that can cause an autosomal recessive disorder are called carriers, because they carry the mutated gene but show no symptoms of the disorder. If both parents are carriers of a mutated gene for Usher syndrome, they will have a one-in-four chance of producing a child with Usher syndrome.

Usually, parents who have normal hearing and vision do not know if they are carriers of an Usher syndrome gene mutation. Currently, it is not possible to determine whether an individual without a family history of Usher syndrome is a carrier. Scientists at the National Institute on Deafness and Other Communication Disorders (NIDCD) are hoping to change this, however, as they learn more about the genes responsible for Usher syndrome.

17. What is the main idea of the passage?
   a. Usher syndrome is an inherited condition that affects hearing and vision.
   b. Some people are carriers of Usher syndrome.
   c. Usher syndrome typically skips a generation.
   d. Scientists hope to develop a test for detecting the carriers of Usher syndrome.

18. What is the meaning of the word *signs* as it is used in the first paragraph?
   a. qualifications
   b. conditions/diseases
   c. subjective markers
   d. measurable indicators

19. Which statement is not a detail from the passage?
   a. Types 1 and 2 Usher syndrome are the most common in the United States.
   b. Usher syndrome affects both hearing and smell.
   c. Right now, there is no way to identify a carrier of Usher syndrome.
   d. Central vision is the ability to see straight ahead.

20. What is the meaning of the word juvenile as it is used in the second paragraph?
   a. bratty
   b. serious
   c. occurring in children
   d. improper

21. What is the meaning of the word mutated as it is used in the third paragraph?
   a. selected
   b. altered
   c. composed
   d. destroyed

Questions 22-27 refer to the following passage:

The immune system is a network of cells, tissues, and organs that defends the body against attacks by foreign invaders. These invaders are primarily microbes—tiny organisms such as bacteria, parasites, and fungi—that can cause infections. Viruses also cause infections but are too primitive to be classified as living organisms. The human body provides an ideal environment for many microbes. It is the immune system's job to keep the microbes out or destroy them.

The immune system is amazingly complex. It can recognize and remember millions of different enemies, and it can secrete fluids and cells to wipe out nearly all of them. The secret to its success is an elaborate and dynamic communications network. Millions of cells, organized into sets and subsets, gather and transfer information in response to an infection. Once immune cells receive the alarm, they produce powerful chemicals that help to regulate their own growth and behavior, enlist other immune cells, and direct the new recruits to trouble spots.

Although scientists have learned much about the immune system, they continue to puzzle over how the body destroys invading microbes, infected cells, and tumors without harming healthy tissues. New technologies for identifying individual immune cells are now allowing scientists to determine quickly which targets are triggering an immune response. Improvements in microscopy are permitting the first-ever observations of living B cells, T cells, and other cells as they interact within lymph nodes and other body tissues.

In addition, scientists are rapidly unraveling the genetic blueprints that direct the human immune response, as well as those that dictate the biology of bacteria, viruses, and parasites. The combination of new technology with expanded genetic information will no doubt reveal even more about how the body protects itself from disease.

22. What is the main idea of the passage?
   a.   Scientists fully understand the immune system.
   b.   The immune system triggers the production of fluids.
   c.   The body is under constant invasion by malicious microbes.
   d.   The immune system protects the body from infection.

23. Which statement is not a detail from the passage?
   a.   Most invaders of the body are microbes.
   b.   The immune system relies on excellent communication.
   c.   Viruses are extremely sophisticated.
   d.   The cells of the immune system are organized.

24. What is the meaning of the word ideal as it is used in the first paragraph?
   a.   thoughtful
   b.   confined
   c.   hostile
   d.   perfect

25. Which statement is not a detail from the passage?
   a.   Scientists can now see T cells.
   b.   The immune system ignores tumors.
   c.   The ability of the immune system to fight disease without harming the body remains mysterious.
   d.   The immune system remembers millions of different invaders.

26. What is the meaning of the word enlist as it is used in the second paragraph?
a. call into service
b. write down
c. send away
d. put across

27. What is the author's primary purpose in writing the essay?
a. to persuade
b. to analyze
c. to inform
d. to entertain

Questions 28-31 refer to the following passage:

The federal government regulates dietary supplements through the United States Food and Drug Administration (FDA). The regulations for dietary supplements are not the same as those for prescription or over-the-counter drugs. In general, the regulations for dietary supplements are less strict.

To begin with, a manufacturer does not have to prove the safety and effectiveness of a dietary supplement before it is marketed. A manufacturer is permitted to say that a dietary supplement addresses a nutrient deficiency, supports health, or is linked to a particular body function (such as immunity), if there is research to support the claim. Such a claim must be followed by the words "This statement has not been evaluated by the Food and Drug Administration. This product is not intended to diagnose, treat, cure, or prevent any disease."

Also, manufacturers are expected to follow certain good manufacturing practices (GMPs) to ensure that dietary supplements are processed consistently and meet quality standards. Requirements for GMPs went into effect in 2008 for large manufacturers and are being phased in for small manufacturers through 2010.

Once a dietary supplement is on the market, the FDA monitors safety and product information, such as label claims and package inserts. If it finds a product to be unsafe, it can take action against the manufacturer and/or distributor and may issue a warning or require that the product be removed from the marketplace. The Federal Trade Commission (FTC) is responsible for regulating product advertising; it requires that all information be truthful and not misleading.

The federal government has taken legal action against a number of dietary supplement promoters or Web sites that promote or sell dietary supplements because they have made false or deceptive statements about their products or because marketed products have proven to be unsafe.

28. What is the main idea of the passage?
a. Manufacturers of dietary supplements have to follow good manufacturing practices.
b. The FDA has a special program for regulating dietary supplements.
c. The federal government prosecutes those who mislead the general public.
d. The FDA is part of the federal government.

Practice Test #2

29. Which statement is not a detail from the passage?

    a. Promoters of dietary supplements can make any claims that are supported by research.

    b. GMP requirements for large manufacturers went into effect in 2008.

    c. Product advertising is regulated by the FTC.

    d. The FDA does not monitor products after they enter the market.

30. What is the meaning of the phrase *phased in* as it is used in the third paragraph?

    a. stunned into silence

    b. confused

    c. implemented in stages

    d. legalized

31. What is the meaning of the word deceptive as it is used in the fifth paragraph?

    a. misleading

    b. malicious

    c. illegal

    d. irritating

Questions 32-35 refer to the following passage:

Anemia is a condition in which there is an abnormally low number of red blood cells (RBCs). This condition also can occur if the RBCs don't contain enough hemoglobin, the iron-rich protein that makes the blood red. Hemoglobin helps RBCs carry oxygen from the lungs to the rest of the body.

Anemia can be accompanied by low numbers of RBCs, white blood cells (WBCs), and platelets. Red blood cells are disc-shaped and look like doughnuts without holes in the center. They carry oxygen and remove carbon dioxide (a waste product) from your body. These cells are made in the bone marrow and live for about 120 days in the bloodstream. Platelets and WBCs also are made in the bone marrow. White blood cells help fight infection. Platelets stick together to seal small cuts or breaks on the blood vessel walls and to stop bleeding.

If you are anemic, your body doesn't get enough oxygenated blood. As a result, you may feel tired or have other symptoms. Severe or long-lasting anemia can damage the heart, brain, and other organs of the body. Very severe anemia may even cause death.

Anemia has three main causes: blood loss, lack of RBC production, or high rates of RBC destruction. Many types of anemia are mild, brief, and easily treated. Some types can be prevented with a healthy diet or treated with dietary supplements. However, certain types of anemia may be severe, long lasting, and life threatening if not diagnosed and treated.

If you have the signs or symptoms of anemia, you should see your doctor to find out whether you have the condition. Treatment will depend on the cause and severity of the anemia.

32. What is the main idea of the passage?

    a. Anemia presents in a number of forms.

    b. Anemia is a potentially dangerous condition characterized by low numbers of RBCs.

    c. Anemia is a deficiency of WBCs and platelets.

    d. Anemia is a treatable condition.

33. Which statement is not a detail from the passage?
   a. There are different methods for treating anemia.
   b. Red blood cells remove carbon dioxide from the body.
   c. Platelets are made in the bone marrow.
   d. Anemia is rarely caused by blood loss.

34. What is the meaning of the word oxygenated as it is used in the third paragraph?
   a. containing low amounts of oxygen
   b. containing no oxygen
   c. consisting entirely of oxygen
   d. containing high amounts of oxygen

35. What is the meaning of the word severity as it is used in the fifth paragraph?
   a. seriousness
   b. disconnectedness
   c. truth
   d. swiftness

Questions 36-39 refer to the following passage:

Contrary to previous reports, drinking four or more cups of coffee a day does not put women at risk of rheumatoid arthritis (RA), according to a new study partially funded by the National Institute of Arthritis and Musculoskeletal and Skin Diseases (NIAMS). The study concluded that there is little evidence to support a connection between consuming coffee or tea and the risk of RA among women.

Rheumatoid arthritis is an inflammatory autoimmune disease that affects the joints. It results in pain, stiffness, swelling, joint damage, and loss of function. Inflammation most often affects the hands and feet and tends to be symmetrical. About one percent of the US population has rheumatoid arthritis.

Elizabeth W. Karlson, M.D., and her colleagues at Harvard Medical School and Brigham and Women's Hospital in Boston, Massachusetts, used the Nurses' Health Study, a long-term investigation of nurses' diseases, lifestyles, and health practices, to examine possible links between caffeinated beverages and RA risk. The researchers were able to follow up more than 90 percent of the original pool of 83,124 participants who answered a 1980 food frequency questionnaire, and no links were found. They also considered changes in diet and habits over a prolonged period of time, and when the results were adjusted for other factors, such as cigarette smoking, alcohol consumption, and oral contraceptive use, the outcome still showed no relationship between caffeine consumption and risk of RA.

Previous research had suggested an association between consuming coffee or tea and RA risk. According to Dr. Karlson, the data supporting that conclusion were inconsistent. Because the information in the older studies was collected at only one time, she says, consideration was not given to the other factors associated with RA, such as cigarette smoking and changes in diet and lifestyle over a follow-up period. The new study presents a more accurate picture of caffeine and RA risk.

36. What is the main idea of the passage?
   a. In the past, doctors have cautioned older women to avoid caffeinated beverages.
   b. Rheumatoid arthritis affects the joints of older women.
   c. A recent study found no link between caffeine consumption and RA among women.
   d. Cigarette smoking increases the incidence of RA.

Practice Test #2

213

37. Which statement is not a detail from the passage?

a. Alcohol consumption is linked with RA.
b. The original data for the study came from a 1980 questionnaire.
c. Rheumatoid arthritis most often affects the hands and feet.
d. This study included tens of thousands of participants.

38. What is the meaning of the word symmetrical as it is used in the second paragraph?

a. affecting both sides of the body in corresponding fashion
b. impossible to treat
c. sensitive to the touch
d. asymptomatic

39. What is the author's primary purpose in writing the essay?

a. to entertain
b. to inform
c. to analyze
d. to persuade

40. This passage describes Toni Morrison's writing as all of the following EXCEPT:

Toni Morrison, who name was originally Chloe Anthony Wofford, is a writer of great distinction who has won many awards, one of which was the Pulitzer Prize in 1988. From her very first novel, *The Bluest Eye*, the writer has portrayed the struggles of black people, and especially black women, in America. Her writing is multifaceted and profound with the distinctive African-American culture as the backbone. Morrison's novels are literary epics with strong, descriptive dialogue and black characters with powerful depth.

a. multifaceted
b. award-winning
c. profound
d. struggling

Verbal

30 minutes, 60 questions

For questions 1-30: Select the synonym. Each question has a word in all capital letters followed by five answer choices in all lower-case letters. Select the answer choice with a definition closest to the capitalized word.

1. OBSCURE:
- a. opinionated
- b. unclear
- c. offensive
- d. benign

2. REMISS:
- a. timely
- b. diligent
- c. negligent
- d. meticulous

3. GRIEVOUS:
- a. casual
- b. frightening
- c. delighted
- d. serious

4. EXHILARATION:
- a. exhalation
- b. aimlessness
- c. curiosity
- d. elation

5. SIEGE:
- a. slip
- b. blockade
- c. severity
- d. odor

6. COURTEOUS:
- a. conscientious
- b. polite
- c. interested
- d. aware

7. RECEDE:
- a. excel
- b. increase
- c. abut
- d. wane

8. BRANDISHED:

a. threw
b. waved menacingly
c. smacked
d. peered

9. BESOTTED:

a. infatuated
b. infuriated
c. perplexed
d. engrossed

10. VICINITY:

a. neighborhood
b. parish
c. mindset
d. idea

11. PROGNOSIS:

a. forecast
b. description
c. outline
d. schedule

12. ABSTAIN:

a. offend
b. retrain
c. to refrain from
d. defenestrate

13. OMINOUS:

a. threatening
b. emboldening
c. destructive
d. insightful

14. INCIDENCE:

a. random events
b. sterility
c. autonomy
d. rate of occurrence

15. OCCLUDED:

a. closed
b. deformed
c. enlarged
d. engorged

16. POTENT:

a. frantic
b. determined
c. feverish
d. powerful

17. PRECIPITOUS:

a. detached
b. sordid
c. encompassed
d. steep

18. INSIDIOUS:

a. stealthy
b. deadly
c. collapsed
d. new

19. PROSCRIBE:

a. anticipate
b. prevent
c. defeat
d. forbid

20. DISTENDED:

a. concave
b. sore
c. swollen
d. empty

21. OVERT:

a. concealed
b. apparent
c. expert
d. delectable

22. CARNIVORE:

a. hungry
b. meat-eating
c. infected
d. demented

23. BELLIGERENT:

a. retired
b. sardonic
c. pugnacious
d. acclimated

Practice Test #2

24. FLACCID:

    a. defended
    b. limp
    c. slender
    d. outdated

25. TERRESTRIAL:

    a. alien
    b. earthly
    c. foreign
    d. domestic

26. ENDOGENOUS:

    a. contagious
    b. painful to the touch
    c. continuous
    d. growing from within

27. DISCRETE:

    a. calm
    b. subtle
    c. hidden
    d. separate

28. EXACERBATE:

    a. implicate
    b. aggravate
    c. heal
    d. decondition

29. HOLISTIC:

    a. insensitive
    b. ignorant
    c. specialized
    d. concerned with the whole rather than the parts

30. REPUGNANT:

    a. destructive
    b. selective
    c. collective
    d. offensive

For questions 31-60: These questions ask you to identify and compare relationships between pairs of words. Select the answer that best completes the comparison.

31. shovel is to dig as spoon is to

    a. stir
    b. knife
    c. silverware
    d. eat

32. shoot is to gun as drive is to

   a. road
   b. way
   c. automobile
   d. golf

33. simmer is to boil as tremor is to

   a. earth
   b. earthquake
   c. shake
   d. nervous

34. intelligent is to stupid as enthusiastic is to

   a. happy
   b. passionate
   c. action
   d. indifferent

35. bouquet is to flowers as recipe is to

   a. success
   b. cookbook
   c. ingredients
   d. chef

36. cool is to freezing as warm is to

   a. boiling
   b. summer
   c. heat
   d. cozy

37. France is to Europe as China is to

   a. Japan
   b. Asia
   c. country
   d. continent

38. fable is to story as sandal is to

   a. strap
   b. summer
   c. foot
   d. shoe

39. shell is to beach as rock is to

   a. roll
   b. stone
   c. mountain
   d. dune

Practice Test #2

40. kitchen is to cook as library is to

    a. peace
    b. read
    c. play
    d. pray

41. rug is to floor as sheet is to

    a. pillowcase
    b. bedspread
    c. sail
    d. bed

42. smokestack is to factory as steeple is to

    a. church
    b. chase
    c. dome
    d. high

43. rain is to wet as fire is to

    a. ash
    b. ember
    c. hot
    d. spark

44. sentence is to paragraph as brick is to

    a. mortar
    b. cement
    c. slate
    d. wall

45. try is to attempt as dare is to

    a. challenge
    b. devil
    c. fear
    d. defy

46. laugh is to joy as sneer is to

    a. snicker
    b. snob
    c. contempt
    d. face

47. hospital is to surgeon as store is to

    a. clerk
    b. inventory
    c. warehouse
    d. customer

48. **weave is to basket as knit is to**

 a. brow
 b. scarf
 c. sew
 d. needle

49. **hungry is to eat as tired is to**

 a. bed
 b. awake
 c. sick
 d. sleep

50. **desert is to dune as ocean is to**

 a. deep
 b. continent
 c. sea
 d. wave

51. **oil is to squeak as salve is to**

 a. burn
 b. medicine
 c. soothe
 d. ointment

52. **nudge is to shove as nibble is to**

 a. morsel
 b. devour
 c. tiny
 d. swallow

53. **cavity is to tooth as wart is to**

 a. hog
 b. blemish
 c. skin
 d. virus

54. **had is to have as saw is to**

 a. tool
 b. sawed
 c. see
 d. wood

55. **racket is to tennis as paddle is to**

 a. hit
 b. punishment
 c. wheel
 d. ping pong

Practice Test #2

56. etch is to glass as paint is to

    a. canvas
    b. draw
    c. color
    d. brush

57. debt is to pay as law is to

    a. obey
    b. break
    c. order
    d. legal

58. president is to government as principal is to

    a. belief
    b. teacher
    c. school
    d. student

59. pearl is to oyster as seed is to

    a. plant
    b. grape
    c. sow
    d. grow

60. rake is to hoe as hammer is to

    a. head
    b. build
    c. pound
    d. screwdriver

Mometrix

Quantitative

Read each question, perform the appropriate calculations, and determine the correct answer.

1. Jason chooses a number that is the square root of four less than two times Amy's number. If Amy's number is 20, what is Jason's number?

    a. 6
    b. 7
    c. 8
    d. 9

2. Fred designs a candy box in the shape of a triangular prism. The base of each triangular face measures 4 inches, while the height of the prism is 7 inches. Given that the length of the prism is 11 inches, what is the volume of the candy box?

    a. 102 in^3
    b. 128 in^3
    c. 154 in^3
    d. 308 in^3

3. Which of the following is equivalent to $4^3 + 12 \div 4 + 8^2 \times 3$?

    a. 249
    b. 393
    c. 211
    d. 259

4. A car holds 12 gallons of gasoline. How many quarts of gasoline does the car hold?

    a. 3 quarts
    b. 48 quarts
    c. $\frac{1}{3}$ quarts
    d. 4 quarts

5. The bar graph shows the number of views a viral video has on four different platforms.

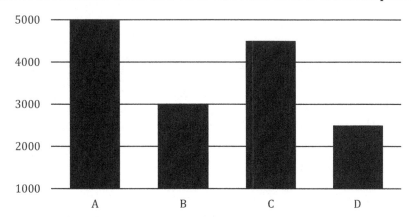

Which statement is supported by the data?

    a. The number of views on platform B is twice the number of views on platform C.
    b. The number of views on platform A is greater than the number of views on platform B and D combined.
    c. The number of views on platform D is half the number of views on platform C
    d. The number of views on platform A is double the number of views on platform D

Practice Test #2

223

6. A farmer has 360 cows. He decides to sell 45. Shortly after, he purchases 85 more cows. How many cows does he have?

    a.   230
    b.   315
    c.   400
    d.   490

7. Four points are graphed on a coordinate grid.

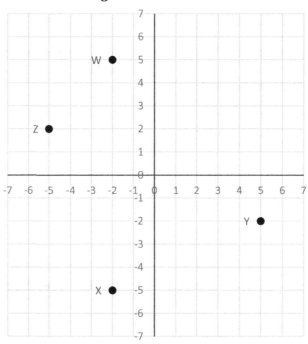

Which point is located at $(-2, 5)$?

    a.   Point W
    b.   Point X
    c.   Point Y
    d.   Point Z

8. Which expression is equivalent to $5^3 + 4 \cdot 7 + 6$?

    a. $(125 + 4) \cdot 13$
    b. $(25 \cdot 5) + (4 \cdot 13)$
    c. $(5 \cdot 5 \cdot 5) + (4 \cdot 7 \cdot 6)$
    d. $25 \cdot 5 + 34$

9. Which expression is equivalent to $3 - (x + 4)$?

    a. $3 + 4x$
    b. $-3 + 4x$
    c. $-x + 4 + 3$
    d. $3 - x - 4$

10. What is the solution for the equation $\frac{x}{24} = -6$?

    a.   4
    b. -4

c. 144
d. −144

11. Antonio wants to buy a roll of border to finish an art project. At four different shops, he found four different borders he liked. He wants to use the widest of the borders. The list shows the width, in inches, of the borders he found.

$$1\frac{7}{10}, 1.72, 1\frac{3}{4}, 1.695$$

Which roll of border should Antonio buy if he wants to buy the widest border?

a. $1\frac{7}{10}$
b. 1.72
c. $1\frac{3}{4}$
d. 1.695

12. Which list includes values that are all equivalent?

a. $20\%, \frac{1}{20}, 0.2$
b. $1.5, 15\%, \frac{15}{100}$
c. $\frac{7}{20}, 35\%, 0.35$
d. $10\%, \frac{1}{10}, 0.01$

13. Which of the following values of x makes this equation a true statement?

$$-2 - 3x = -14$$

a. -4
b. 4
c. 3
d. -5

14. Which of the following is the solution to the equation $320 - 12d = 80$?

a. -20
b. 12
c. 20
d. -12

15. Which equation is true when $x = -4$?

a. $25 = 5x$
b. $x - 36 = 32$
c. $\frac{68}{x} = -17$
d. $17 - x = 13$

16. A mathematics test has a 4:2 ratio of data analysis problems to algebra problems. If the test has 18 algebra problems, how many data analysis problems are on the test?

a. 24
b. 36
c. 38
d. 28

17. A scientist tracked the population of cicadas in an area over 5 years. The table shows the population of cicadas each year in millions.

Year 1	Year 2	Year 3	Year 4	Year 5
4	12	36	108	324

By what scale factor did the population of cicadas increase each year?

    a. 4
    b. 8
    c. 3
    d. 6

18. What expression is NOT equal to 5?

    a. the absolute value of –5
    b. the reciprocal of –5
    c. the absolute value of 5
    d. the opposite of –5

19. The histogram below represents the overall GRE scores for a sample of college students. Which of the following is a true statement?

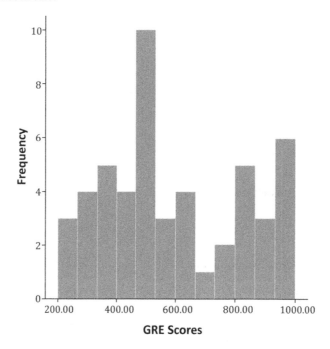

    a. The range of GRE scores is approximately 600.
    b. The average GRE score is 750.
    c. The median GRE score is approximately 500.
    d. The fewest number of college students had an approximate score of 800.

20. A publishing company has been given 29 manuscripts to review. If the company divides the work equally amongst 8 editors, which of the following represents the number of manuscript each editor will review?

    a. $3\frac{3}{5}$

    b. $3\frac{5}{8}$

    c. $3\frac{7}{9}$

    d. $3\frac{2}{3}$

21. Which of the following is equivalent to $-8^2 + (17 - 9) \times 4 + 7$?

    a. -217

    b. 24

    c. -64

    d. -25

22. If 1 mile = 5,280 feet, which of the following proportions can be used to determine the number of miles equal to 26,400 feet?

    a. $\frac{5,280}{1} = \frac{26,400}{x}$

    b. $\frac{5,280}{1} = \frac{x}{26,400}$

    c. $\frac{5,280}{x} = \frac{26,400}{1}$

    d. $\frac{5,280}{26,400} = \frac{x}{1}$

23. Allison is making lemonade. She uses 3 cups of sugar for every 2 gallons of water. Which ratio of sugar to water would make a lemonade with the same sweetness?

    a. $10 : 6$

    b. $2 : 3$

    c. $12 : 8$

    d. $27 : 16$

24. Large boxes of canned beans hold 24 cans of beans and small boxes hold 12 cans. One afternoon, Gerald brought 4 large boxes of canned beans and 6 small boxes of canned beans to the food bank. How many cans of beans did Gerald bring to the food bank that afternoon?

    a. 168

    b. 192

    c. 288

    d. 360

25. Castor collects only baseball and football cards. He has 40 baseball cards and 10 football cards. Which decimal best shows the part of his entire card collection represented by his baseball cards?

    a. 0.8

    b. 0.75

    c. 0.4

    d. 0.25

Practice Test #2

Answer Key and Explanations for Test #2

Quantitative

1. C: One way to find this answer is to set up a proportion: $\frac{6}{10} = \frac{G}{240}$, in which G represents the number of Grade 6 students living within two miles of the school. To solve the proportion, we should cross-multiply. So, 10 times G = 6 times 240. This gives the equation:

$10G = 1,440$. To solve the equation we divide both sides of the equation by 10, which gives $G = 144$.

2. D: The counters represent the expression $-12 + 8$, which equals -4. Using the additive inverse property, the eight negative 1 integers and eight positive 1 integers cancel one another, leaving four negative 1 integers, written as -4.

3. A: The number Akita is thinking of is the opposite of 7. The opposite of a number is the value that is the same distance from zero on the other side of a number line. Akita must be thinking of the number -7. The absolute value of a number is its distance from zero. When looking at a number line, -7 is 7 away from zero, so the absolute value of -7 is 7. The true statements about Akita's number are II: the number is -7, and III: the number has an absolute value of 7.

4. C: The equation that represents the relationship between the position number, n, and the value of the term, a_n, is $a_n = -3n + 8$. Notice each n is multiplied by -3, with 8 added to that value. Substituting position number 1 for n gives $a_n = -3(1) + 8$, which equals 5. Substitution of the remaining position numbers does not provide a counterexample to this procedure.

5. D: The amount charged for miles hauled will require us to multiply the number of miles by \$0.05. The charge for each load of \$80 is not changed by the number of miles hauled. That will be added to the amount charged for miles hauled. So, the equation needs to show 0.05 times miles plus 80, or $c = 0.05m + 80$.

6. B: This problem focuses on equivalent percentages and fractions. There are a few ways to approach this problem. One way would be to convert each fraction to a percentage. Another way would be to convert the percentage to a fraction and simplify. To convert 36% to a fraction, the 36 would be written out of 100 and this fraction can be simplified. $36\% = \frac{36}{100}$, which can be simplified to $\frac{18}{50}$ and $\frac{9}{25}$.

7. B: Let x represent the amount of money saved, \$52 the amount earned mowing yards, and \$14 the amount spent on a birthday present. Then \$52 – \$14 = x. This can be rearranged as $14 + x = 52$. Therefore, choice B is correct. 2.7.10

8. D: The inequality $12.5x \geq 375$ means that 375 is less than or equal to 12.5 times a value x, or a value x times 12.5 is greater than or equal to 375. Option A describes an equation where $12.5x = 375$. Option B describes the inequality $12.5 + x \geq 375$. Option C describes the inequality $12.5x > 375$. Option D describes the inequality $375 \leq 12.5x$ because Desmond makes 12.5 bracelets each day for x days, $12.5x$, and has a goal of making at least 375 bracelets, which means that $12.5x$ must be greater than or equal to 375.

9. A: When setting up a proportion, like quantities need to be placed in the numerators and like quantities need to be placed in the denominators. For this problem, the proportion has the form of $\frac{\text{object}}{\text{shadow}} = \frac{\text{object}}{\text{shadow}}$. The proportion in the correct format is $\frac{x}{4} = \frac{5}{2.5}$. Therefore, choice A is correct.

10. B: The order of operations states that multiplication and division, as they appear from left to right in the expression, should be completed following the evaluation of exponents. Therefore, after evaluating the squared number, that value should be multiplied by 2.

11. C: The first step would be to subtract the $10 he spent on the book from the gift, $40. This gives us $30. This is how much Tomas still has. We add the $35 he earned to the $30 remaining from the gift, which gives $65, the amount Tomas has in total. Then we subtract $65 from the $100 cost of the telescope to find the amount Tomas still needs to save.

12. A: This problem focuses on comparing ratios. There are many ways to compare $3 : 2$ and $5 : 4$. One way would be by finding the unit ratio of coloring to cups using division. Caroline uses a ratio of $3 : 2$ drops to cups, which is equivalent to 1.5 drops to 1 cup because $3 \div 2 = 1.5$. Devon uses a ratio of $5 : 4$ drops to cups, which is equivalent to 1.25 drops to 1 cup because $5 \div 4 = 1.25$. If Caroline uses more drops per cup of water, her water is darker because $3 : 2$ is greater than $5 : 4$.

13. B: This problem focuses on using the area formula of a parallelogram. The reference sheet can be used to find the area formula of a parallelogram: $A = bh$. The height of a parallelogram is the length of a line that connects and is perpendicular to the bases. Based on the diagram, the base of the figure is $12\frac{1}{2}$ inches and the height of the figure is $3\frac{1}{2}$ inches. The equation to find the area is $A = 12\frac{1}{2}$ in $\cdot\, 3\frac{1}{2}$ in $= 43\frac{3}{4}$ in^2.

14. B: Since $\triangle ABE$ and $\triangle ACD$ have two congruent angles (notice that both triangles have $\angle A$ in common, and $\angle B \cong \angle C$ since both angles measure 70°), their third angles must also be congruent. Thus, $\triangle ABE$ is similar to $\triangle ACD$. Since the corresponding sides of similar triangles are proportional, $\frac{AB}{AC} = \frac{AE}{AD}$. However, the lengths BE and CD are not equal. Therefore, choice B is correct.

15. A: This problem focuses on writing situations that represent inequalities. In this example, 36 is less than n divided by 4. This means that a number n is being divided by 4, and this value is greater than 36. The only situation that describes a total, n divided by 4, being greater than 36 is Theresa packaging n number of cupcakes into packages of 4, which makes more than 36 packages.

16. B: There are many ways to approach this problem. One way to solve this would be to review each option and compare them to the given expression. When the expression $9z \cdot z - 27z$ is compared to $9z + (z - 3)$, it is evident that they are not equivalent because $9z \cdot z = 9z^2$ and no term in $9z + (z - 3)$ contains or can be simplified to contain a factor of z^2. When the expression $9z + (z - 3)$ is compared to $(z - 3) + 9z$, it can be observed that these expressions are equivalent because of the commutative property, so the expressions $9z$ and $z - 3$ can be added in any order. When $10z + 3$ is compared to $9z + (z - 3)$, it is evident that these expressions are not equivalent because, while $9z + z = 10z$, the 3 should be subtracted, not added. Lastly, when $(z - 3) - 9z$ is compared to $9z + (z - 3)$, it is evident that these expressions are not equivalent because the sum of $9z$ and $(z - 3)$ is not equivalent to the difference between $(z - 3)$ and $9z$.

17. D: In order to convert the given fraction to a percentage, divide 2 by 7. Doing so gives a decimal of approximately 0.29. The decimal can be converted to a percentage by multiplying by 100, which moves the decimal point two places to the right and gives 29%.

18. D: To correctly write a percent as a decimal, the percent sign is dropped and the number is rewritten with the decimal point two places to the left. This is because a percent is always a value out of 100 and the second place after the decimal point is the hundredths place. So, 70% = 0.70 and the zero at the end after the decimal can be dropped.

19. A: This problem focuses on graphing solutions to inequalities on a number line. Given the inequality $17 - x \geq 9$, this can be solved by isolating x by simplifying the inequality. $17 - x \geq 9$ is simplified by first adding x to each side to get $17 \geq 9 + x$, and this can be further simplified by subtracting 9 from each side to get $8 \geq x$.

This solution can be graphed on a number line using a closed circle over the 8, because x could be equal to 8, and an arrow to the left because if x is not equal to 8, it is less than 8.

20. A: This problem focuses on converting a fraction $\frac{7}{25}$ to a percentage. Converting fractions to percentages can be performed by converting the fraction to a value out of 100, or converting the fraction to a decimal. $\frac{7}{25}$ can be converted to a fraction out of 100 by multiplying the numerator and denominator by 4: $\frac{7}{25} = \frac{28}{100}$, which is equivalent to 28%

21. A: The product of 5 and $\frac{1}{2}$ is the same as the value of $5 \cdot \frac{1}{2}$. The product of a whole number multiplied by a fraction is less than the whole number. 5 times $\frac{1}{2}$ must be less than 5. The product cannot be greater than 5, and the product must be greater than 1 and $\frac{1}{2}$ because $5 \cdot \frac{1}{2} = \frac{5}{2}$ which is greater than 1 and $\frac{1}{2}$.

22. A: This problem focuses on equivalent expressions using exponents and order of operations. There are many ways to approach this problem. One strategy is to simplify each expression and compare. The given expression $81 \div 9 + 36$ is equivalent to 45 because $81 \div 9 = 9$ and $9 + 36 = 45$. The expression in option A, $3^2 + 6^2$, is also equivalent to 45 because $3^2 = 9$, $6^2 = 36$, and $9 + 36 = 45$. The expression in option B, $3 \cdot 3 + 3 \cdot 3 \cdot 3$, is equivalent to 36 because $3 \cdot 3 = 9$, $3 \cdot 3 \cdot 3 = 27$, and $9 + 27 = 36$. The expression in option C, $\frac{9^2}{3^3} + (12 \cdot 3)$, is equivalent to 39 because $9^2 = 81$, $3^3 = 27$, and $\frac{81}{27} = 3$. Then, $12 \cdot 3 = 36$, and finally, $3 + 36 = 39$. The expression in option D, $(9 \cdot 9) \div (3 \cdot 3 \cdot 5)$, is equivalent to 1.8 because $9 \cdot 9 = 81$, $3 \cdot 3 \cdot 5 = 45$, and $81 \div 45 = 1.8$. The only expression that is equivalent to the given expression is the expression $3^2 + 6^2$.

23. D: First, subtract 5 from both sides of the inequality, which yields $-2x > 8$. Then, divide both sides by -2. Remember to reverse the symbol since the inequality is being divided by a negative number. This yields $x < -4$, which is graphed on a number line with an open circle at -4 and shading to the left. Therefore, choice D is correct.

24. D: The volume of a cylinder can be determined by using the following formula: $V = Bh$, where B represents the area of the base and h represents the height. The area of one of the bases refers to the area of one of the circular bases. The area of a circle is determined by πr^2; thus, the area of one of the cylindrical bases is represented by πr^2.

25. D: This problem focuses on the definition of scale factors. If the views on a video increase by a scale factor of 13 each day, this means that the change in views from each day increased by a multiplicative factor of 13. For example, if there are 5 views on day 1, there will be $5 \cdot 13 = 65$ views on day 2 and $65 \cdot 13 = 845$ views on day 3. The number of views increases by multiplying the previous day's total by 13.

Reading Comprehension

1. D: The main idea of this passage is that vaccines help the immune system function properly. Identifying main ideas is one of the key skills tested by the exam. One of the common traps that many test-takers fall into is assuming that the first sentence of the passage will express the main idea. Although this will be true for some passages, often the author will use the first sentence to attract interest or to make an introductory, but not central, point. On this question, if you assume that the first sentence contains the main idea, you will incorrectly choose answer B. Finding the main idea of a passage requires patience and thoroughness; you cannot expect to know the main idea until you have read the entire passage. In this case, a diligent reading will show you that answer choices A, B, and C express details from the passage, but only answer choice D is a comprehensive summary of the author's message.

2. C: This passage does not state that the symptoms of disease will not emerge until the body has learned to fight the disease. The reading comprehension section of the exam will include several questions that require you to identify details from a passage. The typical structure of these questions is to ask you to identify the answer choice that contains a detail not included in the passage. This question structure makes your work a little more difficult, because it requires you to confirm that the other three details are in the passage. In this question, the details expressed in answer choices A, B, and D are all explicit in the passage. The passage never states, however, that the symptoms of disease do not emerge until the body has learned how to fight the disease-causing microbe. On the contrary, the passage implies that a person may become quite sick and even die before the body learns to effectively fight the disease.

3. B: In the third paragraph, the word *virulent* means "malicious." The reading comprehension section of the exam will include several questions that require you to define a word as it is used in the passage. Sometimes the word will be one of those used in the vocabulary section of the exam; other times, the word in question will be a slightly difficult word used regularly in academic and professional circles. In some cases, you may already know the basic definition of the word. Nevertheless, you should always go back and look at the way the word is used in the passage. The exam will often include answer choices that are legitimate definitions for the given word, but which do not express how the word is used in the passage. For instance, the word *virulent* could in some circumstances mean contagious. However, since the passage is not talking about transfer of the disease, but the effects of the disease once a person has caught it, malicious is the more appropriate answer.

4. C: The author's primary purpose in writing this essay is to inform. The reading comprehension section of the exam will include a few questions that ask you to determine the purpose of the author. The answer choices are always the same: The author's purpose is to entertain, to persuade, to inform, or to analyze. When an author is *writing to entertain*, he or she is not including a great deal of factual information; instead, the focus is on vivid language and interesting stories. *Writing to persuade* means "trying to convince the reader of something." When a writer is just trying to provide the reader with information, without any particular bias, he or she is *writing to inform*. Finally, *writing to analyze* means to consider a subject already well known to the reader. For instance, if the above passage took an objective look at the pros and cons of various approaches to fighting disease, we would say that the passage was a piece of analysis. Because the purpose of this passage is to present new information to the reader in an objective manner, it is clear that the author's intention is to inform.

5. A: The subject of this passage is foodborne illnesses. Identifying the subject of a passage is similar to identifying the main idea. Do not assume that the first sentence of the passage will declare the subject. Oftentimes, an author will approach his or her subject by first describing some related, familiar subject. In this passage, the author does introduce the subject of the passage in the first sentence. However, it is only by reading the rest of the passage that you can determine the subject. One way to figure out the subject of a passage is to identify the main idea of each paragraph, and then identify the common thread in each.

6. B: This passage never states that cooked food cannot cause illness. Indeed, the first sentence of the third paragraph states that harmful bacteria can be present on cooked food that is left out for two or more hours. This is a direct contradiction of answer choice B. If you can identify an answer choice that is clearly contradicted by the text, you can be sure that it is not one of the ideas advanced by the passage. Sometimes the correct answer to this type of question will be something that is contradicted in the text; on other occasions, the correct answer will be a detail that is not included in the passage at all.

7. C: In the first paragraph, the word *pathogens* means "disease-causing substances." The vocabulary you are asked to identify in the reading comprehension section of the exam will tend to be health related. The exam administrators are especially interested in your knowledge of the terminology used by doctors and nurses. Some of these words, however, are rarely used in normal conversation, so they may be unfamiliar to you. The best way to determine the meaning of an unfamiliar word is to examine how it is used in context. In the last sentence of the first paragraph, it is clear that pathogens are some substances that cause disease. Note that the pathogens are not diseases themselves; we would not say that an uncooked piece of meat "has a disease," but rather that consuming it "can cause a disease." For this reason, answer choice C is better than answer choice A.

8. A: In the second paragraph, the word *sterile* means "free of bacteria." This question provides a good example of why you should always refer to the word as it is used in the text. The word *sterile* is often used to describe "a person who cannot reproduce." If this definition immediately came to mind when you read the question, you might have mistakenly chosen answer D. However, in this passage the author describes raw foods as *not sterile*, meaning that they contain bacteria. For this reason, answer choice A is the correct response.

9. C: The main idea of the passage is that both the esophagus and the stomach are subject to bleeding problems. The structure of this passage is simple: The first paragraph discusses bleeding disorders of the esophagus, and the second paragraph discusses bleeding disorders of the stomach. Remember that statements can be true, and can even be explicitly stated in the passage, and can yet not be the main idea of the passage. The main idea given in answer choice A is perhaps true but is too general to be classified as the main idea of the passage.

10. B: The passage never states that ulcer disease rarely occurs in the stomach. On the contrary, in the second paragraph the author states that ulcer disease *can* affect the blood vessels in the stomach. The three other answer choices can be found within the passage. The surest way to answer a question like this is to comb through the passage, looking for each detail in turn. This is a time-consuming process, however, so you may want to follow any initial intuition you have. In other words, if you are suspicious of one of the answer choices, see if you can find it in the passage. Often you will find that the detail is expressly contradicted by the author, in which case you can be sure that this is the right answer.

11. A: In the first paragraph, the word *rupture* means "tear." All of the answer choices are action verbs that suggest destruction. In order to determine the precise meaning of *rupture*, then, you must examine its usage in the passage. The author is describing a condition in which damage to a vein causes internal bleeding. Therefore, it does not make sense to say that the vein has *collapsed* or *imploded*, as neither of these verbs suggests a ripping or opening in the side of the vein. Similarly, the word *detach* suggests an action that seems inappropriate for a vein. It seems quite possible, however, for a vein to *tear*: Answer choice A is correct.

12. D: In the second paragraph, the word *erode* means "wear away." Your approach to this question should be the same as for question 11. Take a look at how the word is used in the passage. The author is describing a condition in which ulcers degrade a vein to the point of bleeding. Obviously, it is not appropriate to say that the ulcer has *avoided*, *divorced*, or *contained* the vein. It *is* sensible, however, to say that the ulcer has *worn away* the vein.

13. A: The primary subject of the passage is a new artificial retina. This question is a little tricky, because the author spends so much time talking about the experience of Kathy Blake. As a reader, however, you have to ask yourself whether Mrs. Blake or the new artificial retina is more essential to the story. Would the author still be interested in the story if a different person had the artificial retina? Probably. Would the author have written about Mrs. Blake if she hadn't gotten the artificial retina? Almost certainly not. Really, the story of Kathy Blake is just a way for the author to make the artificial retina more interesting to the reader. Therefore, the artificial retina is the primary subject of the passage.

14. B: In the second paragraph, the word *progressive* means "gradually increasing." The root of the word is *progress*, which you may know means "advancement toward a goal." With this in mind, you may be reasonably certain that answer choice B is correct. It is never a bad idea to examine the context, however. The author is describing *progressive visual loss*, so you might be tempted to select answer choice C or D, since they both suggest loss or diminution. Remember, however, that the adjective *progressive* is modifying the noun *loss*. Since the *loss* is increasing, the correct answer is B.

15. C: The passage never states that retinitis pigmentosa (RP) is curable. This question may be somewhat confusing, since the passage discusses a new treatment for RP. However, the passage never declares that researchers have come up with a cure for the condition; rather, they have developed a new technology that allows people who suffer from RP to regain some of their vision. This is not the same thing as curing RP. Kathy Blake and others like her still have RP, though they have been assisted by this exciting new technology.

16. D: The author's intention in writing this essay is to inform. You may be tempted to answer that the author's intention is to entertain. Indeed, the author expresses his message through the story of Kathy Blake. This story, however, is not important by itself. It is clearly included as a way of explaining the new camera glasses. If the only thing the reader learned from the passage was the story of Kathy Blake, the author would probably be disappointed. At the same time, the author is not really trying to persuade the reader of anything. There is nothing controversial about these new glasses: Everyone is in favor of them. The mission of the author, then, is simply to inform the reader.

17. A: The main idea of the passage is that Usher syndrome is an inherited condition that affects hearing and vision. Always be aware that some answers may be included in the passage but not the main idea. In this question, answer choices B and D are both true details from the passage, but neither of them would be a good summary of the article. One way to approach this kind of question is to consider what you would be likely to say if someone asked you to describe the article in a single sentence. Often, the sentence you come up with will closely mimic one of the answer choices. If so, you can be sure that answer choice is correct.

18. D: In the first paragraph, the word signs means "measurable indicators." The word sign is used frequently in medical contexts, though many people do not entirely understand its meaning. Signs are those objective (measurable) indicators of illness that can be observed by someone besides the person with the illness. A stomachache, for instance, is not technically considered a sign, since it cannot be observed by anyone other than the person who has it, and therefore must be expressed by the individual experiencing it. This would be known as a symptom. Change in vital signs, a failed hearing test, or a low Snellen (vision) chart score, however, would all be considered signs because practitioners can measure or observe them. The best definition for signs, then, is "measurable indicators," that is, objective markers of a disease or condition.

19. B: The passage does not state that Usher syndrome affects both hearing and smell. On the contrary, the passage only states that Usher syndrome affects hearing and vision. You should not be content merely to note that sentence in the passage and select answer choice B. In order to be sure, you need to quickly scan the passage to determine whether there is any mention of problems with the sense of smell. This is because the mention of impaired hearing and vision does not make it impossible for smell to be damaged as well. It is a good idea to practice scanning short articles for specific words. In this case, you would want to scan the article looking for words like *smell* and *nose*.

20. C: In the second paragraph, the word *juvenile* means "occurring in children." Examine the context in which the word is used. Remember that the context extends beyond just the immediate sentence in which the word is found. It can also include adjacent sentences and paragraphs. In this case, the word juvenile is immediately followed by a further explanation of Usher syndrome as it appears in children. You can be reasonably certain, then, that juvenile Usher syndrome is the condition as it presents in children. Although the word *juvenile* is occasionally used in English to describe immature or annoying behavior, it is clear that the author is not here referring to a *bratty* form of Usher syndrome.

21. B: In the third paragraph, the word *mutated* means "altered." This word comes from the same root as mutant; a *mutant* is an organism in which the chromosomes have been changed somehow. The context in which the word is used makes it clear that the author is referring to a scenario in which one of the parent's chromosomes has been altered. One way to approach this kind of problem is to substitute the answer choice into the passage to see if it still makes sense. Clearly, it would not make sense for a chromosome to be *selected*, since chromosomes are passed on and inherited without conscious choice. Neither does it make sense for a chromosome to be destroyed, because a basic fact of biology is that all living organisms have chromosomes.

22. D: The main idea of the passage is that the immune system protects the body from infection. The author repeatedly alludes to the complexity and mystery of the immune system, so it cannot be true that scientists

233

fully understand this part of the body. It is true that the immune system triggers the production of fluids, but this description misses the point. Similarly, it is true that the body is under constant invasion by malicious microbes; however, the author is much more interested in the body's response to these microbes. For this reason, the best answer choice is D.

23. C: The passage never states that viruses are extremely sophisticated. In fact, the passage explicitly states the opposite. However, in order to know this, you need to understand the word *primitive*. The passage says that viruses are too primitive, or early in their development, to be classified as living organisms. A primitive organism is simple and undeveloped—exactly the opposite of sophisticated. If you do not know the word *primitive*, you can still answer the question by finding all three of the answer choices in the passage.

24. D: In the first paragraph, the word *ideal* means "perfect." Do not be confused by the similarity of the word *ideal* to *idea* and mistakenly select answer choice A. Take a look at the context in which the word is used. The author is describing how many millions of microbes can live inside the human body. It would not make sense, then, for the author to be describing the body as a *hostile* environment for microbes. Moreover, whether or not the body is a confined environment would not seem to have much bearing on whether it is good for microbes. Rather, the paragraph suggests that the human body is a perfect environment for microbes.

25. B: The passage never states that the immune system ignores tumors. Indeed, at the beginning of the third paragraph, the author states that scientists remain puzzled by the body's ability to fight tumors. This question is a little tricky, because it is common knowledge that many tumors prove fatal to the human body. However, you should not take this to mean that the body does not at least try to fight tumors. In general, it is best to seek out direct evidence in the text rather than to rely on what you already know. You will have enough time on the exam to fully examine and research each question.

26. A: In the second paragraph, the word *enlist* means "call into service." The use of this word is an example of figurative language, the use of a known image or idea to elucidate an idea that is perhaps unfamiliar to the reader. In this case, the author is describing the efforts of the immune system as if they were a military campaign. The immune system *enlists* other cells, and then directs these *recruits* to areas where they are needed. You are probably familiar with *enlistment* and *recruitment* as they relate to describe military service. The author is trying to draw a parallel between the enlistment of young men and women and the enlistment of immune cells. For this reason, "call into service" is the best definition for *enlist*.

27. C: The author's primary purpose in writing this essay is to inform. As you may have noticed, the essays included in the reading comprehension section of the exam were most often written to inform. This should not be too surprising; after all, the most common intention of any writing on general medical subjects is to provide information rather than to persuade, entertain, or analyze. This does not mean that you can automatically assume that "to inform" will be the answer for every question of this type. However, if you are in doubt, it is probably best to select this answer. In this case, the passage is written in a clear, declarative style with no obvious prejudice on the part of the author. The primary intention of the passage seems to be providing information about the immune system to a general audience.

28. B: The main idea of the passage is that the Food and Drug Administration (FDA) has a special program for regulating dietary supplements. This passage has a straightforward structure: The author introduces his subject in the first paragraph and uses the four succeeding paragraphs to elaborate. All of the other possible answers are true statements from the passage but cannot be considered the main idea. One way to approach questions about the main idea is to take sentences at random from the passage and see which answer choice they could potentially support. The main idea should be strengthened or supported by most of the details from the passage.

29. D: The passage never states that the Food and Drug Administration (FDA) ignores products after they enter the market. In fact, the entire fourth paragraph describes the steps taken by the FDA to regulate products once they are available for purchase. In some cases, questions of this type will contain answer choices that are directly contradictory. Here, for instance, answer choices A and B cannot be true if answer choice D is true. If there are at least two answer choices that contradict another answer choice, it is a safe bet that the contradicted answer choice cannot be correct. If you are at all uncertain about your logic, however, you should refer to the passage.

30. C: In the third paragraph, the phrase *phased in* means "implemented in stages." Do not be tempted by the similarity of this phrase to the word *fazed*, which can mean "confused or stunned." The author is referring to manufacturing standards that have already been implemented for large manufacturers and are in the process of being implemented for small manufacturers. It would make sense, then, for these standards to be implemented in *phases*: that is, to be *phased in*.

31. A: In the fifth paragraph, the word *deceptive* means "misleading." The root of the word *deceptive* is the same as for the words *deceive* and *deception*. Take a look at the context in which the word is used. The author states that the FDA prevents certain kinds of advertising. It would be somewhat redundant for the author to mean that the FDA prevents *illegal* advertising; this goes without saying. At the same time, it is unlikely that the FDA spends its time trying to prevent merely *irritating* advertising; the persistent presence of such advertising makes this answer choice inappropriate. Left with a choice between *malicious* and *misleading* advertising, it makes better sense to choose the latter, since being mean and nasty would be a bad technique for selling a product. It is common, however, for an advertiser to deliberately mislead the consumer.

32. B: The main idea of the passage is that anemia is a potentially dangerous condition characterized by low numbers of RBCs (red blood cells). All of the other answer choices are true (although answer C leaves out RBCs), but only answer choice C expresses an idea that is supported by the others. When you are considering a question of this type, try to imagine the answer choices as they would appear on an outline. If the passage above were placed into outline form, which answer choice would be the most appropriate title? Which answer choices would be more appropriate as supporting details? Try to get in the habit of imagining a loose outline as you are reading the passages on the exam.

33. D: The passage never states that anemia is rarely caused by blood loss. On the contrary, in the first sentence of the fourth paragraph the author lists three causes of anemia, and blood loss is listed first. Sometimes, answer choices for this type of question will refer to details not explicitly mentioned in the passage. For instance, answer choice A is true without ever being stated in precisely those terms. Since the passage mentions several different treatments for anemia, however, you should consider the detail in answer choice A to be in the passage. In other words, it is not enough to scan the passage looking for an exact version of the detail. Sometimes, you will have to use your best judgment.

34. D: In the third paragraph, the word *oxygenated* means "containing high amounts of oxygen." This word is not in common usage, so it is absolutely essential for you to refer to its context in the passage. The author states in the second paragraph that anemia is in part a deficiency of the red blood cells that carry oxygen throughout the body. Then in the first sentence of the third paragraph, the author states that anemic individuals do not get enough oxygenated blood. Given this information, it is clear that *oxygenated* must mean carrying high amounts of oxygen, because it has already been stated that anemia consists of a lack of oxygen-rich blood.

35. A: In the fifth paragraph, the word *severity* means "seriousness." This word shares a root with the word *severe*, but not with the word *sever*. As always, take a look at the word as it is used in the passage. In the final sentence of the passage, the author states that the treatment for anemia will depend on the *cause and severity* of the condition. In the previous paragraph, the author outlined a treatment for anemia and indicated that the proper response to the condition varies. The author even refers to the worst cases of anemia as being *severe*. With this in mind, it makes the most sense to define *severity* as seriousness.

36. C: The main idea of the passage is that a recent study found no link between caffeine consumption and rheumatoid arthritis (RA) among women. As is often the case, the first sentence of the passage contains the

235

Answer Key and Explanations for Test #2

main idea. However, do not assume that this will always be the case. Furthermore, do not assume that the first sentence of the passage will only contain the main idea. In this passage, for instance, the author makes an immediate reference to the previous belief in the correlation between caffeine and RA. It would be incorrect, however, to think that this means answer choice A is correct. Regardless of whether or not the main idea is contained in the first sentence of the passage, you will need to read the entire text before you can be sure.

37. A: The passage never states that alcohol consumption is linked with RA. The passage does state that the new study took into account alcohol consumption when evaluating the long-term data. This is a good example of a question that requires you to spend a little bit of time rereading the passage. A quick glance might lead you to believe that the new study had found a link between alcohol and RA. Tricky questions like this make it even more crucial for you to go back and verify each answer choice in the text. Working through this question by using the process of elimination is the best way to ensure the correct response.

38. A: In the second paragraph, the word *symmetrical* means "affecting both sides of the body in corresponding fashion." This is an example of a question that is hard to answer even after reviewing its context in the passage. If you have no idea what *symmetrical* means, it will be hard for you to select an answer: All of them sound plausible. In such a case, the best thing you can do is make an educated guess. One clue is that the author has been describing a condition that affects the hands and the feet. Since people have both right and left hands and feet, it makes sense that inflammation would be described as *symmetrical* if it affects both the right and left hand or foot.

39. B: The author's primary purpose in writing this essay is to inform. You may be tempted to select answer choice D on the grounds that the author is presenting a particular point of view. However, there is no indication that the author is trying to persuade the reader of anything. One clear sign that an essay is written to persuade is a reference to what the reader already thinks. A persuasive essay assumes a particular viewpoint held by the reader and then argues against that viewpoint. In this passage, the author has no allegiance to any idea; he or she is only reporting the results of the newest research.

40. D: Although the passage does use the word "struggles" in the second sentence, the word does not describe the writing. The struggles are ones that Morrison's characters are dealing with rather than a description of Morrison's writing.

Verbal

1. B: The word "obscure" means "unclear" and "difficult to understand."

2. C: The word "remiss" means "negligent or forgetful."

3. D: Serious most closely means the same thing as grievous.

4. D: Elation most closely means the same thing as exhilaration.

5. B: Blockade most closely means the same thing as siege.

6. B: Polite most closely means the same things as courteous.

7. D: Wane most closely means the same thing as recede.

8. B: Brandish means to wave menacingly.

9. A: Besotted means infatuated.

10. A: Vicinity means neighborhood.

11. A: The best definition for the word *prognosis* is "forecast."

12. C: The best definition for the word *abstain* is "to refrain from."

13. A: The best synonym for *ominous* is "threatening."

14. D: The word *incidence* means "rate of occurrence."

15. A: The closest meaning for the word *occluded* is "closed."

16. D: The best definition for the word *potent* is "powerful."

17. D: The word *precipitous* means "steep."

18. A: The best definition of the word *insidious* is "stealthy."

19. D: The word *proscribe* means "forbid."

20. C: The word *distended* means "swollen."

21. B: The word *overt* means "apparent."

22. B: The word *carnivore* means "meat-eating."

23. C: The word *belligerent* means "pugnacious." *Pugnacious* means "ready to fight."

24. B: The best description for the word *flaccid* is "limp.

25. B: The word *terrestrial* means "earthly."

26. D: The word *endogenous* means "growing from within."

27. D: The best description for the word *discrete* is "separate."

28. B: The word *exacerbate* means "aggravate."

Answer Key and Explanations for Test #2

29. D: The word *holistic* means "concerned with the whole rather than the parts."

30. D: The word *repugnant* means "offensive, especially to the senses or the morals."

31. A: A shovel is used to dig and a spoon is used to stir. While a spoon can also be used to eat, it isn't the direct instrument of eating in the way that a shovel is the direct instrument of digging.

32. C: Shoot is an action done with a gun and drive is an action done with an automobile.

33. B: Simmer is a milder form of boil and tremor is a milder form of earthquake.

34. D: Intelligent is the opposite of stupid and enthusiastic is the opposite of indifferent.

35. C: A bouquet is made up of flowers and a recipe is made up of ingredients.

36. A: Cool is a mild temperature and freezing is extreme; warm is a mild temperature and boiling is extreme.

37. B: France is a country on the continent of Europe and China is a country on the continent of Asia.

38. D: A fable is a type of story and a sandal is a type of shoe.

39. C: A shell can be found on the beach and a rock can be found on a mountain.

40. B: You cook in a kitchen and you read in a library.

41. D: A rug covers the floor and a sheet covers a bed.

42. A: A smokestack extends from the roof of a factory and a steeple extends from the roof of a church.

43. C: Rain feels wet and fire feels hot.

44. D: Sentences make up a paragraph and bricks make up a wall.

45. A: Try is another word for attempt and challenge is another word for dare.

46. C: To laugh is to show joy and to sneer is to show contempt.

47. A: A surgeon works in a hospital and a clerk works in a store.

48. B: A basket can be made by weaving and a scarf can be made by knitting.

49. D: To eat is a solution to being hungry and to sleep is a solution to being tired.

50. D: A dune is a feature of the desert and a wave is a feature of the ocean.

51. A: Oil is applied to relieve a squeak and salve is applied to relieve a burn.

52. B: A nudge is less extreme as compared to a shove and nibble is less extreme as compared to devour.

53. C: A cavity is a flaw in a tooth and a wart is a flaw on the skin.

54. C: Had is the past tense of have and saw is the past tense of see.

55. D: A racket is used to play tennis and a paddle is used to play ping pong.

56. A: To etch is to embellish glass and to paint is to embellish a canvas.

57. A: A debt must be paid and a law must be obeyed.

58. C: A president heads the government and a principal heads the school.

59. B: A pearl can be found inside an oyster and a seed can be found inside a grape.

60. D: A rake and a hoe are both tools for gardening and a hammer and a screwdriver are both tools for building.

Quantitative

1. A: Jason's number can be determined by writing the following expression: $\sqrt{2x - 4}$, where x represents Amy's number. Substitution of 20 for x gives $\sqrt{2(20) - 4}$, which simplifies to $\sqrt{36}$, or 6. Thus, Jason's number is 6. Jason's number can also be determined by working backwards. If Jason's number is the square root of 4 less than 2 times Amy's number, Amy's number should first be multiplied by 2 with 4 subtracted from that product and the square root taken of the resulting difference.

2. C: The volume of a triangular prism can be determined using the formula $V = \frac{1}{2}bhl$, where b represents the length of the base of each triangular face, h represents the height of each triangular face, and l represents the length of the prism. Substitution of the given values into the formula gives $V = \frac{1}{2} \cdot 4 \cdot 7 \cdot 11$, which equals 154. Thus, the volume of the candy box is 154 cubic inches.

3. D: The order of operations states that numbers with exponents must be evaluated first. Thus, the expression can be rewritten as $64 + 12 \div 4 + 64 \times 3$. Next, multiplication and division must be computed as they appear from left to right in the expression. Thus, the expression can be further simplified as $64 + 3 + 192$, which equals 259.

4. B: This problem focuses on converting measurements. The conversion sheet can be used to find that 1 gallon is equivalent to 4 quarts. This means that $\frac{4 \text{ quarts}}{1 \text{ gallon}} = \frac{x}{12 \text{ gallons}}$, which is equivalent to $x = 4 \cdot 12$ quarts = 48 quarts.

5. D: This problem focuses on interpreting data from a bar graph. Based on the bar graph, the number of views on platform A is 5,000, platform B is 3,000, platform C is 4,500, and platform D is 2,500. These values should be compared to the statements to find the statement that is supported by the data. 3,000 is not twice the value of 4,500. 5,000 is not greater than $3,000 + 2,500 = 5,500$. 2,500 is not half of 4,500. 5,000 is double 2,500.

6. C: First, calculate how many cows he has after selling 45.

$$360 - 45 = 315$$

Then, calculate how many cows he has after buying 85 more.

$$315 + 85 = 400$$

The farmer now has 400 cows.

7. A: This problem focuses on identifying parts and coordinate points on a graph. The given coordinates are $(-2,5)$, which describe a point that is 2 units to the left of the origin, and 5 units above the x-axis. The point that fits this description and is located at $(-2,5)$ is point W.

8. D: This problem focuses on equivalent expressions using order of operations and exponents. There are many strategies that can be used to solve this problem. One way to solve this problem is to gradually simplify the expression and compare to the options. The first step to simplify the given expression is to simplify the exponents. The expression 5^3 is equivalent to many expressions, including $5 \cdot 5 \cdot 5$, $25 \cdot 5$, and 125. Each option includes an equivalent expression to 5^3. The next step to simplifying the expression is to multiply 4 and 7, which is 28. Option A shows the expression $(125 + 4) \cdot 13$, where addition is performed before multiplication when $7 + 6$ is solved before multiplying 4 and 7. Option B shows the expression $(25 \cdot 5) + (4 \cdot 13)$, where, again, addition is performed before multiplication when $7 + 6$ is solved before multiplying 4 and 7. Option C shows the expression $(5 \cdot 5 \cdot 5) + (4 \cdot 7 \cdot 6)$ where the addition operation $7 + 6$ is changed to multiplication. Option D shows the expression $25 \cdot 5 + 34$ where each operation is performed in the correct order when the multiplication of 4 and 7 is performed and then 6 is added to the product.

9. D: This problem focuses on equivalent expressions using the associative and distributive properties. There are many ways to approach this problem. One place to start would be to use the distributive property and distribute the negative sign, or −1. This can be done because $3 - (x + 4)$ can also be written as $3 - 1(x + 4)$ and because we can distribute the −1 in this problem. This means that $3 - (x + 4)$ is equivalent to $3 - x - 4$ because $-1 \cdot x = -x$ and $-1 \cdot 4 = -4$.

10. D: This problem focuses on solving equations with one variable. To solve the equation $\frac{x}{24} = -6$, the goal is to isolate x, or have x alone on one side of the equal sign. To isolate x, each side of the equal sign should be multiplied by 24. $\frac{x}{24} = -6$ can be simplified to $24 \cdot \frac{x}{24} = -6 \cdot 24$, which is further simplified to $x = -144$.

11. C: To answer this question correctly, convert all numbers to decimal form to make them easy to compare. Since two of the numbers are already in decimal form, we only need to convert $1\frac{7}{10}$ and $1\frac{3}{4}$ to decimal form.

$$7 \div 10 = 0.7, \text{ so } 1\frac{7}{10} = 1.7$$
$$\text{and } 3 \div 4 = 0.75, \text{ so } 1\frac{3}{4} = 1.75$$

Therefore, by comparing place values from left to right of 1.7, 1.72, 1.75 and 1.695, we see that 1.695 is least, 1.7 is next greatest, 1.72 is next, and 1.75 is greatest. So, Antonio should buy the border that is $1\frac{3}{4}$ inches wide.

12. C: This problem involves finding equivalent fractions, decimals, and percentages. To solve this problem, each value in the list should be compared to identify if they are equivalent. 20% is equivalent to 0.2, but is not equivalent to $\frac{1}{20}$, which is equivalent to 5%. 15% is equivalent to $\frac{15}{100}$, but is not equivalent to 1.5, which is equivalent to 150%. $\frac{7}{20}$ is equivalent to $\frac{35}{100}$ which is equivalent to 35% and 0.35. 10% is equivalent to $\frac{1}{10}$ and 0.1, but it is not equivalent to 0.01.

13. B: The first step in solving $-2 - 3x = -14$ is to add 2 to both sides. This results in $-3x = -12$. Dividing both sides by -3 yields $x = 4$. Therefore, choice B is correct.

14. C: Subtracting 320 from both sides yields $-12m = -240$. Dividing both sides by -12 yields $m = 20$. Therefore, choice C is correct.

15. C: This problem focuses on testing equations with a known value in order to identify a variable. In this case, $x = -4$, so −4 will replace each x value to see if −4 is a solution. First, $25 \neq 5 \cdot -4$ because $5 \cdot -4 = -20$. Next, $-4 - 36 \neq 32$ because $-4 - 36 = -40$. Next, $\frac{68}{-4} = -17$ because $68 \div -4 = -17$. Last, $17 - (-4) \neq 13$ because $17 - (-4) = 17 + 4 = 21$.

16. B: The proportion can be written as $\frac{4}{2} = \frac{x}{18}$. Solving for x gives $x = 36$. Thus, there are 36 data analysis problems on the test.

17. C: This problem focuses on scale factors. According to the table, the population of cicadas increased each year. From year 1 to year 2, the population increased from 4 to 12 million. The population increased by a factor of 3 because $4 \cdot 3 = 12$. From year 2 to year 3, the population increased from 12 to 36 million; $12 \cdot 3 = 36$. From year 3 to year 4, $36 \cdot 3 = 108$. From year 4 to year 5, $108 \cdot 3 = 324$. Each year the population increases by a scale factor of 3.

18. B: The absolute value of −5 is 5 because the absolute value represents a number's distance from zero on a number line. The reciprocal of −5 is $-\frac{1}{5}$. The absolute value of 5 is 5. The opposite of −5 is also 5.

19. C: The score that has approximately 50% above and 50% below is approximately 500 (517 to be exact). The scores can be manually written by choosing either the lower or upper end of each interval and using the frequency to determine the number of times to record each score, i.e., using the lower end of each interval shows an approximate value of 465 for the median; using the upper end of each interval shows an approximate value of 530 for the median. A score of 500 (and the exact median of 517) is found between 465 and 530.

20. B: In order to determine the number of manuscripts each editor will review, the total number of manuscripts should be divided by the number of editors; $29 \div 8$ can be written as $\frac{29}{8}$, which simplifies to the mixed fraction $3\frac{5}{8}$. Notice that the quotient is 3 with a remainder of 5.

21. D: The order of operations requires evaluation of the expression inside the parentheses as a first step. Thus, the expression can be re-written as $-8^2 + 8 \times 4 + 7$. Next, the integer with the exponent must be evaluated. Doing so gives $-64 + 8 \times 4 + 7$. The order of operations next requires all multiplications and divisions to be computed as they appear from left to right. Thus, the expression can be written as $-64 + 32 + 7$. Finally, the addition may be computed as it appears from left to right. The expression simplifies to $-32 + 7$, or -25.

22. A: When setting up a proportion, it's important to remember that like quantities must be placed in the numerators, and like quantities must be placed in the denominators. The general idea for a problem like this is $\frac{\text{feet}}{\text{miles}} = \frac{\text{feet}}{\text{miles}}$. The correct proportion is $\frac{5,280}{1} = \frac{26,400}{x}$. Therefore, choice A is correct.

23. C: In the story, Allison is making lemonade and uses a ratio of 3 cups of sugar to every 2 gallons of water, or $3 : 2$. A lemonade with the same sweetness would have a ratio that is equivalent to $3 : 2$. One way to solve this problem is to find equivalent ratios using multiplication. $3 : 2$ is equivalent to $6 : 4, 9 : 6, 12 : 8, 15 : 10, 18 : 12, 21 : 14, 24 : 16$, and so on. $12 : 8$ is equivalent to $3 : 2$.

24. A: Multiply 24 by 4 to get 96 and multiply 12 by 6 to get 72. Then, add 96 and 72 to get the correct answer, 168.

25. A: In order to answer this question, we add the number of baseball and football cards to realize that there are 50 total cards in Castor's collection, 40 of which are baseball cards. To convert this to a decimal, we need to divide 40 by 50. This gives the correct answer, 0.8.

Practice Test #3

Writing

25 Minutes

Instructions: Read the following prompt, taking a few moments to plan a response. Then, write your response in essay form.

<u>Prompt</u>: *A professional athlete should be held to a higher standard in his or her personal life than the average citizen.*

Do you agree or disagree with this statement? Use examples from history, literature, or your own personal experience to support your point of view.

Quantitative

Read each question, perform the appropriate calculations, and determine the correct answer.

1. 148% is equivalent to what fraction?

   a. $\frac{148}{1}$

   b. $\frac{37}{25}$

   c. $\frac{50}{74}$

   d. $\frac{1}{148}$

2. The cost of tickets to a community event is shown in the table below. Which of the following is the unit rate?

Number of tickets	5	10	20	30
Cost ($)	30	60	120	180

   a. $\frac{6}{1}$

   b. $\frac{1}{6}$

   c. $\frac{5}{1}$

   d. $\frac{1}{5}$

3. Enrique used a formula to find the total cost, in dollars, for repairs he and his helper, Jenny, made to a furnace. The expression below shows the formula he used, with 4 being the number of hours he worked on the furnace and 2 being the number of hours Jenny worked on the furnace.

$$20 + 35(4 + 2) + 47$$

What is the total cost for repairing the furnace?

   a. $189

   b. $269

   c. $277

   d. $377

4. Triangle A has side lengths of 12 cm, 8 cm, and 16 cm. Triangle B is related to Triangle A by a scale factor of $\frac{1}{4}$. Which of the following represents the dimensions of Triangle B?

   a. 4 cm, 2 cm, 8 cm

   b. 2 cm, 3 cm, 8 cm

   c. 3 cm, 2 cm, 4 cm

   d. 6 cm, 4 cm, 8 cm

5. Sha is packaging cupcakes in packs of 12. Which expression does NOT express the relationship between packages, p, and cupcakes, c?

   a. $12c = p$

   b. $p = \frac{c}{12}$

   c. $c = 12p$

   d. $\frac{c}{p} = 12$

6. Elaine represents an equation using the algebra tiles shown below

Given that ▭ represents x, □ represents positive 1, and ■ represents negative 1, which of the following represents the solution to the equation?

 a. $x = -6$
 b. $x = 4$
 c. $x = 12$
 d. $x = -4$

7. Petra installed 10 light fixtures at a new warehouse that was being built. Each of the fixtures required 3 light bulbs. The bulbs come in packages of 5 and cost $8 per package. What was the total cost for the bulbs required for all of the fixtures Petra installed at the warehouse?

 a. $16
 b. $48
 c. $120
 d. $240

8. A unit of liquid measure in the English System of Measure is the gill. The table, shown here, gives conversions from gills to fluid ounces.

Conversion Table

Gills	Fluid Ounces
2	8
4	16
5	20
6	24
10	40

Which equation best describes the relationship between gills, g, and fluid ounces, f?

 a. $f = 8g - 8$
 b. $f = 2g + 4$
 c. $f = 4g$
 d. $4f = g$

9. Two rectangles are similar. The length and the width of the first rectangle is 3 meters by 6 meters. The second rectangle is similar by a scale factor of $\frac{1}{2}$. What are length and width of the second rectangle?

 a. 1.5 meters by 3 meters
 b. 3.5 meters by 6.5 meters
 c. 6 meters by 12 meters
 d. 1 meter by 2.5 meters

10. Which of the following is the correct representation for the solution of $x + 2 = 5$?

a.

-4 -3 -2 -1 0 1 2 3 4

b.

-4 -3 -2 -1 0 1 2 3 4

c.

-4 -3 -2 -1 0 1 2 3 4

d.

-4 -3 -2 -1 0 1 2 3 4

11. Tommy is 4 years older than Gianna. Which equation represents the relationship between Tommy's age, t, and Gianna's age, g?

a. $4 + t = g$
b. $t = 4 + g$
c. $4 - t = g$
d. $g - t = 4$

12. Charlie wrote a story to match the graph below.

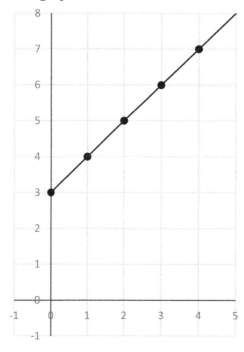

Which story below could be the story that Charlie wrote?

a. Damien is 3 years older than Jackson.
b. Damien sold 3 times as many candy bars as Jackson.
c. Damien didn't make any money for 3 weeks and then made 1 dollar each week.
d. Damien read 3 pages each day for 4 days.

246

13. In Δ*RST*, shown here, *m∠S* is 20° less than *m∠R*.

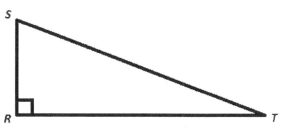

What is the measure of ∠*T*?
 a. 110°
 b. 70°
 c. 50°
 d. 20°

14. The dot plot shows the number of sandwiches sold each day by a sandwich shop.

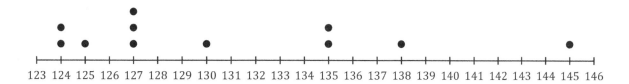

Which statement is best supported by the data?
 a. The sandwich shop sold 135 sandwiches more often than they sold 124 sandwiches.
 b. The sandwich shop sold more than 129 sandwiches on 5 days.
 c. The sandwich shop sold sandwiches for only 10 days.
 d. The sandwich shop sold fewer than 130 sandwiches exactly half of the time.

15. Kimi is saving to buy a pair of earbuds that cost $195. She makes money mowing lawns and earns $10 for each lawn she mows. Which inequality illustrates how many lawns, *x*, Kimi needs to mow to make at least $195?
 a. $195 < 10x$
 b. $195 > 10x$
 c. $195 \leq 10x$
 d. $195 \geq 10x$

16. A grocery store received a delivery of 250 apples. 14 apples from the delivery were rotten and could not be sold. Which equation could NOT be used to find the number of apples, *a*, that could be sold?
 a. $a - 14 = 250$
 b. $14 = 250 - a$
 c. $a = 250 - 14$
 d. $a + 14 = 250$

17. Four points are graphed on a coordinate plane.

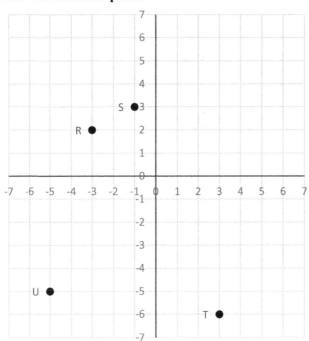

What ordered pair best represents point T?

    a. $(-3, 6)$
    b. $(6, -3)$
    c. $(-6, 3)$
    d. $(3, -6)$

18. A social media company creates 75 posts per hour. Which graph represents the relationship between the number of posts, y, and hours worked, x?

a.

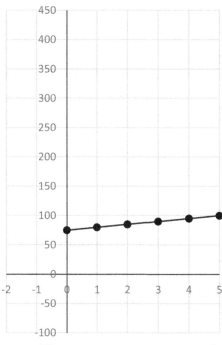

c.

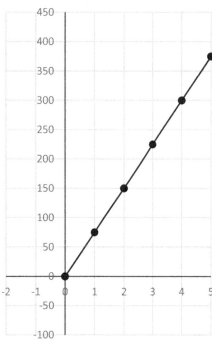

b.

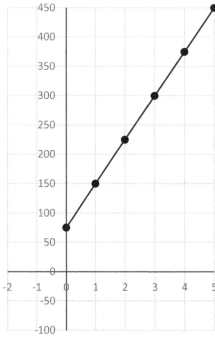

d.

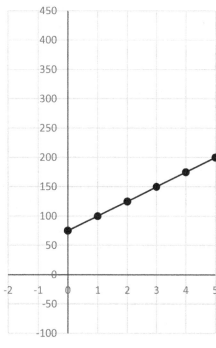

19. Which of the following options makes this inequality a true statement?

$$30b < 372$$

    a. $b = 30$
    b. $b = 22$
    c. $b = 14$
    d. $b = 12$

20. A round trip airline ticket costs \$406. The airline Aidan is using charges \$35 per checked bag. Which of the following equations represents the total cost for the ticket and checked bag(s)?

    a. $y = 35 + 406x$

    b. $y = 441x$

    c. $y = \dfrac{406}{35}x$

    d. $y = 406 + 35x$

21. Amanda has finished 80% of a grant proposal. Which of the following fractions represents the amount she has finished?

    a. $\dfrac{3}{4}$

    b. $\dfrac{7}{9}$

    c. $\dfrac{4}{5}$

    d. $\dfrac{6}{7}$

22. If 1 mile = 5,280 feet, which of the following proportions can be used to determine the number of miles equal to 26,400 feet?

    a. $\dfrac{5,280}{1} = \dfrac{26,400}{x}$

    b. $\dfrac{5,280}{1} = \dfrac{x}{26,400}$

    c. $\dfrac{5,280}{x} = \dfrac{26,400}{1}$

    d. $\dfrac{5,280}{26,400} = \dfrac{x}{1}$

23. Robert secures three new clients every eight months. After how many months has he secured 24 new clients?

    a.   64

    b.   58

    c.   52

    d.   66

24. Tanya is painting the kitchen wall and has chosen a paint mixture that has a ratio of 3 ounces of green paint to 8 ounces of white paint. To complete Tanya's paint order, how many ounces of green paint are in a container that has 192 ounces of white paint?

    a.   52

    b.   64

    c.   24

    d.   72

25. Which of the following statements is true regarding the circumference (C) and the diameter (d) of a circle?

    a. $\pi = C + d$

    b. $\pi = Cd$

    c. $\pi = \dfrac{C}{d}$

    d. $\pi = \dfrac{d}{C}$

Reading Comprehension

Read each passage closely and answer the associated questions. Be sure to choose the answer that BEST answers the question being asked.

Questions 1-4 refer to the following passage:

Protozoa are microscopic, one-celled organisms that can be free-living or parasitic in nature. They are able to multiply in humans, a factor which contributes to their survival and also permits serious infections to develop from just a single organism. Transmission of protozoa that live in the human intestine to another human typically occurs by a fecal-oral route (for example, contaminated food or water, or person-to-person contact). Protozoa that thrive in the blood or tissue of humans are transmitted to their human hosts by an arthropod vector (for example, through the bite of a mosquito or sand fly).

Helminths are large, multicellular organisms that are generally visible to the naked eye in their adult stages. Like protozoa, helminths can be either free-living or parasitic in nature. In their adult form, helminths cannot multiply in humans. There are three main groups of helminths (derived from the Greek word for worms) that are human parasites:

1. Flatworms (platyhelminths) – these include the trematodes (flukes) and cestodes (tapeworms).
2. Thorny-headed worms (acanthocephalins) – the adult forms of these worms reside in the gastrointestinal tract. The acanthocephala are thought to be intermediate between the cestodes and nematodes.
3. Roundworms (nematodes) – the adult forms of these worms can reside in the gastrointestinal tract, blood, lymphatic system or subcutaneous tissues. Alternatively, the immature (larval) states can cause disease through their infection of various body tissues.

1. As used in this passage, the word "parasite" means

a. a person who lives in Paris
b. an organism that live on or in another organism
c. microscopic insects
d. a person who takes advantage of the generosity of others

2. According to the passage, adult Roundworms can live in

a. the arthropod vector
b. fecal matter
c. the subcutaneous tissue of humans
d. contaminated water

3. You can infer from this passage that

a. larval stages of parasites are more dangerous than the adult forms
b. mosquitoes do not transmit parasites
c. worms cannot infect humans
d. clean sanitary conditions will keep you free of protozoa

4. According to the passage, which of the following is true?

I. Protozoa live in the blood or tissue of humans.
II. Adult helminthes cannot reproduce in humans.
III. Adult thorny-headed worms live in the intestinal tract.

a. I only
b. II only
c. I and II only
d. I, II, and III

Questions 5-9 refer to the following passage:

What do you think is the biggest American holiday? The most significant and uniquely American holiday would have to be the Fourth of July, the day when the United States celebrates its independence from Britain. You might think that the Fourth of July became a holiday immediately after the signing of the Declaration of Independence on July 4, 1776, but actually it didn't become a tradition until after the War of 1812.

By the 1870s, the Fourth of July was the most important nonreligious holiday on the calendar. All across the country, on that day, towns and cities held celebrations with parades, barbecues, and fireworks displays.

Back in the 1870s, the Fourth of July was "the big event of the year," according to Nettie Spencer, a pioneer from Portland, Oregon. The holiday included a parade with floats, a band, and a speaker. "First, the speaker would challenge England to a fight and berate the King and say that he was a skunk. In the afternoon, we had what we called the 'plug uglies'--funny floats and clowns who took off on the political subjects of the day," said Spencer. At that time, the Fourth of July made people think about what it meant to be independent from Britain.

More than 200 years have passed since the signing of the Declaration of Independence, and our independence from Britain is sometimes taken for granted.

Today, the Fourth of July holiday is still a popular day for celebrations with family and friends. The holiday's importance has inspired the creation of everything from the lyrics to "Yankee Doodle Dandy" ("I'm a Yankee Doodle Dandy ...born on the Fourth of July...") to movies like *Independence Day*. America's independence has always been an important concept of our country, and Americans will protect it from I any and all challenges facing it.

5. The author wrote this passage to

a. tell about the Declaration of Independence
b. encourage the reader to watch movies about America's independence
c. give the reader the history of an American holiday
d. explain why America's independence from Britain is taken for granted

6. This passage is primarily about

a. the most important nonreligious holiday in America
b. how the Fourth of July did not become a tradition until after the War of 1812
c. how Americans will always protect their independence
d. how the Fourth of July no longer makes people think about independence from Britain

7. According to the passage, when did Americans first begin celebrating the Fourth of July?

a. Immediately after signing the Declaration of Independence
b. After the War of 1812
c. In the 1870s
d. Two hundred years after the Declaration of Independence was signed

8. The word "berate" in the third passage can best be replaced with

a. compliment
b. praise
c. inform
d. scold

9. The tone of this passage can best be described as

a. confused
b. neutral
c. admiring
d. condescending

Questions 10-13 refer to the following passage:

Nutria (Myocastor coypu) are large rodents that look like beavers with long, thin tails. Nutria may weigh up to 20 lbs. but on average weigh between 12-15 lbs. with males slightly larger than females. They have dense, grayish under-fur overlaid by long, glossy guard hairs that vary in color from dark brown to yellowish brown. Their large front teeth are yellow-orange to orange-red on the outer surface. The forepaws have four well-developed clawed toes and one non-functional toe. The hind feet have five clawed toes: four webbed and one that hangs free. Nutria have several other adaptations to help them in the water. Their eyes, ears and nostrils are set high on their heads. The nostrils and mouth have valves that seal out water while swimming, diving or feeding underwater. The female's teats are located high on her sides to allow the young to suckle while in the water. Nutria are primarily nocturnal (active at night), with peak activity occurring near midnight. When food is abundant, nutria rest and groom during the day and feed at night. When food is limited, daytime feeding increases, especially in wetlands free from disturbance.

Nutria inhabit fresh and brackish marshes, rivers, bayous, farm ponds, freshwater impoundments, drainage canals, swamps and various other types of wetlands. Although found in sixteen US states, nutria are native to South America. Their original range includes Argentina, Chile, Bolivia, Uruguay, Paraguay and southern Brazil. After escaping from captivity in the US and elsewhere, they now inhabit a much greater area. Nutria were first imported into the United States between 1899 and 1930 in an attempt to establish a fur farm industry. Many of the fur farms failed in the late 1940s because fur prices fell and nutria did not reproduce well in captivity. Many nutria were released into the wild. Nutria are now reported in every Maryland Eastern Shore county and are found from Bombay Hook National Wildlife Refuge in Delaware through the Delmarva Peninsula to Virginia's Eastern Shore. They have also been reported on the western shore of Maryland in the Potomac and Patuxent Rivers and in Virginia as far south as the Northern Neck near the Rappahanock River.

Nutria are highly prolific and breed all year. Reproductive peaks occur in late winter, early summer, and mid-autumn. Reproduction and survival may be influenced by extreme weather conditions. Nutria reach sexual maturity at four to six months. Sexually mature male nutria can breed throughout the year. Females are pregnant from 128 to 130 days and are ready to breed within forty-eight hours after giving birth. Litters average four to five young; however, nutria can have up to thirteen young per litter and may have three litters per year. Young are born

253

fully furred and active, weighing 8 oz. at birth. They can swim and eat vegetation shortly thereafter, still feeding on mother's milk for up to eight weeks. Within five days of life, nutria can survive away from the mother.

10. Where would you most likely find this passage?

    a. In a tourist guidebook
    b. In a history textbook
    c. In an online encyclopedia
    d. In a comic book

11. It can be inferred from the passage that nutrias' eyes, ears, and nostrils are set high on their heads

    a. so they can see their young while they are in the water
    b. to prevent water from getting in them while they are swimming
    c. so that they can eat at night
    d. so that they are balanced with the rest of their body

12. According to the passage, how long does it take for nutria to reach sexual maturity?

    a. 4 to 6 months
    b. 128 to 130 days
    c. 48 hours
    d. 8 weeks

13. The author states that fur farms failed in the 1940s because

    a. nutria were released into the wild
    b. of limited amounts of food for the nutria
    c. nutria are highly prolific
    d. nutria did not reproduce well in captivity

Questions 14-18 refer to the following passage:

Born Ehrich Weiss, Harry Houdini was a master of illusion. Houdini earned an international reputation as an escape artist who dramatically freed himself from ropes, shackles, and handcuffs. He was married to Wilhelmina Rahner, who, as Beatrice Houdini, was his stage assistant. He performed on vaudeville and was also in many motion pictures.

In 1899, when Houdini decided to stop doing traditional magic and instead concentrate on escapes, his career took off. He created several dramatic escape tricks. In 1908, in St. Louis, Houdini introduced his escape from a giant milk can filled with water. It became a very popular trick and he took it on tour throughout the US, England, and Germany. What kind of escape could top this?

For his next escape, Houdini had to come up with something even more dramatic than the Giant Milk Can Escape, and he did. His new trick, which he began to perform in 1913, was known as the Upside Down Water Torture Cell. In this trick, Houdini's ankles were secured in a brace and he was put under water, upside down, and locked in place in full view of the audience. From this position, he freed himself and escaped from the water cell. Another escape was called the underwater burial. Houdini called this "the greatest feat I have ever attempted."

Some magicians might make a rabbit jump out of a hat or a bird disappear into thin air, but that was too easy for Houdini. He had to work with an elephant! In 1918, in the middle of the brightly lit stage of the Hippodrome Theater in New York City, Houdini made a 10,000-pound elephant named Jennie disappear. The act was called "The Vanishing Elephant," and when

Houdini fired a pistol, Jennie vanished from view. Houdini had created a sensation. This incredible trick helped make Houdini a world-famous master of illusion.

14. The best title for this passage is

    a. Hippodrome Theater

    b. The Giant Milk Can Escape

    c. The Master of Illusion

    d. Rabbit in the Hat

15. The author wrote this passage to

    a. inform the reader

    b. entertain the reader

    c. persuade the reader

    d. humor the reader

16. Who was Beatrice Houdini?

    a. A 10,000 pound elephant

    b. Houdini's mother

    c. The owner of Houdini's vaudeville show

    d. Wilhelmina Rahner, Houdini's wife

17. According to the passage, what was Houdini's most sensational act?

    a. The Giant Milk Can Escape

    b. The Upside Down Water Torture Cell

    c. The Vanishing Elephant

    d. Escape from Handcuffs

18. Which word best replaces the word "feat" in the fourth paragraph without changing the meaning?

    a. exploit

    b. failure

    c. discovery

    d. surrender

Questions 19-22 refer to the following passage:

Volcanoes destroy and volcanoes create. The catastrophic eruption of Mount St. Helens on May 18, 1980, made clear the awesome destructive power of a volcano. Yet, over a time span longer than human memory and record, volcanoes have played a key role in forming and modifying the planet upon which we live. More than 80 percent of the earth's surface--above and below sea level--is of volcanic origin. Gaseous emissions from volcanic vents, scoring and shaping the earth over hundreds of millions of years, formed the earth's earliest oceans and atmosphere, and supplied the ingredients vital to generate and sustain life. Over geologic eons, countless volcanic eruptions have produced mountains, plateaus, and plains, which subsequent erosion and weathering have sculpted into majestic landscapes and fertile soils.

Ironically, these volcanic soils and inviting terrains have attracted people, and continue to attract people, to an existence on the flanks of volcanoes. Thus, as population density increases in regions of active or potentially active volcanoes, mankind must become increasingly aware of the hazards and learn not to "crowd" the volcanoes. People living in the shadow of volcanoes must live in harmony with them, expecting and planning for periodic violent unleashings of their pent-up energy.

19. According to the passage, how were the earth's early oceans and atmosphere formed?

a. By gaseous emissions from volcanic vents
b. Through erosion and weathering
c. By volcanic eruptions
d. By hurricanes

20. According to the context of the passage, "crowd" means

a. a group of people gathered in one spot
b. to press or throng into a space
c. a group of people with something in common
d. the common people

21. This passage would most likely be found in

a. an almanac
b. a science textbook
c. a social studies textbook
d. a novel

22. How does erosion and weathering affect the earth's surface?

a. They create mountains and plateaus
b. They create volcanic emissions
c. They destroy the landscape
d. They help to form fertile soils

Questions 23-27 refer to the following passage:

Jazz singer Billie Holiday, later nicknamed "Lady Day," was born on April 7, 1915, in Baltimore, Maryland. In her autobiography, "Lady Sings the Blues," Holiday says, "Mom and Pop were just a couple of kids when they got married; he was 18, she was 16, and I was three." Despite a challenging childhood and no formal musical training, Billie Holiday made her professional singing debut in Harlem nightclubs in 1931. By 1933, she had made her first recordings. Do you think her parents really named her "Billie?"

Born Eleanora Fagan, she gave herself the stage name Billie after Billie Dove, an early movie star. While becoming a star, Holiday faced racism. Laws at that time created separate facilities, public spaces, and seats on public buses for black people and, in the private sector, there were restaurants that would serve only white people. As a result, Holiday sometimes found herself singing in clubs that refused service to black people. Her 1939 version of "Strange Fruit," a song about lynching, was described in the album's liner notes as the most haunting and sad "expression of protest against man's inhumanity to man that has ever been made in the form of vocal jazz."

Billie Holiday worked with many jazz greats including Count Basie and Benny Goodman. She sang in small clubs, large concert halls, and in the film *New Orleans*. She even arranged and composed her own songs such as "I Love My Man" and "God Bless the Child." Many people mourned the loss of "Lady Day" when she died in New York at the age of 44.

23. The best title for this passage is

a. Mom and Pop
b. Harlem
c. Lady Day Sings the Blues
d. Jazz in the 1930s

24. According to the passage, which of the following is true?

   I. Billie Holiday had no formal musical training.
   II. Billie Holiday's parents were very young when they got married.
   III. Billie Holiday sang in clubs that refused service to white people.

   a. I only
   b. II only
   c. I and II only
   d. I, II, and III

25. It can be inferred from the passage that Holiday

   a. felt strongly about racism
   b. despised her given name, Eleanora Fagan
   c. preferred singing in large concert halls
   d. died of a heart attack

26. The author wrote this passage to

   a. tell a story
   b. make the reader laugh
   c. describe the life of a famous singer
   d. convince the reader to buy a Billie Holiday CD

27. When did Billie Holiday make her professional singing debut in Harlem?

   a. 1915
   b. 1931
   c. 1933
   d. 1939

Questions 28-31 refer to the following passage:

When you think of a web, you probably don't think of earthworms, do you? What comes to mind? A spider web? The World Wide Web? How about a duck's webbed feet? Well, there's another kind of web you might not know about. It's the soil food web.

The soil food web is the set of organisms that work underground to help plants grow. There are billions of organisms that make up the soil food web. These include bacteria, fungi, protozoa, nematodes, arthropods and earthworms. Each type of organism plays an important role in keeping the soil healthy for all living things.

Earthworms eat just about every other organism in the soil. They're miniature topsoil factories—all the soil you have ever seen has passed through the stomachs of lots of earthworms. When they eat, they leave behind "castings," which are high in organic matter and plant nutrients and are a valuable fertilizer.

Earthworms move through the soil creating tunnels—areas that can be filled by air and water. Fields that are "tilled" by earthworm tunneling can absorb water at a rate 4 to 10 times that of fields without worm tunnels. This reduces water runoff, restores groundwater, and helps store more water for dry spells.

This burrowing also helps nutrients enter the subsoil at a faster rate and opens up pathways for roots to grow into. During droughts, the tunnels allow plant roots to penetrate more deeply, enabling them to reach the water they need to thrive.

Earthworms help keep soil healthy by moving organic matter from the surface into the soil. Normally, a tree leaf may take three to five years to decompose and be incorporated into the soil. In forests infested with night crawlers, this process can take as little as four weeks! By speeding up the breakdown of plant material, earthworms also speed up the rate at which nutrients are recycled back to the plants.

Earthworms and other soil organisms are a necessary part of the soil food web. Without them, all the organic matter would build up on the soil surface and never get down into the soil. To grow healthy, productive plants, you need healthy, productive soil. Organisms in the soil provide the food for plants—when they need it and in a form they can use!

28. The tone of this passage can be described as

a. confused
b. neutral
c. mournful
d. positive

29. Which of the following are part of the soil food web?

   I. bacteria
   II. protozoa
   III. nematodes

a. I only
b. II only
c. I and II only
d. I, II, and III

30. According to the context of the passage, "tilled" means

a. plowed
b. hardened
c. moistened
d. destroyed

31. What benefits do earthworms provide by burrowing in the soil?

a. They provide valuable fertilizer
b. They open pathways for roots to grow in
c. They slow the decomposition rate
d. They allow bacteria into the soil

Questions 32-36 refer to the following passage:

The Missouri territory came to the United States as part of the 1803 Louisiana Purchase, one of the best real estate deals the United States ever made. Before Missouri became the 24th state on August 10, 1821, certain compromises had to be made to keep a balance in the Union between the slave and non-slave states. Those compromises would later turn neighbor against neighbor.

Under the Missouri Compromise of 1820, designed by statesman Henry Clay, Missouri entered the Union as a slave state, and Maine entered as a free state, thus keeping the number of slave and non-slave states equal at 12 each.

John F. Smith recalled in an interview an incident when Jayhawkers, a group opposed to slavery, came to his house in 1861. One of the Jayhawkers threatened to shoot his father, a Missouri slave owner. "... (then) we heard a shout and looked up the road... The man dropped his gun to his side, when Judge Myers rode up, he was shaking his head and his eyes were blazing fire...All the Jayhawkers turned around and sulked off like whipped dogs."

The Civil War continued to divide Missourians. Although the state remained with the Union, some of its citizens chose to fight for the Confederacy. Smith's father and his rescuer, Judge Myers, remained best friends despite their conflicting views on slavery, but the two ended up fighting on opposite sides of the war.

32. This passage would most likely be found in a(n)

a. World history textbook
b. American history textbook
c. Ancient history textbook
d. Art history textbook

33. According to the passage, how did the Missouri Territory become part of the United States?

a. Through the Missouri Compromise
b. Through the defeat of the Confederacy
c. Through the Louisiana Purchase
d. As a result of a Jayhawkers revolt

34. What can you infer from the statement "Those compromises would later turn neighbor against neighbor" at the end of the first paragraph?

a. All Missourians wanted a free state
b. All Missourians wanted a slave state
c. Missourians disagreed on the issue of slave ownership
d. Neighbors were arguing over property lines

35. According to the passage, Jayhawkers were

a. part of the Ku Klux Klan
b. a slavery opposition group
c. Confederate soldiers
d. judges

36. What is the author most likely to discuss next?

a. Missouri's role in the Civil War
b. Different judges' rulings on slavery
c. The biography of Henry Clay
d. The history of the Jayhawkers

Questions 37-40 refer to the following passage:

Corals in the deep sea? When asked to describe corals, most people think of those that make up tropical, shallow-water reefs like the Great Barrier Reef. However, there are corals that live in much deeper, colder waters where there is no sunlight. Over the past 8 years, my colleagues and I have been studying these deep-sea corals in North Atlantic waters deeper than 1,000 meters.

Between 2003-2005, we visited a previously unexplored group of extinct underwater volcanoes in the western North Atlantic—the New England Seamounts and Corner Rise Seamounts—looking for deep-sea coral communities living between 1,000 and 2,500 meters. Our explorations revealed some spectacular assemblages of bamboo corals, bubblegum corals, black corals, and a variety of other sea fan and sea whip species.

Living amidst the corals were a myriad of animals, including shrimp, crabs, snake stars, sea stars, feather stars, scale worms and many species of deep-sea fish. Most of the species we found were new to science, while others (or their close relatives) were known only from the eastern North Atlantic and were being observed in the western Atlantic for the first time.

As a follow-up to those discoveries, we planned this expedition to explore the deep slopes of the northern Bahamas. In the western North Atlantic, a major deep-sea current flows from north to south along the slope of the continental USA, but as it approaches the tropics, it encounters deep, cold water flowing northward from Antarctica. Our goal is to determine if the coral species, and their associated fauna, living in the subtropical Bahamas are the same as those on the seamounts to the north, or will we begin to see a different group of species reflecting a southern influence?

37. The best title for this passage is
   a. Underwater Volcanoes
   b. The Western North Atlantic
   c. Bubblegum Coral
   d. Coral Reefs in the Deep Sea

38. Deep sea coral reefs are unique because
   a. they are less than 1,000 meters deep
   b. they survive where there is no sunlight
   c. they are found in tropical waters
   d. they are composed of shallow water reefs

39. This passage was written in
   a. first person
   b. second person
   c. third person
   d. fourth person

40. What is the goal of the next expedition?
   a. To reach deep-sea communities at 2,500 meters
   b. To visit an unexplored group of extinct underwater volcanoes
   c. To determine if the corals living in the Bahamas are the same as those on the seamounts to the north
   d. To discover crabs, snake stars, sea stars, feather stars, and scale worms

Verbal

30 minutes, 60 questions

For questions 1-30: Select the synonym. Each question has a word in all capital letters followed by five answer choices in all lower-case letters. Select the answer choice with a definition closest to the capitalized word.

1. ENTHRALL:

    a. extreme
    b. fascinate
    c. devote
    d. bizarre

2. COWARD:

    a. gutless
    b. boor
    c. judge
    d. brave

3. NOVICE:

    a. expert
    b. nurse
    c. beginner
    d. naught

4. TEMPERATE:

    a. extreme
    b. lenient
    c. taut
    d. moderate

5. AUTHENTIC:

    a. genuine
    b. colorful
    c. flimsy
    d. laughable

6. SALVAGE:

    a. bless
    b. slobber
    c. swagger
    d. recover

7. VERNACULAR:

    a. poison
    b. language
    c. veracity
    d. ballad

8. ATTEST:
- a. bewitch
- b. accommodate
- c. vouch
- d. heed

9. DERELICT:
- a. abandoned
- b. corrupted
- c. dispirited
- d. depressed

10. ORDAIN:
- a. arrange
- b. create
- c. command
- d. adorn

11. HAUGHTY:
- a. obscure
- b. arrogant
- c. perilous
- d. bitter

12. LAPSE:
- a. prank
- b. margin
- c. error
- d. award

13. NAUSEATE:
- a. rival
- b. crave
- c. annoy
- d. repulse

14. PALTRY:
- a. cheap
- b. peaceful
- c. severely
- d. lurid

15. REFINED:
- a. aromatic
- b. blatant
- c. cultured
- d. frightened

16. VIRTUAL:

   a. real
   b. visible
   c. potent
   d. simulated

17. LOATHE:

   a. fear
   b. hate
   c. exist
   d. charge

18. MIMIC:

   a. recall
   b. delve
   c. imitate
   d. curtail

19. BRITTLE:

   a. fragile
   b. radical
   c. broad
   d. smooth

20. WRETCHED:

   a. wicked
   b. awry
   c. absorbed
   d. miserable

21. VEHEMENT:

   a. troubled
   b. intense
   c. changeable
   d. obstinate

22. DIATRIBE:

   a. criticism
   b. apology
   c. commend
   d. merit

23. COGITATE:

   a. surprise
   b. endanger
   c. confuse
   d. deliberate

24. INVIDIOUS:

    a. offensive
    b. pleasant
    c. ornate
    d. infectious

25. HYPERBOLE:

    a. reference
    b. amendment
    c. exaggeration
    d. demarcation

26. INNOCUOUS:

    a. harmful
    b. innocent
    c. scandalous
    d. hidden

27. CAPRICIOUS:

    a. steady
    b. unpredictable
    c. pleasant
    d. violent

28. INTERMITTENT:

    a. occasional
    b. intense
    c. frequent
    d. bursts

29. SOLITARY:

    a. single
    b. solid
    c. sturdy
    d. stoic

30. PRECIPITOUS:

    a. rugged
    b. dangerous
    c. steep
    d. wet

For questions 31-60: These questions ask you to identify and compare relationships between pairs of words. Select the answer that best completes the comparison.

31. surgeon is to operating room as

    a. chiropractor is to doctor
    b. novelist is to panel
    c. conductor is to symphony hall
    d. truck driver is to rest stop

32. opinionated is to indecisive as

a. diffident is to shy
b. frugal is to spendthrift
c. conspicuous is to obvious
d. thoughtful is to thought-provoking

33. pleased is to overjoyed as

a. dirty is to squalid
b. thrilled is to happy
c. determined is to decided
d. perceptive is to unaware

34. punitive is to punishment as

a. spatial is to measurement
b. exhausted is to sleep
c. perplexed is to answer
d. complimentary is to praise

35. considerable is to extensive as

a. enormous is to vacant
b. diminutive is to microscopic
c. outlandish is to undistinguished
d. descriptive is to straightforward

36. insipid is to boredom as

a. tasty is to craving
b. gratuitous is to freedom
c. morose is to rebellion
d. jovial is to optimistic

37. sedentary is to sit as

a. descry is to lampoon
b. espoused is to belief
c. perseverance is to endurance
d. peripatetic is to wander

38. querulous is to amiable as

a. sequential is to serial
b. ponderous is to insubstantial
c. illicit is to forbidden
d. pugnacious is to truculent

39. abstemious is to restraint as

a. discerning is to awareness
b. servile is to aggression
c. avowal is to affirm
d. exhilarate is to enlivened

40. Motorcycle is to bicycle as speedboat is to:

a. Motor
b. Paddleboat
c. Float
d. Transportation

41. Apple is to seed as person is to

a. Parent
b. Embryo
c. Nourishment
d. Cell

42. Fraction is to whole as slice is to

a. Pie
b. Cut
c. Part
d. Element

43. Temperature is to heat as pound is to

a. Weight
b. Height
c. Measurement
d. Heavy

44. Bank is to savings as safe is to

a. Valuables
b. Combination
c. Crack
d. Vault

45. Island is to sea as star is to

a. Light
b. Night
c. Celestial
d. Space

46. Inattention is to accidents as practice is to

a. Improvement
b. Performance
c. Discipline
d. Repetition

47. Sight is to sense as gravity is to

a. Weight
b. Pounds
c. Distance
d. Force

48. Dexterity is to skill as English is to

- a. Language
- b. Literature
- c. Japanese
- d. Linguistics

49. Coach is to team as teacher is to

- a. Knowledge
- b. School
- c. Students
- d. Principal

50. Article is to magazine as chapter is to

- a. Verse
- b. Book
- c. Number
- d. Paragraph

51. House is to neighborhood as tree is to

- a. leaf
- b. timber
- c. forest
- d. limb

52. Wallet is to money as envelope is to

- a. mail
- b. letter
- c. address
- d. post office

53. German shepherd is to dog as strawberry is to

- a. red
- b. vine
- c. seeds
- d. fruit

54. Joyful is to sad as empty is to

- a. bare
- b. crowded
- c. productive
- d. vacant

55. Automobile is to garage as dish is to

- a. plate
- b. food
- c. cupboard
- d. spoon

56. Doctor is to medicine as teacher is to

  a. student
  b. teaching
  c. education
  d. school

57. Chirp is to tweet as jump is to

  a. leap
  b. rope
  c. high
  d. street

58. Sleeping is to tired as drinking is to

  a. glass
  b. thirsty
  c. swallow
  d. water

59. Four-leaf clover is to luck as arrow is to

  a. bow
  b. Cupid
  c. shoot
  d. direction

60. Question is to answer as problem is to

  a. mathematics
  b. solution
  c. worry
  d. trouble

Quantitative

Read each question, perform the appropriate calculations, and determine the correct answer.

1. André drew a data table that represents the relationship between x and y where $y = 3x$. Which table could NOT be the data table that André drew?

a.

x	1	3	5
y	3	6	8

b.

x	2	4	6
y	6	12	18

c.

x	1.5	2	2.5
y	4.5	6	7.5

d.

x	1	10	50
y	3	30	150

2. Simplify the expression.

$$\frac{(-9 + 3)}{2}$$

  a. 6
  b. −6
  c. 3
  d. −3

3. Tavario made 32 t-shirts for his customers and is packaging them in sets of 4. He wants to know how many packages he will have. Which option is NOT a way that Tavario can express this division problem?

  a. $4\overline{)32}$
  b. $\frac{4}{32}$
  c. $32 \div 4$
  d. 32 divided by 4

4. Which equation CANNOT be used to find the area of a square?

  a. $A = s^2$
  b. $A = s \cdot s$
  c. $A = s + s + s + s$
  d. $A = bh$

5. Which of the following expressions is equivalent to $2(a + 3) + 3a + 4$?

   a. $5a + 10$
   b. $5a + 7$
   c. $4a + 10$
   d. $12a$

6. The table shows the rate a babysitter charges for babysitting services.

Hours	Dollars
3	30
5	50
6	60
8	80

Which best represents the dependent variable in the table?

   a. Hours
   b. Dollars
   c. Dollars per hour
   d. $10 per hour

7. What is the measure of angle *A*?

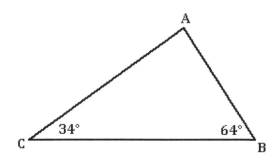

   a. 86°
   b. 82°
   c. 78°
   d. 92°

8. The table shows a relationship between _s_ and _t_, where _s_ is the independent value.

s	t
1	4
2	8
7	28
9	36

Which equation represents the relationship between _s_ and _t_?

   a. $s = t + 4$
   b. $s = 4t$
   c. $t = 4s$
   d. $t = s + 4$

9. Jordan owns a jewelry business and listed the wire options for their customers below using fraction measurements.

$$\frac{1}{8}, \frac{1}{4}, \frac{3}{8}, \frac{1}{2}$$

Which list correctly lists the wire options in decimal form?

   a. 0.12, 0.25, 0.266, 0.5
   b. 1.8, 1.4, 3.8, 1.2
   c. 0.8, 0.4, 0.38, 0.2
   d. 0.125, 0.25, 0.375, 0.5

10. The list below represents a set of data points.

     1, 1, 1, 2, 2, 2, 0, 1, 1, 1, 2, 2, 2, 0, 0, 0, 2, 1, 1, 1

What is the mode of the data set?

   a. 0
   b. 1
   c. 1.5
   d. 2

11. The length of a classroom is 7.3 meters. Which length is equivalent to 7.3 meters?

   a. 0.0073 kilometers
   b. 7,300 centimeters
   c. 0.073 kilometers
   d. 73 millimeters

12. A recipe calls for 5 cups of flour for every 2 cups of sugar. Azah wrote a proportion to find the amount of sugar needed with 8 cups of flour. Which proportion could Azah have written?

   a. $\dfrac{2}{5} = \dfrac{8}{x}$
   b. $\dfrac{2}{8} = \dfrac{x}{5}$
   c. $\dfrac{5}{8} = \dfrac{2}{x}$
   d. $\dfrac{5}{2} = \dfrac{8}{x}$

13. Nadia is working summer jobs. She earns $5 for every dog she walks, $2 for bringing back a trashcan, $1 for checking the mail, and $5 for watering the flowers. Nadia walks 3 dogs, brings back 5 trashcans, checks the mail for 10 neighbors, and waters the flowers at 6 houses. Which expression can be used to find out how much money Nadia earned?

    a. $2(5) +$6(10) + $1
    b. $10(6) + $1 + $5
    c. $5(3+6) + $2(5) + $1(10)
    d. $15 + $10 + $16

14. The dimensions of a trapezoid are given in centimeters.

What is the area of the trapezoid?

    a. 100 cm^2
    b. 60 cm^2
    c. 21.5 cm^2
    d. 22.5 cm^2

15. Jason wants to put dry fertilizer on the grass in his front yard. The yard is 20 feet wide and 45 feet long. Each pound of the fertilizer he plans to use is enough for 150 square feet. Which procedure could Jason use to determine the correct amount of fertilizer to use on the entire yard?

    a. Divide 150 by 20 and divide 150 by 45, and then add those quotients together
    b. Add 20 and 45, double that total, and then divide that total by 150
    c. Multiply 20 by 45, and then subtract 150 from that product
    d. Multiply 20 by 45, and then divide that product by 150

16. Which statement is true about the examples below?

Example 1	Example 2
$2x + 4 - x$	$2x - x = -4$

    a. Example 1 is an equation and Example 2 is an equation.
    b. Example 1 is an expression and Example 2 is an expression.
    c. Example 1 is an expression and Example 2 is an equation.
    d. Example 1 is an equation and Example 2 is an expression.

17. Steven has $50 to buy snacks for his party. He plans to spend $10 on soda and the rest on pizza. If each pizza costs $8, which of the following inequalities represent the number (n) of pizzas Steven can buy?

    a. $50n \geq 8n - 10$
    b. $8n + 10 \leq 50$
    c. $10n - 8 \leq 50$
    d. $8n \leq 50 - 10n$

18. What is the volume of this rectangular prism?

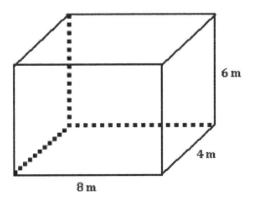

6 m

4 m

8 m

    a.   18 m³

    b.   192 m³

    c.   206 m³

    d.   186 m³

19. Which of the following describes all requirements of similar polygons?

    a.   Similar polygons have congruent corresponding angles and proportional corresponding sides

    b.   Similar polygons have congruent corresponding angles and congruent corresponding sides

    c.   Similar polygons have proportional corresponding sides

    d.   Similar polygons have congruent corresponding angles

20. Elyse wrote a list of values.

$$0.23, \frac{20}{100}, 45\%, 0.6, \frac{2}{5}$$

Which list correctly orders the values from greatest to least?

    a. $45\%, \frac{2}{5}, \frac{20}{100}, 0.6, 0.23$

    b. $0.6, 45\%, \frac{2}{5}, 0.23, \frac{20}{100}$

    c. $0.6, 45\%, 0.23, \frac{2}{5}, \frac{20}{100}$

    d. $45\%, 0.6, \frac{2}{5}, 0.23, \frac{20}{100}$

21. In the formula for the volume of the figure shown below, written as $V = B \cdot h$, h represents the height of the prism when it rests one of its bases. What does the B represent?

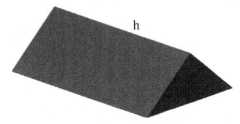

h

    a. $\frac{1}{3}bh$, where b represents the length of the triangle's base and h represents the triangle's height

    b. bh, where b represents the length of the triangle's base and h represents the triangle's height

    c. $2bh$, where b represents the length of triangle's base and h represents the triangle's height

    d. $\frac{1}{2}bh$, where b represents the length of triangle's base and h represents the triangle's height

22. The table shows the portion of bowls of food each puppy ate at a doggy day camp.

Puppy Food Chart	
Puppy Name	**Portion of bowls eaten**
Athena	$\frac{2}{5}$
Buddy	$\frac{7}{8}$
Rufus	80%
Sparky	33%
Spot	$\frac{3}{4}$

Which list shows the puppies in order from greatest to least amount of food eaten?

a. Buddy, Rufus, Spot, Athena, Sparky
b. Sparky, Athena, Spot, Rufus, Buddy
c. Sparky, Athena, Rufus, Buddy, Spot
d. Buddy, Rufus, Athena, Spot, Sparky

23. Which of the following statements is true for this set of similar triangles?

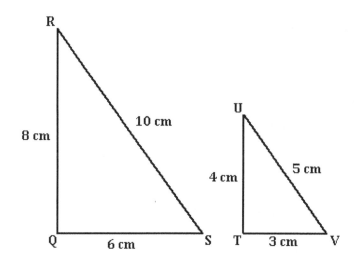

a. $\frac{RQ}{RS} = \frac{UT}{TV}$
b. $\frac{RS}{QS} = \frac{UV}{UT}$
c. $\frac{QS}{RS} = \frac{TV}{UV}$
d. $\frac{RQ}{QS} = \frac{UT}{UV}$

24. Which of the following statements is true?

a. All triangles are similar.
b. All trapezoids are similar.
c. All polygons are similar.
d. All squares are similar.

25. Bella is limiting her social media time to no more than 420 minutes per week. If she spends the same amount of time on social media each day, which inequality describes all possible numbers of m minutes Bella could spend each day of the week on social media?

    a. $60 \geq m$
    b. $60 \leq m$
    c. $60 < m$
    d. $60 > m$

Answer Key and Explanations for Test #3

Quantitative

1. B: This problem focuses on equivalent fractions and percentages. A percentage is a part out of 100, so 148% is equivalent to $\frac{148}{100}$. This fraction can be simplified by dividing the numerator and denominator by the greatest common factor. $\frac{148}{100} = \frac{148 \div 4}{100 \div 4} = \frac{37}{25}$.

2. A: The unit rate is determined by the ratio $\frac{\text{Cost(\$)}}{\text{Number of tickets}}$. Using the data from the first column from the table, the unit rate is $\frac{30}{5}$ or $\frac{6}{1}$. Therefore, choice A is correct.

3. C: To solve this formula, follow the order of operations. First, add what is in the parenthesis, $4 + 2$, to get 6. Then, multiply the 6 by 35 to get 210. Last, we should add $20 + 210 + 47$ to get 277.

4. C: Since the lengths of Triangle B are related to the lengths of Triangle A by a scale factor of $\frac{1}{4}$, each side length of Triangle A should be multiplied by the factor $\frac{1}{4}$: $12 \times \frac{1}{4} = 3$; $8 \times \frac{1}{4} = 2$; $16 \times \frac{1}{4} = 4$. The side lengths of Triangle B measure 3 cm, 2 cm, and 4 cm, respectively.

5. A: If each package holds 12 cupcakes, the relationship between packages and cupcakes is that the number of cupcakes is 12 times the number of packages. This can be expressed by many equivalent equations: $c = 12p$, $p = \frac{c}{12}$, "and" $\frac{c}{p} = 12$. $12c = p$ would express the reverse relationship, that the number of packages is 12 times the number of cupcakes.

6. B: The equation represented by the algebra tiles is $3x - 8 = 4$. Solving for x gives $3x = 12$, so $x = 4$. The equation can be visually solved by adding 8 green tiles to each side, and using the additive inverse property to isolate the $3x$. The equation can then be written as $3x = 12$. Each x can be mapped to 4 positive integer tiles. Thus, $x = 4$.

7. B: To answer this question, find the total number of bulbs required by multiplying 10 by 3. The number of packages of bulbs required can be found by dividing this total number of bulbs, 30, by 5, to find that 6 packages are needed. Then, multiplying 6 by the cost per package, 8, we find that the total cost for all the bulbs needed was $48.

8. C: Looking at the chart, a pattern can be seen in the relationship between the number of gills and the number of fluid ounces. Each number of gills in the first column, when multiplied by 4, gives the number of fluid ounces in the second column. So, f equals 4 times g, or $f = 4g$.

9. A: Since the scale factor is less than 1, the second rectangle is smaller than the first rectangle. To find the dimensions of the second rectangle, multiply each dimension of the first rectangle by $\frac{1}{2}$ or 0.5. Since $(0.5)(3)$ is 1.5, and $(0.5)(6)$ is 3, the dimensions of the second rectangle are 1.5 meters by 3 meters. Therefore, choice A is correct.

10. A: The equation $x + 2 = 5$ can be solved by subtracting 2 from both sides of the equation. This results in $x = 3$. This is represented by a solid circle at 3 on a number line. Therefore, choice A is correct.

11. B: Tommy's age is 4 more than Gianna's age. For example, if Tommy is 13 years old, Gianna is 9 years old. Tommy's age, t, is Gianna's age, g, plus 4. The equation $t + 4 = g$ is the only equation listed that represents the relationship in the story.

12. A: This problem focuses on writing situations to match a graph. There are many strategies that can be used to solve this problem. One strategy is to identify an equation to match the graph and then match the story to the equation. The graph includes the points (0,3), (1,4), (2,5), (3,6), and (4,7) where each y value is 3 more than each x value. The equation that matches the graph is $y = x + 3$. The story that represents the relationship is option A, where Damien is 3 years older than Jackson.

13. D: The box symbol shown at $\angle R$ means that $\angle R$ measures 90°. Since we are told $m\angle S$ is 20° less than $m\angle R$, subtract 90 −20 to get 70. This means that $m\angle S = 70°$. The sum of $m\angle R$ and $m\angle S$ is found by adding: 90 +70 = 160. The sum of all angles in a triangle always adds up to 180°, so subtracting 180 − 160 results in a difference of 20. So, $m\angle T$ is 20°.

14. B: This problem focuses on interpreting data from a dot plot. Based on the data, the sandwich shop sold 135 sandwiches on two days and sold 124 sandwiches on two days, so the first statement is not supported by the data. The sandwich shop sold more than 129 sandwiches on 5 days, so the second statement is supported by the data. The sandwich shop sold sandwiches for 11 days, so the third statement is not supported by the data. The sandwich shop sold fewer than 130 sandwiches $\frac{6}{11}$ of the times, so the fourth statement is not supported by the data.

15. C: If Kimi makes $10 for each lawn, where x is the number of lawns, then the expression $10x$ describes the number of dollars Kimi makes. If the earbuds Kimi wants cost $195, she needs at least $195 to buy the earbuds. If Kimi needs at least $195, that means that she can make more than $195 to get the earbuds but cannot make less than $195. This means that the number of dollars made, $10x$, must be more than or equal to $195. The expression that represents this is $10x \geq 195$, or $195 \leq 10x$.

16. A: This problem focuses of writing equations that represent a problem. If a grocery store received 250 apples and 14 could not be sold, $250 - 14$ equals the number of apples that can be sold. This means that $a = 250 - 14$. Two equivalent equations to $a = 250 - 14$ are $a + 14 = 250$ and $250 - a = 14$.

17. D: This problem focuses on identifying the ordered pair representation of a point on a coordinate plane. Point T is located 3 units to the right of the origin and 6 units down from the x-axis, so the ordered pair that best represents point T is $(3, -6)$.

18. C: This problem focuses on graphs that represent relationships in a story. If a company creates 75 posts each hour, the equation that represents the story is $y = 75x$, where each y value is 75 times the corresponding x value. This means that after 0 hours, the company would create 0 posts. After 1 hour, the company would create 75 posts. After 2 hours, the company would create 150 posts, and so on. Graph C is the only graph that appropriately represents this relationship.

19. D: This problem can be solved by substituting each option into the inequality: substituting $b = 12$ results in $(30)(12) < 372$, or $360 < 272$, which is a true statement. Alternatively, solve the inequality for b by dividing both sides by 30, which yields $b < 12.4$; of the choices, only 12 is less than 12.4. Therefore, choice D is correct.

20. D: The total cost y includes the constant price of the airline ticket plus the price of the baggage, which varies depending on the number of checked bags. The total cost y can be represented by the equation $y = 406 + 35x$, where x represents the number of checked bags

21. C: The fraction $\frac{4}{5}$ can be converted to a decimal by dividing 4 by 5. Doing so gives 0.80, which is equal to 80%.

22. A: When setting up a proportion, it's important to remember that like quantities must be placed in the numerators, and like quantities must be placed in the denominators. The general idea for a problem like this is $\frac{\text{feet}}{\text{miles}} = \frac{\text{feet}}{\text{miles}}$. The correct proportion is $\frac{5,280}{1} = \frac{26,400}{x}$. Therefore, choice A is correct.

Answer Key and Explanations for Test #3

23. A: The following proportion can be used to solve the problem: $\frac{3}{8} = \frac{24}{x}$. Solving for x gives: $3x = 192$, which simplifies to $x = 64$.

24. D: This problem focuses on equivalent ratios. The ratio of green to white paint is $3 : 8$, so solving the equation $3 : 8 = x : 192$ will provide the number of ounces of green paint to 192 ounces of white paint. $8 \cdot 24 = 192$, and $3 \cdot 24 = 72$, so $3 : 8 = 72 : 192$. There are 72 ounces of green paint to every 192 ounces of white paint in the paint mixture that Tanya ordered.

25. C: The ratio of the circumference of a circle to the diameter of the circle is pi. This can be written as $\frac{C}{d} = \pi$. Therefore, choice C is correct.

Reading Comprehension

1. B: As used in this passage, the word "parasite" means an organism that lives on or in another organism, Choice B. Choice A and C are obviously wrong, since the passage mentions nothing of Paris or insects. Choice D is another definition for "parasite," but does not fit the context of the word used in this passage.

2. C: According to the description of Roundworms, they can live in the subcutaneous tissue of humans, Choice C. Choices A, B, and D describe where protozoa live and how they are transmitted.

3. D: According to the first paragraph, protozoa are transmitted through food and water contaminated by fecal matter. It can then be inferred that clean sanitary conditions will prevent the spread of protozoa, Choice D. Choice A is an incorrect inference because the passage discusses both larval and adult forms of parasites that infect humans. Choice B is an incorrect inference, since the first paragraph states that protozoa are transmitted by mosquitoes. Choice C is an incorrect inference because the second paragraph is about worms that infect humans.

4. D: To answer this question, you will need to verify all three statements in the passage. All three of these statements are true and are supported by the passage.

5. C: This passage was written to give the reader the history of the American holiday, the Fourth of July, Choice C. With regard to Choice A, the Declaration of Independence is mentioned in the passage, but the main purpose of the passage does not focus on it. The same is true for Choice B. The passage does talk about movies associated with the Fourth of July, but the main purpose of the passage is not to encourage the reader to watch those movies. In Choice D, the passage does mention that independence from Britain is taken for granted, but the passage does not explain why.

6. A: This passage is primarily about the most popular American holiday, the Fourth of July, Choice A. The passage does relate to some extent to the other choices, but these do not reflect the main idea of the passage.

7. B: This detailed question offers four time periods mentioned in the passage as possible answer choices. Use caution when choosing the answer. Look back at the passage. The end of paragraph one offers the correct choice, Choice B.

8. D: As used in this passage, "berate" means to scold or rebuke, Choice D. Choices A and B are antonyms. Choice C does not fit the meaning.

9. C: The last sentence of the passage gives the best clue to the tone of the passage: "American independence has always been an important concept in our country, and Americans will protect it from any and all challenges facing it." Of the four options given, *admiring* would best describe the tone.

10. C: You could possibly find this passage in a tourist guidebook, Choice A, but you would most likely find the passage in an online encyclopedia, Choice C. Choices B and D can be eliminated, since a history text book and a comic book are the least likely choices.

11. B: The passage explains that nutria have several adaptations to help them in the water. The logical inference is that their eyes, ears, and nostrils are high on their heads to prevent water from entering them while they are swimming, Choice B.

12. A: Use caution when answering this detailed question, since all the choices given are quantitative possibilities used in the passage. According to the third paragraph, nutria reach sexual maturity in four to six months, Choice A.

13. D: Look back to the passage to answer this detailed question. According to the second paragraph, fur farms failed due to the drop in prices of fur and nutrias' failure to reproduce well in captivity, Choice D.

Answer Key and Explanations for Test #3

14. C: This passage is about Harry Houdini. In both the first paragraph and the last paragraph, the author refers to Houdini as a master of illusion. The best choice is Choice C. Choices A and D are both mentioned in the passage, but are not the main idea of the passage. Although Choice B seems like a possibility because a whole paragraph focuses on the escape, several other escapes are also described, making this a poor choice.

15. A: This passage gives facts and details about the life of Harry Houdini and was written in order to inform the reader, Choice A. Although the passage could be considered entertaining, its main purpose is to inform. There are no persuasive techniques used in the passage, nor is it humorous, making Choices C and D incorrect.

16. D: According to the first paragraph, Beatrice Houdini was Harry Houdini's stage assistant and wife, Choice D.

17. C: To answer this detail question, look back at the passage. The last paragraph states that "Houdini had created a sensation" with The Vanishing Elephant act, Choice C. Choices A and B are acts discussed in the passage, but they are not described as his most sensational. Choice D is not an actual act discussed in the passage, and therefore, an incorrect choice.

18. A: Choice A, "exploit" is a synonym for "feat." Choice B, "failure," is an antonym. Choices C and D do not fit the context of the sentence. The correct answer is Choice A.

19. A: The first paragraph describes how gaseous emissions from volcanic vents formed the early oceans and atmosphere, Choice A.

20. B: Although all of the answer choices point to the word "crowd," Choice B is the only logical choice based how the word is used in the context of the passage.

21. B: Of the choices given, this passage would most likely be found in a science textbook, Choice B.

22. D: The second paragraph states that erosion and weathering have sculpted "majestic landscapes and formed fertile soils", Choice D.

23. C: The best title for this passage is Choice C. The first paragraph tells the reader that Billie Holiday's nickname was Lady Day. The entire passage focuses on her career as a Jazz singer.

24. C: To answer this question, you will need to find supporting statements in the passage. Only the first two statements are supported by the passage, Choice C.

25. A: The second paragraph describes the racism that blacks were facing in the 1930s. It supports this inference, stating that one of Holiday's songs was a sad "expression of protest against man's inhumanity to man that has ever been made in the form of vocal jazz." There is no support in the passage for the other three answer choices. Choice A is the correct answer.

26. C: The purpose of this passage is to inform the reader. Choice C is the correct answer.

27. B: The answer choices are all dates from the passage. Refer back to the passage to check each date. The first paragraph gives the correct answer, Choice B.

28. D: Scan the passage for words that reveal how the author feels about the subject. The author states that Earthworms have an "important role" and play a "necessary part" in the soil food web. These words have a positive connotation. The last paragraph also exudes a positive feeling towards earthworms. Choice D is the correct answer.

29. D: To answer this question, you will need to verify all three options in the passage. The second paragraph lists all three organisms as members of the soil food web, Choice D.

30. A: To till means to plow or cultivate, Choice A. The other answer choices do not fit the context of the sentence.

31. B: According to the fifth paragraph, burrowing helps nutrients enter the subsoil at a faster rate and opens up pathways for roots to grow into, Choice B.

32. B: Because this passage is about how the Missouri Territory became a part of the United States, the most likely place to find this passage is in an American history textbook, Choice B.

33. C: According to the first paragraph, the Missouri Territory became part of the United States through the 1803 Louisiana Purchase, Choice C.

34. C: First, determine what the compromise was. According to the passage, compromises had to be made to keep a balance in the Union between the slave and non-slave states. An accurate inference would be that Missourians disagreed on the issue of slavery, Choice C.

35. B: According to the third paragraph, Jayhawkers were members of a group opposed to slavery.

36. A: All the answer choices are related to the passage in some way. However, the last paragraph of the passage begins discussing Missourians and the Civil War. The most logical choice, then, would be Choice A, a continued discussion of Missouri's role in the Civil War.

37. D: Although the first three answer choices are mentioned in the passage, the last answer choice is best in summarizing the passage as a whole. The correct answer is choice D.

38. B: All choices, except Choice B, describe shallow water coral reefs. According to the passage, deep sea coral reefs are found where sunlight does not reach, making them unique. The correct answer is Choice B.

39. A: This passage was written in the first-person format. The author refers to himself or herself with the pronouns "we" and "I." A passage written in second person would include the pronouns "you." A passage written in the third person would have a narrator telling the story, but not part of the events. There is no fourth person narrative. The correct answer is Choice A.

40. C: Answer Choices A, B, and D all refer back to the first expedition. The end of the passage clearly states that the next goal is to "determine if the coral species, and their associate fauna, living in the subtropical Bahamas are the same as those on the seamounts to the north." The correct answer is Choice C.

Verbal

1. B: To enthrall is to fascinate or mesmerize.

2. A: A coward is someone who is gutless, or lacks courage when facing danger.

3. C: A novice is someone who is new to the circumstances, or a beginner.

4. D: Temperate means to be moderate or restrained.

5. A: Something authentic is genuine or true.

6. D: To salvage something is to save or recover it from wreckage, destruction or - loss.

7. B: Vernacular is the speech or language of a place.

8. C: To attest is to vouch for or to certify.

9. A: Derelict means to be neglected or abandoned, e.g., "a derelict old home."

10. C: To ordain is to order or command.

11. B: To be haughty is to be proud or arrogant.

12. C: A lapse is an error or mistake, e.g., "a lapse of memory."

13. D: To nauseate is to disgust or repulse.

14. A: Something paltry is cheap, base, or common.

15. C: To be refined is to be cultured and well-bred.

16. D: Virtual means to be simulated, especially as related to computer software.

17. B: To loathe is to hate or abhor.

18. C: When you mimic, you imitate or copy someone or something.

19. A: Something brittle is fragile and easily damaged or destroyed.

20. D: Wretched means miserable or woeful.

21. B: Vehement most closely means the same thing as intense.

22. A: Diatribe most closely means the same thing as criticism.

23. D: Cogitate most closely means the same thing as deliberate.

24. A: Invidious most closely means the same thing as offensive.

25. C: Hyperbole most closely means the same thing as exaggeration.

26. B: Innocuous most closely means the same thing as innocent.

27. B: The word "capricious" means "unpredictable" or "changeable."

28. A: The word "intermittent" also means "occasional" or "discontinuous."

29. A: Solitary can mean a number of different things, but one meaning is single. For example, if you said there was a solitary tree in a yard, you would mean that there was a single tree.

30. C: The word "precipitous" means "steep."

31. C: The relationship sought is one of a professional to the place in which he/she performs his/her professional work. The only answer that has that relationship is that of conductor to symphony hall.

32. B: The relationship sought is that of antonyms. The only answer that has that relationship is that of frugal to spendthrift.

33. A: The relationship sought is one of an adjective to another adjective that is a stronger form of the first word. The only answer that has that relationship is that of dirty to squalid.

34. D: The relationship sought is one of an emotional state to the action taken as a result of being in that state. The only answer that has that relationship is that of complimentary to praise.

35. B: The relationship sought is that of synonyms. The only answer that has that relationship is that of diminutive to microscopic.

36. A: The relationship sought is one of an adjective to the state of mind something modified by that adjective creates. The only answer that has that relationship is that of tasty to craving.

37. D: The relationship sought is one of an adjective to the action which the state of being described by the adjective necessitates. The only answer that has that relationship is that of peripatetic to wander.

38. B: The relationship sought is that of antonyms. The only answer that has that relationship is that of ponderous to insubstantial.

39. A: The relationship sought is that of an adjective and an action or state of being exhibited by one accurately described by that adjective. The only answer that has that relationship is that of discerning to awareness.

40. B: A motorcycle is a motorized bicycle; a speedboat is a motorized paddleboat.

41. B: An apple develops from a seed; a person develops from an embryo.

42. A: A fraction is a part of a whole; a slice is a part of a pie.

43. A: Temperature is used to measure heat; pounds are used to measure weight.

44. A: A bank is a place to keep one's savings; a safe is a place to keep one's valuables.

45. D: An island is surrounded by the sea; a star is surrounded by space.

46. A: Inattention can lead to accidents; practice can lead to improvement.

47. D: Sight is an example of a sense; gravity is an example of a force.

48. A: Dexterity is a kind of skill; English is a kind of language.

49. C: A coach is in charge of a team; a teacher is in charge of students.

50. B: An article is a section of a magazine; a chapter is a section of a book.

51. C: A house is a part of the neighborhood and a tree is a part of the forest.

52. B: A wallet holds money and an envelope holds a letter.

53. D: A German shepherd is a type of dog and a strawberry is a type of fruit.

54. B: Joyful is an opposite of sad and empty is an opposite of crowded.

55. C: An automobile is stored in the garage and a dish is stored in a cupboard.

56. C: A doctor works in the field of medicine and a teacher works in the field of education.

57. A: Chirp is a similar action to tweet and jump is a similar action to leap.

58. B: Sleeping is a solution for being tired and drinking is a solution for being thirsty.

59. D: A four-leaf clover is a symbol of luck and an arrow is a symbol of direction.

60. B: A question requires an answer and a problem requires a solution.

Quantitative

1. A: To solve this problem, the relationship between x and y needs to be identified for each data table. The relationship in data table A is that y is 3 more than x: $y = x + 3$. The relationship in data table B is that y is 3 times as much as x: $y = 3x$. The relationship in data table C is that y is 3 times as much as x: $y = 3x$. The relationship in data table D is that y is 3 times as much as x: $y = 3x$. Data table B, C, and D could be the table that André drew, and A could not be the table that he drew.

2. D: This problem focuses on solving problems with integers and using the order of operations. The first step is to solve the addition problem in the parentheses, so $-9 + 3 = -6$. The next step is to simplify the fraction $\frac{-6}{2}$ using division, so $-6 \div 2 = -3$.

3. B: This problem focuses on the different ways to represent division. In the story given, Tavario has 32 shirts and is packaging them in sets of 4. He can express the division problem in many ways, but no matter the representation, this problem explains that 32 shirts are divided into piles of 4, or 32 divided by 4. Division can be represented using long division, a fraction, the division symbol, and word form. Each representation expresses the division problem from the story except option B, which represents 4 divided by 32 instead of 32 divided by 4.

4. C: This problem focuses on the formula for the area of a square. A square is a type of rectangle where all sides are the same length. Because a square is a rectangle, the formula for the area of a rectangle, $A = bh$, can be used to find the area of a square. Also, because a square has equivalent side lengths, the base and height are equal and can be described as side length, s. This means that the area of a square is $A = s \cdot s$. Also, a value multiplied by itself can be represented as the square of that value, so $A = s \cdot s$ is equivalent to $A = s^2$. The formula $A = s + s + s + s$ would add all the side lengths of a square, which is used not to find the area, but to find the perimeter.

5. A: Applying the distributive property to $2(a + 3) + 3a + 4$ yields $2a + 6 + 3a + 4$. Combining like terms yields $5a + 10$. Therefore, choice A is correct.

6. B: In this table, the x values represent the number of hours and the y values represent the number of dollars. The number of hours is the independent value because the number of dollars is dependent on the number of hours.

7. B: The sum of the angles of a triangle is 180°. The measure of angle A can be found by 180° − (34° + 64°), or 180° − 98°, which is 82°. Therefore, choice B is correct.

8. C: This problem focuses on writing equations from a table. In this table, s is the independent value which means that an operation is being performed on s to get t. In this example, each s value is multiplied by 4 to get the t value, which is expressed by the equation $t = 4s$.

9. D: This problem focuses on converting fractions to decimals. There are a couple strategies that can be used to convert fractions to decimals. One way would be through using division. $\frac{1}{8}$ is equivalent to 0.125, $\frac{1}{4} = 0.25$, $\frac{3}{8} = 0.375$, and $\frac{1}{2} = 0.5$.

10. B: This problem focuses on identifying the mode of a data set. The mode of a data set is the value that appears the most. In this example, the value 0 appears 4 times, the value 1 appears 9 times, and the value 2 appears 7 times. The mode of the data set is 1.

11. A: This problem focuses on converting measurements. The conversion sheet can be used to find that 1 meter is equivalent to 100 centimeters, so 7.3 meters is equivalent to 730 centimeters because $7.3 \cdot 100 = 730$. Also, 1 centimeter is equivalent to 10 millimeters, so 7.3 meters is equivalent to 7300 millimeters because $7.3 \cdot$

285

1,000 = 7,300. Lastly, 1 kilometer is equivalent to 1,000 meters, so 7.3 meters is equivalent to 0.0073 kilometers because 7.3 ÷ 1,000 = 0.0073.

12. D: This problem focuses on using proportions to solve a problem. If a recipe calls for 5 cups of flour for every 2 cups of sugar, the ratio of flour to sugar is $\frac{5}{2}$. If Azah needs to know the number of cups of sugar used for 8 cups of flour, this ratio of flour to sugar can be expressed by $\frac{8}{x}$, where x represents the number of cups of sugar. The ratio of flour to sugar stays proportional, which means that $\frac{5}{2} = \frac{8}{x}$.

13. C: Since she earns $5 for walking dogs and watering flowers, this term can be combined to simplify the equation. The other terms for bringing back trashcans and checking the mail are straight multiplication.

14. B: This problem focuses on using the area formula to find the area of a trapezoid. The reference sheet can be used to find the formula for the area of a trapezoid, $A = \frac{1}{2}(b_1 + b_2)h$. Based on the diagram, $b_1 = 15$ cm, $b_2 = 25$ cm, and $h = 3$ cm. These values can be inserted into the trapezoid formula, where $A = \frac{1}{2}(15 + 25) \cdot 3 = \frac{1}{2}(40) \cdot 3 = 20 \cdot 3 = 60$.

15. D: This procedure first finds the area to be fertilized, by multiplying the length and width of the rectangular yard. Then, it divides that area by the area each pound of fertilizer will cover.

16. C: This problem focuses on the difference between an equation and an expression. An expression is a number, variable, or group of numbers, variables, and operations. Expressions are often meant to be simplified, can stand alone, and can be found on one side of an equal sign. An equation is a group of expressions separated by an equal sign. Equations are often meant to be solved, usually solving for a variable. In this problem, $2x + 4 - x$ is a group of numbers, variables, and operations that does not include an equal sign, so Example 1 is an expression. $2x - x = -4$ is a set of expressions; $2x - x$ and -4 are both expressions. These expressions are separated by an equal sign, so Example 2 is an equation.

17. B: The total cost of the soda and pizza must be less than or equal to $50. Since each pizza cost $8, $8n$ represents the cost of n pizzas, and since Steven plans to spend $10 on soda, $8n + 10$ represents the cost of the pizza and soda together, which must be less than or equal to $50. The correct inequality is $8n + 10 \le 50$. Therefore, choice B is correct.

18. B: The volume of the rectangular prism is found by multiplying the area of the base times the height, or Volume = length × width × height. So, $V = (8m)(4m)(6m) = 192$ m^3. Therefore, choice B is correct.

19. A: Similar polygons must have congruent corresponding angles and proportional corresponding sides. Both requirements must be fulfilled in order to declare similarity in polygons.

20. B: There are many ways to order the given values. One way is to convert all values to decimals. 0.23 and 0.6 are already in decimal form. $\frac{20}{100}$ is equivalent to 0.2, 45% is equivalent to 0.45, and $\frac{2}{5}$ is equivalent to 0.4. These decimal values listed from greatest to least are 0.6, 0.45, 0.4, 0.23, 0.2.

21. D: The B in the formula $V = Bh$ represents the area of the triangular base. The formula for the area of a triangle is $\frac{1}{2}bh$, where b represents the length of the triangle's base and h represents the triangle's height.

22. A: There are many strategies that can be used to correctly order these values from greatest to least. One way to approach this problem would be to use number sense and conversions. By reviewing the table and using some number sense, identify the largest or smallest values. The largest values in the table are $\frac{7}{8}$ and 80%. To appropriately compare these values to find the greatest value, they should be converted to a similar format, like decimals. The decimal form of $\frac{7}{8}$ can be found using division, where 7 divided by 8 equals 0.875, and 80% is equivalent to 0.8. Based on this comparison $\frac{7}{8}$ is the greatest value, followed by 80%. By understanding fractions, percents, and decimals, it can be identified that $\frac{3}{4}$ is equivalent to 0.75, or 75%, so $\frac{3}{4}$ is the next greatest number. The remaining values are 33% and $\frac{2}{5}$. These values can be converted to decimals. 33% is equivalent to 0.33 and $\frac{2}{5}$ is equivalent to 0.4, so 0.33 is the smallest value. The correct list from greatest to least is represented by option A: $\frac{7}{8}$, 80%, $\frac{3}{4}$, $\frac{2}{5}$, 33%.

23. C: The corresponding sides of similar triangles are proportional. In these triangles, *RQ* corresponds to *UT*, *QS* corresponds to *TV*, and *RS* corresponds to *UV*. Therefore, $\frac{QS}{RS} = \frac{TV}{UV}$.

Choice C is correct.

24. D: Similar figures have the same shape, and corresponding angles of the similar figures are congruent. Since all squares are quadrilaterals with four right angles and four congruent sides, all squares are similar. Not all triangles, trapezoids, or polygons are similar. Therefore, choice D is correct.

25. A: This problem focuses on solutions to inequalities. The story expresses the inequality $420 \geq 7m$ because Bella doesn't want to spend more than 420 minutes on social media during each week, which means that she could spend 420 minutes but cannot go over 420 minutes. This inequality can be simplified by using division. $420 \geq 7m$ is equivalent to $\frac{420}{7} \geq \frac{7m}{7}$, which can be simplified to $60 \geq m$.

How to Overcome Test Anxiety

Just the thought of taking a test is enough to make most people a little nervous. A test is an important event that can have a long-term impact on your future, so it's important to take it seriously and it's natural to feel anxious about performing well. But just because anxiety is normal, that doesn't mean that it's helpful in test taking, or that you should simply accept it as part of your life. Anxiety can have a variety of effects. These effects can be mild, like making you feel slightly nervous, or severe, like blocking your ability to focus or remember even a simple detail.

If you experience test anxiety—whether severe or mild—it's important to know how to beat it. To discover this, first you need to understand what causes test anxiety.

Causes of Test Anxiety

While we often think of anxiety as an uncontrollable emotional state, it can actually be caused by simple, practical things. One of the most common causes of test anxiety is that a person does not feel adequately prepared for their test. This feeling can be the result of many different issues such as poor study habits or lack of organization, but the most common culprit is time management. Starting to study too late, failing to organize your study time to cover all of the material, or being distracted while you study will mean that you're not well prepared for the test. This may lead to cramming the night before, which will cause you to be physically and mentally exhausted for the test. Poor time management also contributes to feelings of stress, fear, and hopelessness as you realize you are not well prepared but don't know what to do about it.

Other times, test anxiety is not related to your preparation for the test but comes from unresolved fear. This may be a past failure on a test, or poor performance on tests in general. It may come from comparing yourself to others who seem to be performing better or from the stress of living up to expectations. Anxiety may be driven by fears of the future—how failure on this test would affect your educational and career goals. These fears are often completely irrational, but they can still negatively impact your test performance.

Elements of Test Anxiety

As mentioned earlier, test anxiety is considered to be an emotional state, but it has physical and mental components as well. Sometimes you may not even realize that you are suffering from test anxiety until you notice the physical symptoms. These can include trembling hands, rapid heartbeat, sweating, nausea, and tense muscles. Extreme anxiety may lead to fainting or vomiting. Obviously, any of these symptoms can have a negative impact on testing. It is important to recognize them as soon as they begin to occur so that you can address the problem before it damages your performance.

The mental components of test anxiety include trouble focusing and inability to remember learned information. During a test, your mind is on high alert, which can help you recall information and stay focused for an extended period of time. However, anxiety interferes with your mind's natural processes, causing you to blank out, even on the questions you know well. The strain of testing during anxiety makes it difficult to stay focused, especially on a test that may take several hours. Extreme anxiety can take a huge mental toll, making it difficult not only to recall test information but even to understand the test questions or pull your thoughts together.

Effects of Test Anxiety

Test anxiety is like a disease—if left untreated, it will get progressively worse. Anxiety leads to poor performance, and this reinforces the feelings of fear and failure, which in turn lead to poor performances on subsequent tests. It can grow from a mild nervousness to a crippling condition. If allowed to progress, test anxiety can have a big impact on your schooling, and consequently on your future.

Test anxiety can spread to other parts of your life. Anxiety on tests can become anxiety in any stressful situation, and blanking on a test can turn into panicking in a job situation. But fortunately, you don't have to let anxiety rule your testing and determine your grades. There are a number of relatively simple steps you can take to move past anxiety and function normally on a test and in the rest of life.

Physical Steps for Beating Test Anxiety

While test anxiety is a serious problem, the good news is that it can be overcome. It doesn't have to control your ability to think and remember information. While it may take time, you can begin taking steps today to beat anxiety.

Just as your first hint that you may be struggling with anxiety comes from the physical symptoms, the first step to treating it is also physical. Rest is crucial for having a clear, strong mind. If you are tired, it is much easier to give in to anxiety. But if you establish good sleep habits, your body and mind will be ready to perform optimally, without the strain of exhaustion. Additionally, sleeping well helps you to retain information better, so you're more likely to recall the answers when you see the test questions.

Getting good sleep means more than going to bed on time. It's important to allow your brain time to relax. Take study breaks from time to time so it doesn't get overworked, and don't study right before bed. Take time to rest your mind before trying to rest your body, or you may find it difficult to fall asleep.

Along with sleep, other aspects of physical health are important in preparing for a test. Good nutrition is vital for good brain function. Sugary foods and drinks may give a burst of energy but this burst is followed by a crash, both physically and emotionally. Instead, fuel your body with protein and vitamin-rich foods.

Also, drink plenty of water. Dehydration can lead to headaches and exhaustion, especially if your brain is already under stress from the rigors of the test. Particularly if your test is a long one, drink water during the breaks. And if possible, take an energy-boosting snack to eat between sections.

Along with sleep and diet, a third important part of physical health is exercise. Maintaining a steady workout schedule is helpful, but even taking 5-minute study breaks to walk can help get your blood pumping faster and clear your head. Exercise also releases endorphins, which contribute to a positive feeling and can help combat test anxiety.

When you nurture your physical health, you are also contributing to your mental health. If your body is healthy, your mind is much more likely to be healthy as well. So take time to rest, nourish your body with healthy food and water, and get moving as much as possible. Taking these physical steps will make you stronger and more able to take the mental steps necessary to overcome test anxiety.

Mental Steps for Beating Test Anxiety

Working on the mental side of test anxiety can be more challenging, but as with the physical side, there are clear steps you can take to overcome it. As mentioned earlier, test anxiety often stems from lack of preparation, so the obvious solution is to prepare for the test. Effective studying may be the most important weapon you have for beating test anxiety, but you can and should employ several other mental tools to combat fear.

First, boost your confidence by reminding yourself of past success—tests or projects that you aced. If you're putting as much effort into preparing for this test as you did for those, there's no reason you should expect to fail here. Work hard to prepare; then trust your preparation.

Second, surround yourself with encouraging people. It can be helpful to find a study group, but be sure that the people you're around will encourage a positive attitude. If you spend time with others who are anxious or cynical, this will only contribute to your own anxiety. Look for others who are motivated to study hard from a desire to succeed, not from a fear of failure.

Third, reward yourself. A test is physically and mentally tiring, even without anxiety, and it can be helpful to have something to look forward to. Plan an activity following the test, regardless of the outcome, such as going to a movie or getting ice cream.

When you are taking the test, if you find yourself beginning to feel anxious, remind yourself that you know the material. Visualize successfully completing the test. Then take a few deep, relaxing breaths and return to it. Work through the questions carefully but with confidence, knowing that you are capable of succeeding.

Developing a healthy mental approach to test taking will also aid in other areas of life. Test anxiety affects more than just the actual test—it can be damaging to your mental health and even contribute to depression. It's important to beat test anxiety before it becomes a problem for more than testing.

Study Strategy

Being prepared for the test is necessary to combat anxiety, but what does being prepared look like? You may study for hours on end and still not feel prepared. What you need is a strategy for test prep. The next few pages outline our recommended steps to help you plan out and conquer the challenge of preparation.

STEP 1: SCOPE OUT THE TEST

Learn everything you can about the format (multiple choice, essay, etc.) and what will be on the test. Gather any study materials, course outlines, or sample exams that may be available. Not only will this help you to prepare, but knowing what to expect can help to alleviate test anxiety.

STEP 2: MAP OUT THE MATERIAL

Look through the textbook or study guide and make note of how many chapters or sections it has. Then divide these over the time you have. For example, if a book has 15 chapters and you have five days to study, you need to cover three chapters each day. Even better, if you have the time, leave an extra day at the end for overall review after you have gone through the material in depth.

If time is limited, you may need to prioritize the material. Look through it and make note of which sections you think you already have a good grasp on, and which need review. While you are studying, skim quickly through the familiar sections and take more time on the challenging parts. Write out your plan so you don't get lost as you go. Having a written plan also helps you feel more in control of the study, so anxiety is less likely to arise from feeling overwhelmed at the amount to cover.

STEP 3: GATHER YOUR TOOLS

Decide what study method works best for you. Do you prefer to highlight in the book as you study and then go back over the highlighted portions? Or do you type out notes of the important information? Or is it helpful to make flashcards that you can carry with you? Assemble the pens, index cards, highlighters, post-it notes, and any other materials you may need so you won't be distracted by getting up to find things while you study.

If you're having a hard time retaining the information or organizing your notes, experiment with different methods. For example, try color-coding by subject with colored pens, highlighters, or post-it notes. If you learn better by hearing, try recording yourself reading your notes so you can listen while in the car, working out, or simply sitting at your desk. Ask a friend to quiz you from your flashcards, or try teaching someone the material to solidify it in your mind.

STEP 4: CREATE YOUR ENVIRONMENT

It's important to avoid distractions while you study. This includes both the obvious distractions like visitors and the subtle distractions like an uncomfortable chair (or a too-comfortable couch that makes you want to fall asleep). Set up the best study environment possible: good lighting and a comfortable work area. If background music helps you focus, you may want to turn it on, but otherwise keep the room quiet. If you are using a computer to take notes, be sure you don't have any other windows open, especially applications like social media, games, or anything else that could distract you. Silence your phone and turn off notifications. Be sure to keep water close by so you stay hydrated while you study (but avoid unhealthy drinks and snacks).

Also, take into account the best time of day to study. Are you freshest first thing in the morning? Try to set aside some time then to work through the material. Is your mind clearer in the afternoon or evening? Schedule your study session then. Another method is to study at the same time of day that you will take the test, so that your brain gets used to working on the material at that time and will be ready to focus at test time.

STEP 5: STUDY!

Once you have done all the study preparation, it's time to settle into the actual studying. Sit down, take a few moments to settle your mind so you can focus, and begin to follow your study plan. Don't give in to distractions or let yourself procrastinate. This is your time to prepare so you'll be ready to fearlessly approach the test. Make the most of the time and stay focused.

Of course, you don't want to burn out. If you study too long you may find that you're not retaining the information very well. Take regular study breaks. For example, taking five minutes out of every hour to walk briskly, breathing deeply and swinging your arms, can help your mind stay fresh.

As you get to the end of each chapter or section, it's a good idea to do a quick review. Remind yourself of what you learned and work on any difficult parts. When you feel that you've mastered the material, move on to the next part. At the end of your study session, briefly skim through your notes again.

But while review is helpful, cramming last minute is NOT. If at all possible, work ahead so that you won't need to fit all your study into the last day. Cramming overloads your brain with more information than it can process and retain, and your tired mind may struggle to recall even previously learned information when it is overwhelmed with last-minute study. Also, the urgent nature of cramming and the stress placed on your brain contribute to anxiety. You'll be more likely to go to the test feeling unprepared and having trouble thinking clearly.

So don't cram, and don't stay up late before the test, even just to review your notes at a leisurely pace. Your brain needs rest more than it needs to go over the information again. In fact, plan to finish your studies by noon or early afternoon the day before the test. Give your brain the rest of the day to relax or focus on other things, and get a good night's sleep. Then you will be fresh for the test and better able to recall what you've studied.

How to Overcome Test Anxiety

STEP 6: TAKE A PRACTICE TEST

Many courses offer sample tests, either online or in the study materials. This is an excellent resource to check whether you have mastered the material, as well as to prepare for the test format and environment.

Check the test format ahead of time: the number of questions, the type (multiple choice, free response, etc.), and the time limit. Then create a plan for working through them. For example, if you have 30 minutes to take a 60-question test, your limit is 30 seconds per question. Spend less time on the questions you know well so that you can take more time on the difficult ones.

If you have time to take several practice tests, take the first one open book, with no time limit. Work through the questions at your own pace and make sure you fully understand them. Gradually work up to taking a test under test conditions: sit at a desk with all study materials put away and set a timer. Pace yourself to make sure you finish the test with time to spare and go back to check your answers if you have time.

After each test, check your answers. On the questions you missed, be sure you understand why you missed them. Did you misread the question (tests can use tricky wording)? Did you forget the information? Or was it something you hadn't learned? Go back and study any shaky areas that the practice tests reveal.

Taking these tests not only helps with your grade, but also aids in combating test anxiety. If you're already used to the test conditions, you're less likely to worry about it, and working through tests until you're scoring well gives you a confidence boost. Go through the practice tests until you feel comfortable, and then you can go into the test knowing that you're ready for it.

Test Tips

On test day, you should be confident, knowing that you've prepared well and are ready to answer the questions. But aside from preparation, there are several test day strategies you can employ to maximize your performance.

First, as stated before, get a good night's sleep the night before the test (and for several nights before that, if possible). Go into the test with a fresh, alert mind rather than staying up late to study.

Try not to change too much about your normal routine on the day of the test. It's important to eat a nutritious breakfast, but if you normally don't eat breakfast at all, consider eating just a protein bar. If you're a coffee drinker, go ahead and have your normal coffee. Just make sure you time it so that the caffeine doesn't wear off right in the middle of your test. Avoid sugary beverages, and drink enough water to stay hydrated but not so much that you need a restroom break 10 minutes into the test. If your test isn't first thing in the morning, consider going for a walk or doing a light workout before the test to get your blood flowing.

Allow yourself enough time to get ready, and leave for the test with plenty of time to spare so you won't have the anxiety of scrambling to arrive in time. Another reason to be early is to select a good seat. It's helpful to sit away from doors and windows, which can be distracting. Find a good seat, get out your supplies, and settle your mind before the test begins.

When the test begins, start by going over the instructions carefully, even if you already know what to expect. Make sure you avoid any careless mistakes by following the directions.

Then begin working through the questions, pacing yourself as you've practiced. If you're not sure on an answer, don't spend too much time on it, and don't let it shake your confidence. Either skip it and come back later, or eliminate as many wrong answers as possible and guess among the remaining ones. Don't dwell on these questions as you continue—put them out of your mind and focus on what lies ahead.

Be sure to read all of the answer choices, even if you're sure the first one is the right answer. Sometimes you'll find a better one if you keep reading. But don't second-guess yourself if you do immediately know the answer. Your gut instinct is usually right. Don't let test anxiety rob you of the information you know.

If you have time at the end of the test (and if the test format allows), go back and review your answers. Be cautious about changing any, since your first instinct tends to be correct, but make sure you didn't misread any of the questions or accidentally mark the wrong answer choice. Look over any you skipped and make an educated guess.

At the end, leave the test feeling confident. You've done your best, so don't waste time worrying about your performance or wishing you could change anything. Instead, celebrate the successful completion of this test. And finally, use this test to learn how to deal with anxiety even better next time.

> **Review Video: Test Anxiety**
> Visit mometrix.com/academy and enter code: 100340

Important Qualification

Not all anxiety is created equal. If your test anxiety is causing major issues in your life beyond the classroom or testing center, or if you are experiencing troubling physical symptoms related to your anxiety, it may be a sign of a serious physiological or psychological condition. If this sounds like your situation, we strongly encourage you to seek professional help.

How to Overcome Test Anxiety

Additional Bonus Material

Due to our efforts to try to keep this book to a manageable length, we've created a link that will give you access to all of your additional bonus material:

mometrix.com/bonus948/ssatmiddle

Made in United States
Orlando, FL
27 March 2025

59905483R00168